THE GREAT WHITE WAY

THE UNIVERSITY OF
WINCHESTER

Martial Rose Library
Tel: 01962 827306

To be returned on or before the day marked above, subject to recall.

THE GREAT WHITE WAY

RACE AND THE BROADWAY MUSICAL

Warren Hoffman

RUTGERS UNIVERSITY PRESS
NEW BRUNSWICK, NEW JERSEY, AND LONDON

Library of Congress Cataloging-in-Publication Data
Hoffman, Warren, 1976–
The Great White Way : race and the Broadway musical / Warren Hoffman.
pages cm
Includes bibliographical references and index.
ISBN 978-0-8135-6335-0 (hardcover : alk. paper) — ISBN 978-0-8135-6334-3 (pbk. : alk.
paper) — ISBN 978-0-8135-6336-7 (e-book)
Race in musical theater. 2. Music and race. 3. Musical theater—Social aspects—United
States—History—20th century. 4. Musical theater—Social aspects—United States—History—
21st century. 5. Musical theater—Political aspects—United States—History—20th century. 6.
Musical theater—Political aspects—United States—History—21st century. I. Title.
ML3918.M85H64 2014
792.6089'0097471—dc23
2013013412
A British Cataloging-in-Publication record for this book is available from the British Library.
For permissions see page 241.

Visit our website: http://rutgerspress.rutgers.edu
Manufactured in the United States of America

In memory of my grandma,
Laura Wildman,
whose favorite musical was
La Cage aux Folles

Contents

Acknowledgments

It dawns on me that I never actually asked Angela Davis if she likes Broadway musicals, but without her wisdom and amazing generosity, this book might not have come to be. As a student of Dr. Davis at the University of California–Santa Cruz, first in her seminar on racial theory, and then in a private tutorial on whiteness studies, I was given the remarkable opportunity to learn from one of the country's most erudite and eloquent individuals on the topic of race. To combine this experience with my own lifelong passion for the American musical has been a wonderful journey, but one that I could not have completed without the help and support of many people.

Senior Music Specialist Mark Eden Horowitz at the Library of Congress's Music Division was an unending source of historical information about musical theater and always pointed me to interesting archival materials that I might not have discovered on my own. The entire staff, especially Jeremy McGraw, at the New York Public Library for the Performing Arts was also more than eager to assist me in my many requests. Thanks too to Ron Mandelbaum at Photofest for help with many of the images in this book.

Many estates and rights holders kindly gave me permission to reprint and publish lyrics, libretto excerpts, and letters in this book. I want to thank Christopher Pennington at the Jerome Robbins Foundation, Linda Kline of the Edward Kleban Estate, Sargent Aborn at Tams-Witmark, Stephen Sondheim, Damon Booth at Notable Music, Bruce Pomahac and Sebastian Fabal at the Rodgers and Hammerstein Organization, Michael Gibbons, Maarten Kooij at ICM, Jonathan Lomma at William Morris, Carol Rosegg, Joan Marcus, and Paul Meloccaro. For detailed information, please see the permissions section at the end of the book.

The writing process of this book stretched over many years, and I had the great fortune of having multiple friends and colleagues offer feedback on these chapters. I am honored to call Andrea Most, whose work has transformed the field of musical theater studies, both a friend and colleague. Her advice throughout the writing and entire publication process was extremely helpful. Two close friends, Tim White and Steven Capsuto, took time to read various chapters and offered smart and insightful criticisms that made this a better piece of scholarship. Hands down, the person who scores the most points for most chapters read is Jason Fitzgerald, one of the smartest and kindest people I know. Despite having his own heavy workload of reading and writing, Jason continually made time for my project, and I cannot thank him enough for his generosity. I also want to thank Beth Wenger for inviting me to be part of a Jewish studies writing group in Philadelphia. Having the ability to share my work with other scholars was not only helpful but also morale boosting. I especially want to thank those individuals who gave feedback on chapters, including Lila Corwin Berman, Dianne Ashton, Rebecca Alpert, Arthur Kiron, Reena Friedman, and Deborah Waxman.

The stress of writing and research can sometimes be overwhelming, and the emotional support and encouragement of friends and family kept me focused on the goal. Murray Baumgarten and Michael Cowan, grad school advisers where this work had its genesis, have remained faithful cheerleaders since the beginning. In Philadelphia, I have been surrounded by a warm cadre of friends, especially Miriam Steinberg-Egeth, Gershon Cattan, Mitch Ginsburgh, Rebecca Bar, and Ilana Emmett, who were always there to lend a reassuring ear.

This book would not have been possible without the support of Leslie Mitchner at Rutgers University Press, who truly understood and backed my vision. I also want to thank India Cooper for her crackerjack job of copyediting the manuscript.

I want to thank my parents, especially my mom, who instilled in me a love of the arts, particularly musical theater, from a young age. I am so lucky as well to have the love and support of my sister, Deena, and her entire family. Finally, my grandma never hesitated to ask me "how the book is going," and knowing that she cared made all the difference.

Thanks to everyone who buys and reads this book, especially musical theater lovers, strange lot that we are.

And now, on with the show!

THE GREAT WHITE WAY

Overture

All Singin'! All Dancin'! All White People?

When I was nine, my parents took me to see my first musical: the national tour of *42nd Street*, the hit 1980 show that had taken Broadway by storm and five years later was still doing boffo business in New York and on the road. We took our seats at the Playhouse Theatre in Wilmington, Delaware, and what I saw for the next two and a half hours changed my life forever. As I followed the story of young chorus hopeful Peggy Sawyer and the backstage drama of *Pretty Lady*, the 1933 Broadway musical that producer Julian Marsh is trying to turn into a hit, I was transported to a world of music, dance, and spectacle that I had never before experienced. An opening number had all these people dancing together in perfect unison. How did they do that, and how did their feet make that metallic rapping sound? One number called "Dames" had beautiful women in spectacular multicolored gowns parading about, while "Shuffle Off to Buffalo" featured a train onstage! My favorite moment, though, was a song called "We're in the Money," in which the chorus, costumed in matching shiny outfits to evoke coins, tap danced on giant 1933 Mercury dimes. I even got my first cast album that day; its bold red cover with the show's logo—a sexy woman staring coquettishly at me—opened up to reveal photos from the original Broadway production. I would spend hours poring over the images in the days that followed as I listened to the album again and again, re-creating in my head what I had witnessed live onstage.

42nd Street was the first of many musicals I would see in what would become a passion of mine, but that particular show has left a lasting impression to this day. Not only do I retain strong memories—the staging of "Go into Your Dance" remains as distinct as if I saw it yesterday—but more than that, I was mesmerized by the magic of the musical itself. It was pure entertainment: fantastic singing and dancing coupled with lavish costumes and sets. To say I was dazzled would be an understatement. The show depicted a world where everyone was cheerful and happy endings reigned supreme. If that was what musicals were, I was sold. It is probably this utopian vision coupled with the visceral liveness of performance that explains my lifelong love affair with this art. Yes, straight plays have a magical quality as well, but as much as I like them, they lack the *jouissance* that a musical provides, taking the dramatic action to more transcendent, more emotional highs. When the characters in a show sing and dance, I am transported to what can only be termed "musical theater heaven," a state of bliss that few other art forms can compete with.

And yet, despite all this, we have been duped. The happy-go-lucky, toe-tapping, belt-to-the-rafters Broadway musical has blinded us with its songs and dances, making us think that it is the most innocent of art forms when, in fact, it is one of America's most powerful, influential, and even at times polemical arts *precisely* because it often seems to be about nothing at all.

Take again *42nd Street*. It may be one of the giddiest shows in the canon of musical theater, but it's also a vehicle that promulgates white privilege and white racial favoritism. *42nd Street* has us believe that any talented understudy can get the "big break" and become a star like Peggy Sawyer from Allentown, PA, but the truth is, if Peggy Sawyer were black, or any race other than white, she would never have gotten the job; she wouldn't even have been given the chance to audition.

For some, this observation may seem incidental, even irrelevant. *42nd Street* doesn't involve any dialogue that explicitly discusses race, so how can it be an issue? This isn't *Show Boat* or *South Pacific*, whose racial ideologies and narratives are writ large. But that is precisely one of the grossest misreadings of musicals, that because they seem so frivolous, they can only be about race, gender, class, or other issues of social importance when they explicitly tell us that they are. In fact, many musicals reveal a great deal about such topics, even when they don't appear to, and that's what makes the American musical such a deceptively potent form. It sings, dances, and performs its politics in plain sight, but we the audience are so mesmerized by the spectacle that a show's social context and ideologies may become difficult to see.

While a number of serious musicals do exist, the stereotype of the genre as a whole is that musicals are fanciful, silly, throwaway entertainments that have nothing profound to offer.[1] As the theater historian Gerald Mast has said, the common perception of musicals is that they are "essentially frivolous and silly diversions: lousy drama and lousy music."[2] People typically say they go to musicals because they want to be entertained or because they want to escape from the real world for a few hours, but many of Broadway's best and most famous shows do more than provide a lighthearted evening of song and dance; they tell us profound truths about the world in which we live.

While the musical engages with a variety of social topics, the issue of race takes precedence. It is no coincidence that the American musical comes into its own in the twentieth century, a time of great racial upheaval. African American scholar and activist W.E.B. Du Bois wrote presciently in his 1903 book *The Souls of Black Folk* that "the problem of the Twentieth Century is the problem of the color-line."[3] Du Bois made this statement just a few years into the century, not knowing what the future would hold, but his was an observation that would more than ring true in a hundred years of civil rights battles, immigration influx, multicultural political correctness, and color-blind affirmative action. The musical finds its own history intersecting with the legacy of popular music in America from ragtime to jazz to rock and roll, musical forms that are infused with the cultural contributions of African Americans and immigrants, especially Jews. And yet, ironically, there are few blacks, Jews, or other minorities of any stripe to be seen onstage; rather the musical seems to be, at least on the surface, the domain of white people. Plainly put, the history of the American musical is the history of white identity in the United States.

The Great White Way is a journey into the depths of the Broadway musical to reveal its complicated racial layers. The book examines major works of the American musical canon and the ways in which white identity has been shaped, protected, and upheld by this art form for over one hundred years. Despite the seeming silence about race, we don't have to look too hard to see that the musical has always been interested in questions of race and ethnicity, sometimes in ways that were quite forthright (*South Pacific*) and sometimes in ways that were more subtle (*The Music Man*). In fact, if you make a list of the key shows that are said to have revolutionized the American musical theater—*Show Boat, Oklahoma!, West Side Story,* and *A Chorus Line*—each one is about race on one level or another. And those are only the watershed musicals. Other popular works like *Annie Get Your Gun, Flower Drum Song,* and *The Will Rogers Follies* also engage with racial matters. The topic is most interesting, counterintuitively perhaps, with shows like *Hello, Dolly!, 42nd Street,* and *The Music Man* that are populated mainly if not exclusively with white people and don't seem to have anything to do with race. Paradoxically, their silence about race actually speaks volumes and reveals that it is frequently difficult for white identity to mark itself at all in this country.

Further complicating this whole mix is the fact that the Broadway musical is one of the few art forms, aside from jazz and film, that is homegrown in America. The musical has its roots in European forms including opera, operetta, British pantomime, and the music hall, but it also emerges out of the American tradition of vaudeville and the racist practice of minstrel shows with their use of blackface. Like the racial histories that constitute America itself from slavery to immigration, so too is the American musical a mélange of influences and styles, ultimately taking shape as a popular, middlebrow cultural art form that aimed to be accessible to the masses in ways that seemed quite appropriately democratic.

Yet despite the presumed "all-Americanness" of the genre, even a quick perusal of most musicals reveals that "all Americans" are not well represented by this art. This despite the theater historian Stuart Hecht claiming that "blacks, women, gays, and Latino/Latinas" also used the musical as a mode of integration into American society, and that the Broadway musical is "our 'cultural Ellis Island' as it provides access to U.S. culture not unlike how Ellis Island once welcomed immigrants to America's New York shores."[4] Hecht's assertion, comparing the histories of blacks, gays, and women to those of immigrants, though, is neither true nor defensible. While gay men have made major contributions to musical theater, the other groups have not been granted full access to creating Broadway shows, let alone succeeded in putting fair representations of themselves onstage.[5] No, to be quite specific about it, the musical, with few exceptions, is written *by* white people, *for* white people, and is *about* white people.[6] From its creators to its consumers, the musical firmly reflects a white outlook on American life.[7] All this only holds, of course, if we can agree that musicals are "white" at all. Often they are presented as being raceless or "universal" in content. "As long as race is something only applied to non-white people," writes Richard Dyer in his book *White*, "as long as white people are not racially seen and named, they/we function as a human norm. Other people are raced, we are just people."[8]

Though there is a tenacious white hold on this art form, few scholars and even fewer aficionados have considered the genre as a site of manipulative racial politics. And why would they? It's sometimes hard to see beyond the perfectly executed tap dancing and sleek costumes. Instead, the American musical is repeatedly written off as inconsequential, because it would appear that the all-singin', all-dancin' musical is too occupied with entertaining its middlebrow masses to articulate any sort of politics, racial or otherwise. The musical's seeming simplicity and apparent lack of seriousness becomes the cover that serves to mask its more complicated and even insidious political views. The musical, after all, is marked by a vague white anxiety about race, a point substantiated by the theater historian David Savran, who, remarking about the connection among middlebrow culture, anxiety, and the Cold War, claims that "middlebrow cultural producers, consumers, and critics alike are always looking over their shoulders; always fearful of encroachments from above or below."[9] While Savran doesn't discuss race as an "anxiety" issue, one might argue that the 1950s, falling right in the heart of the Golden Age of the Broadway musical and intersecting at a moment in which postwar white suburbia was the new American Dream, were a time in which anxiety about nonwhites was a more than present concern.

How do we explain, though, the connection between whiteness and the American musical, as well as the stubborn love that many individuals like myself have for the art? Are those points at all connected? The fact that in terms of their content and structure musicals are often about community, about people coming together, both onstage to sing and dance and in the audience to watch, partially explains the form's appeal. Musicals are also often utopic, imagining a world in which nothing is wrong, or if something *is* wrong, it's nothing that can't be fixed with a little soft shoe or a high-belting anthem. But it's these two facets, the sense of community and utopic promise, that have race built into them, albeit tacitly. Community really means *white* community, while people of color are often absent from the utopia that many musicals present.

I admit that part of my own love for these shows stems from the musical's unabashed naïveté, wearing its heart on its sleeve, pronouncing its emotions loudly and boldly wherever it goes. However, the musical resonates not just on this "sappy" personal level but on a larger macro level as well. If our country's national narrative is in part predicated on the American Dream, the belief that America is the land of opportunity, community, happiness, and freedom, then the Broadway musical might be the art form that best captures these desires and hopes. The Broadway musical, after all, *is* about America, but it's an imaginary America, one in which the country's real problems—poverty, social inequality, racism, and misogyny—often disappear. The musical by its nature indulges in flights of fancy, a world in which people bursting into song is not the exception but its defining characteristic.

What we love about musicals is the songs, and musicals, unlike straight plays or film, operate on at least two levels: the spoken and the sung, which are then combined, sometimes with dance, to create a seamless work of art that we know today as the "integrated musical." The musical theater scholar Scott McMillin, however, challenges the concept of the "integrated musical" and argues that "the [musical] numbers interrupt our normal sense of character and plot with song and dance, and what we are left with is not the 'one' but the 'multiple.'"[10] Musicals *always* work on multiple levels, McMillin believes, but rather than becoming a unified integrated whole, song and dance actually pull us *out* of the moment, stopping the progression of narrative time so we can enjoy the song. Song in a musical becomes an enhanced level of emotional expression, a cathartic moment for the character and potentially for the audience as well. When a character can no longer fully express herself in dialogue, she erupts into song, revealing what is in her heart. *Carousel*'s "If I Loved You," *Les Misérables*'s "On My Own," and *My Fair Lady*'s "I Could Have Danced All Night" take the character and audience to new transcendent levels and serve as moments of deep confession, intense sadness, and unadulterated joy. Yet apropos of this discussion of race, Richard Dyer argues: "Bursting from the confines of life by singing your heart out and dancing when you feel like it—this is the joy of the musical. Where the musical most disturbingly constructs a vision of race is in the fact that it is whites' privilege to be able to do this, and what that tells us about the white dream of being in the world."[11] In fact, musicals even have a formulaic way of expressing this longing known as the "I want" song, which allows a character to announce what he or she desires.[12] With few exceptions, though, nonwhite characters, unless they are the main characters in a show such as *Dreamgirls* or *Flower Drum Song*, are not given "I want" songs. Musicals, then, are about freedom of expression, about longings, but only for a select group of people.

Despite the fact that the key element that defines the modern musical is the integration of the score with the libretto, the songs, regardless of what anyone says, still occupy the prime place of importance. A character may sing when he is excited or when he wants to divulge a secret either to other characters or to us in soliloquy fashion. Because of this function, songs are where subtext is revealed. This is different from a straight play in which, with only one level (the spoken word) to contend with, the subtext remains just that: unspoken if not altogether hidden from view, left to percolate between the lines. In a play, if one character is in love with another character but is too shy to say anything, the attraction may be hinted at but never fully announced. In a musical, the character does just the opposite. She sings about the attraction as an unburdening of what she feels. With this logic, it would appear that there is no further subtext to reveal, because everything has already been expressed. Scott McMillin suggests:

> Often a number seems to express a character's deep feeling, as though song and dance can reach into the area of subtext and transform the private motivations found there into performability. . . . If the subtext is to be explored by the realistic actor in the legitimate theater, it is to be changed into accessible song and dance formats in the musical. *There is no subtext the musical cannot get to*, and once gotten to, the hidden motive will be obvious to everyone, transformed into a different beat, into a melody that can be shared, into a lyric others can join.[13]

Where does this leave the issue of race? In a musical, if something is important, it is sung about, and musicals are rarely places for subtlety. They just tell us what we need to know, and unless a musical chooses to offer a song about racial ideology (an arguably tedious and didactic move indeed), there is no easy way to give ideology its due. Given this, the musical is often silent, literally, about race. If a moment is deemed worthy of a song, we are meant to sit up and take notice. The question remains: what happens to the moments that aren't musicalized? Do they matter less? How does the rift between what is sung, what is spoken, and what is silent alter what we perceive to be the musical's driving dramatic force? Or, more significantly, do racial ideologies that remain hidden and unvoiced actually have more power because they are left to propagate their ideas in ways that are much more subversive because they go unchallenged and unquestioned?

Musicals are all about heightened expression, and yet the thematic of race is typically given the silent treatment, with one major exception: *nonwhite* characters frequently engage race and ethnicity via song, from Joe in *Show Boat's* "Ol' Man River" to the company of *Flower Drum Song* in "Chop Suey." In *West Side Story*, the Sharks sing "America," which contrasts life in Puerto Rico with their new lives in America, but the Jets, the Sharks' rival gang, never get a song that explicitly addresses their racial identity, despite the fact that the librettist Arthur Laurents describes them as "an anthology of what is called 'American.'"[14] The Jets' own racial identity might be best termed "newly white" or "off-white" given that they are second-generation Americans, whose parents—Poles, Italians, and other white ethnics—are new to the country, hardly "pristine" Anglo Saxons. Yet, despite the immigrant status of both gangs, only the Sharks are racialized within the framework of the musical. The erasure of whiteness in this show contributes to the conception that race is not something that marks or affects whites. We only think about race when it is explicitly pointed out to us. In the musical, whites control racial discourse, and people of color are situated as "problems" to be solved.

The power of the musical derives from the notion that everything is in plain sight. Thus, the common audience perception of the musical as "simplistic" or "unsophisticated" is in part derived from the fact that it has nothing to conceal. This tactic of appearing to hide nothing is the same strategy employed by whiteness; whiteness marks itself and its concomitant politics as invisible. Whiteness just "is." It is the norm, it is all surface. Of course, whiteness is not this bland monolithic entity, devoid of substance. The ability for whiteness to constantly erase itself, to make it appear as if it is nothing at all, is precisely where its power comes from.[15] Whiteness, like the American musical, is a paradox. It insinuates its politics of normativity and racial privilege by not announcing its presence. The novelist Toni Morrison suggests that "the act of enforcing racelessness in literary discourse is itself a racial act."[16] When whites do not draw attention to their racial identity, it is not a simple omission, but a move in which rendering whiteness invisible has the effect of downplaying whiteness's cultural and political influence and power.[17]

Pushing further on this similarity, musicals mirror the nature of racism in the United States, which George Lipsitz, the author of *The Possessive Investment in Whiteness*, sees as divided along individual and collective lines. Lipsitz elucidates: "As long as we define social life as the sum total of conscious and deliberative individual activities, we will be able to discern as racist only *individual* manifestations of personal prejudice and hostility. Systemic, collective, and coordinate group behavior consequently drops out of sight."[18] In other words, it's easier to identify and condemn individual acts of racism, such as hate speech, than to combat societal and institutional racism, despite the latter's being more pervasive, because systemic racism is harder to see. Following this model, in a musical, songs like *South Pacific*'s "You've Got to Be Carefully Taught" that explicitly reference racism are the "individual acts," while the show's unspoken yet racialized ideologies occupy the site of collective racialized behavior that remains hidden. Whites, whether in life or in musicals, are only deemed "racist" if they explicitly discriminate against nonwhites, while institutional racisms go unpunished and whiteness goes unmarked.

Consider further the following example. English professor Mike Hill opens his book *After Whiteness*, an examination into the vicissitudes of white identity in the early twenty-first century, by describing his visit to the 2002 American Renaissance (AR) conference. American Renaissance is a white nationalist organization that wants to protect the future and "interests" of white people against the encroaching "dangers" of an increasingly nonwhite population in the United States. If AR is not outwardly violent,

Hill still sees it as exemplifying a new strain of white supremacy in America, racist at its core.[19] Here's the question, though. To what extent is *The Music Man* (or better yet a current-day revival of the show) any different from AR? American Renaissance is invested in a reactionary, nostalgic view of American society in which the formation of a homogeneous white community is the norm. Is this not what *The Music Man*, a musical that celebrates small-town white America at the turn of the twentieth century, is also about? I'm being purposely provocative here to make a point. The line between AR and *The Music Man* is more unclear and diffuse than we might think. We tend to think of racism as outright, explicit calls for white superiority, but is not an *unspoken* worldview that propagates white exclusivity essentially the same thing? I'm not trying to paint *Music Man* creator Meredith Willson as some vile racist, but clearly there is a racial ideology at work in this show that needs to be examined. *The Music Man* might be just one show, but if we consider that Broadway musicals of the forties, fifties, and sixties, many of which privilege all-white communities, make up a large preponderance of Broadway's revival offerings in the last thirty years, we have to ask, isn't Broadway in its own way advocating for a nostalgic return to white America? While the theater scholar Jill Dolan sees theater as a place of utopia, a potential site of hope and promise, the musical occupies a position that is simultaneously utopic *and* nostalgic.[20] A paradox to be sure, but not an impossibility. Most of us cringe at the politics of American Renaissance because they outwardly repulse us, but we continue to sing along to *The Music Man* and plunk down good hard-earned dollars to see the show without questioning what it is that we're watching.

The thematic of white privilege that informs many musicals often goes muted, which actually allows these works to enact a form of white supremacy. You might scratch your head over this. Is Ado Annie secretly a neo-Nazi? Maybe you're picturing the cast of *Bye Bye Birdie* in KKK hoods. Or a gang of skinheads producing a wholesome revival of *She Loves Me*. While the concept of "white supremacy" is used at its most extreme as a marker of Aryan racial superiority or virulent racist prejudice, I am more interested in the way in which George Lipsitz looks at white supremacy and what he has termed "the possessive investment in whiteness." He writes: "The adjective 'possessive' [is used] to stress the relationship between whiteness and asset accumulation in our society, to connect attitudes to interests, to demonstrate that white supremacy is usually less a matter of direct, referential, and snarling contempt than a system for protecting the privileges of whites by denying communities of color opportunities for asset accumulation and upward mobility."[21] In this articulation, white supremacy is not some sort of rabid, explicit version of racial hatred but a more subtle yet fiercely pervasive social and economic ideology. At times this belief system may be imperceptible, so embedded are its machinations in our country's national psyche. Arguably, in addition to being the great all-American art form, the musical is uniquely positioned, given its combination of music and text, to carefully hide its hegemonic racial politics in plain view of its audiences. Beyond the obvious details of white creators, characters, and consumers, the musical maintains its power and force as a major cultural white art form by carefully erasing its racial investments and refocusing its sights elsewhere, namely on nonwhites, while white identity and American identity are rolled into one normative indistinguishable package.

Keeping with this line of thinking, I want to offer a larger metareading of the musical and make a case for why the study and analysis of musical theater has been so neglected until quite recently.[22] The majority of studies on the musical have emphasized its structural history, tracing its origins and development from opera and operetta through several major watershed moments: (1) *Show Boat* in 1927, (2) *Oklahoma!* in 1943, (3) the Golden Age of Broadway in the 1940s, 1950s, and 1960s, (4) rock musicals and the work of Stephen Sondheim in the 1970s, and (5) revivals and the decline of Broadway in the 1980s and beyond.[23] Essentially wiping out all other contextual concerns that have impinged on the musical, including sexual, gender, and racial issues, the history of the musical has come to resemble the plot of a Broadway show itself: a rags-to-riches story in which a highbrow European art form, combined with immigrant contributions, assimilates and becomes the all-American middlebrow musical comedy. If the topic of minority identity is addressed at all, it is engaged either as a problem to be solved (the Sharks in *West Side Story*) or as a rallying point around which to build communal pride (Asian identity in *Flower Drum Song*). To read the musical for its normative whiteness might seem either an obvious choice or a nonissue, but the absence of such a critique speaks to just how powerful and pervasive this ideology has been in shaping the content and structure of this art form.[24]

While some theater scholars have looked at nonwhite racial issues in the Broadway musical, as Richard Wright, the author of *Native Son*, reminds us in his insightful inversion of American racial politics: "There isn't any Negro problem; there is only a white problem."[25] This book applies the strategies of whiteness studies to the American musical so as to make a case for reading the racial content of musicals beyond the world of minority politics. In doing so, I show how musicals create images of America that uphold, even inadvertently, white supremacy. The plots of many musicals are predicated on the belief that true love, a good job, and/ or wealth will come to everyone in due time, but the musical perpetrates notions of white supremacy by speciously pretending that such rewards are available to all when in fact they are accessible only to some. Color-blind casting might be a partial remedy for this problem, but ignoring a musical's historical context or assuming that white shows *are* universal propagates white normativity and overlooks the specific challenges that people of color have had to face in the United States.

To further explain how musicals strategically underline their whiteness, I want to address some misconceptions that have often erroneously defined the musical's form and reception, and thereby have subsequently reinforced the perceived racelessness of the musical. While some critics are finally beginning to treat the musical with a level of academic rigor and sophistication previously missing, an overly nostalgic and quaint approach to the musical still defines much writing about the genre, which is a symptom of the belief that musicals don't have much to say in the first place about race, or anything else for that matter.

Myth #1: All Musicals Are Happy

Despite the fact that a major development in the history of the Broadway musical has been the introduction and handling of serious thematic content, the general perception of the musical is that it is light, frothy fare. Such a notion is well satirized by the 2001 Broadway musical *Urinetown*, which pokes fun at musicals and the way in which characters burst into song at the drop of a hat without winking at the audience. In *Urinetown*, a comic if dystopic view of the future where a water shortage wreaks havoc on society, Little Sally, the young optimistic voice of the show, asks the corrupt Officer Lockstock in a metatheatrical moment:

> What kind of musical is this?! The good guys finally take over and then everything starts falling apart?!
> OFFICER LOCKSTOCK. Like I said, Little Sally, this isn't a happy musical.
> LITTLE SALLY. But the music's so happy!
> (LOCKSTOCK *chuckles*.)
> OFFICER LOCKSTOCK. Yes, Little Sally. Yes it is.[26]

Urinetown is a highly entertaining and funny show, but its underlying plot (supported by Mark Hollman and Greg Kotis's dark Kurt Weill–esque score) is actually a satiric comment on corporate culture and greed. While much hysterical mayhem ensues, multiple characters die or are murdered. This, however, doesn't stop the characters from singing and dancing, all in the most upbeat fashion. Little Sally attempts a final self-aware plea at the show's finale, asking, "Can't we do a happy musical next time?"[27] Little Sally believes, as probably most audiences do, that the musical by definition is an optimistic art form and that something seems amiss when the plot becomes grim.

In this current age of terrorism, economic instability, and widespread unemployment, many Americans, especially when paying $130 or more per ticket to see a Broadway show, want to be taken out of their troubles, not immersed in them. It's no wonder that *42nd Street* with its army of hoofers, *The Lion King* with its spectacular puppets, and *Mamma Mia!* with its catchy, hummable ABBA pop tunes have found success on Broadway. Contrast those shows with three critically acclaimed but topic-heavy box office flops: *Parade*, about the lynching of Jewish American Leo Frank in 1915; *Caroline, or Change*, a musical about a Jewish family and their black maid in Louisiana in the 1960s; and *The Scottsboro Boys*, the real-life story about nine African American young men unjustly accused of raping two white women. It's not difficult to fathom why those shows were not financial blockbusters.[28]

This is not to say that musicals should be gloomy, dull, or labored work meant to teach moral lessons. The German playwright and theorist Bertolt

Brecht, known for his political theater, including the musical *The Three-penny Opera*, states in "A Short Organum for the Theatre" that

> from the first it has been the theatre's business to entertain people, as it also has of all the other arts. It is this business which always gives it its particular dignity; it needs no other passport than fun, but this it has got to have. We should not by any means be giving it a higher status if we were to turn it e.g. into a purveyor of morality; it would on the contrary run the risk of being debased, and this would occur at once if it failed to make its moral lesson enjoyable, and enjoyable to the senses at that: a principle, admittedly, by which morality can only gain.[29]

Theater must be pleasurable, and most Broadway musicals excel at this, but audiences become so hungry for entertainment that they willingly gloss over deeper issues, particularly racial themes, contained within. If a musical does dare to explicitly engage with race, the show often handles the topic in a way that simplifies matters and makes its audiences (white liberals?) feel good about themselves for thinking either that they are not racist or that they have defeated racism.[30]

What's even stranger, particularly given all the pleasure associated with the musical, is all the dead bodies that have littered the plots of shows that profess to be upbeat. Take *Oklahoma!*, for example. Audiences never seemed fazed by the fact that the villain, Jud Fry (who doesn't read as fully white), is killed five minutes before the show's conclusion, and his gruesome demise—he falls on his own knife—is quickly washed away by a cheerful reprise of "Oh, What a Beautiful Mornin'." Everything might be "goin' their way" for Curly, Laurey, and the rest of the white characters in *Oklahoma!*, but Jud and the musical's never seen or referenced Native Americans who are stripped of their land by white settlers could hardly share in such heady optimism.

Characters in many of Rodgers and Hammerstein's other shows don't fare much better. Lt. Joe Cable is killed in an airplane crash in *South Pacific*; Billy Bigelow, the raffish carousel barker, kills himself in *Carousel*; and the eponymous king of *The King and I* succumbs to natural causes at the end of that show. Throw in the deaths of Tony, Riff, and Bernardo in *West*

Side Story, the demise of Latino transvestite Angel in *Rent*, and all the characters who die in Stephen Sondheim's *Into the Woods*, and suddenly the classics of the American musical, both Golden Age and contemporary, don't seem such friendly places anymore.

And it's not just death that marks many of these shows. The 1927 musical *Show Boat* contains plot threads of spousal abandonment, miscegenation, alcoholism, and racism. *Fiddler on the Roof* and *Cabaret* both involve violent outbursts of anti-Semitism. *Man of La Mancha*, based on Cervantes's *Don Quixote*, even features a rape scene. Yet despite the heavy thematics of such works, audiences often willfully look past these depressing moments and embrace the genre as a whole with the rationale that if it's a musical, it must be happy. Racial matters, the cause of much conflict in this country, are often overlooked by viewers or not taken seriously because such issues are not typically seen as fitting the stereotype of what the Broadway musical is.

Myth #2: Show Tunes Are Just Pretty Music

The 1946 musical biopic about Broadway composer Jerome Kern, *Till the Clouds Roll By*, concludes with a strange final sequence. Perched upon a white pedestal, Frank Sinatra, dressed in a white tuxedo and surrounded by a large orchestra and all-white chorus, also attired completely in white, sings one of Kern's most famous songs, "Ol' Man River" from *Show Boat*. It is an uncanny moment as Sinatra, not changing any of the lyrics, sings about lifting bales of cotton, toting barges, and ending up drunk in jail. Forgoing for the moment any discussion of how well these lyrics actually define the black characters of *Show Boat*, here the words are ludicrous, if not downright insulting, coming out of Sinatra's mouth. Sinatra performs the number in his inimitable fashion, which is to say he doesn't have the least idea of what he is singing about. As the song reaches its soaring climax, the camera pulls back and we see the huge white set, resembling a wedding cake, on which Sinatra and the musicians are perched, an enormous stage designed to look like some fantastic interpretation of musical comedy heaven. The visual clash of the sequence's overwhelming whiteness, from its scenery and costumes to numerous white bodies, with the song's original function as a comment on the mistreatment of African Americans is unsettling. Sinatra is not to be blamed for this sad parody.

The explanation is simply that "Ol' Man River" has achieved that coveted status of "classic show tune," divorced from its original context and left to circulate in the air as "pretty music."

When show tunes enter the canon of popular music, they are freed from the confines of narrative and story, and in this scenario, the lyric may become less important and all we hear is the melody. The modern musical might have given us the "integrated form," but it hasn't stopped songs from being excerpted from their scores. Indeed, when the musical was in its Golden Age in the mid-twentieth century (and even before, for that matter), show tunes were popular hits that easily circulated outside the show, potentially making them seem as if they lacked a context. Thus, one can sit in a dentist's office and listen to "One" from *A Chorus Line* and "America" from *West Side Story* as Muzak and enjoy the songs without the messy encumbrance of the show itself.

The significance of severing songs from their shows is profound. The political ideologies contained in such songs, whether they be race-, sex-, or class-based, temporarily disappear, and the show tunes are free to disseminate into popular culture as "harmless" and "inconsequential" music that people can hum without having to process the accompanying context. When show tunes are covered by pop artists, turned into elevator music, or sung at piano bars or karaoke lounges, their racial content is disrupted. While it might seem as if this would attenuate the power of the musical, all it does is encourage the belief that musicals have nothing to say in the first place. As Barbara Fields says about the construction of race, "ideas about color, like ideas about anything else, derive their importance, indeed their very definition, from their context."[31] If we accept the idea, as many historians and scholars before me have suggested, that race is a socially constructed, historically specific, and contextualizable category whose meanings change over time, insofar as the musical is a marker and reflection of racial identity, it too only retains meaning when placed in a specific context. While such a statement could perhaps be made of any art form, show tunes are untethered from their contexts more often than other works of art, free-floating in the pop culture ether as if they lacked origin, history, or even a specific story. If race is all about context, what happens when that context goes missing?

Myth #3: Musicals Don't Matter outside New York

Without a doubt, New York is the musical theater epicenter of the world. I still remember my first trip to the Big Apple from Philadelphia in the early 1990s to see *The Phantom of the Opera*. I was wowed as a young high school student, but my trip to *Phantom* was hardly my first foray to the theater. I might have been late in getting to New York, but compared to many of my friends, I saw a lot of theater as a child, often a variety of musicals that passed through Philadelphia and nearby Wilmington, Delaware.

True, the musical's roots are in New York City. This is due in part to the city's ethnic makeup; it's a city of immigrants and ethnic minorities. Jewish Americans, in particular, contributed directly to the development of musical theater, precisely at the time of its growth and maturation. Where other jobs or industries were closed off to Jews, musical theater was a place, still in its early twentieth-century infancy, where individuals without status could secure footing and break into this burgeoning field.[32] This, combined with the fact that New York has a centralized theater district, Times Square, made New York the birthplace of the American musical.

Theater still remains one of the largest draws for tourists in New York, but it would be wrong to equate musical theater solely with the ten square blocks or so of Times Square. According to the League of American Theaters and Producers, which publishes statistics about audience makeup, gross ticket sales, and other economic facets of the "biz," in 2010–2011, Broadway road and touring companies earned a gross of $804 million and saw an audience of 13.1 million people. During that same year, the League calculated that Broadway itself brought in $1.080 billion, an amount that exceeded touring shows presumably because of the higher prices that Broadway charges, but only playing to 12.53 million people. These numbers far exceed the profits and attendance records of twenty-five years ago; for the 1984–1985 touring season, gross profits totaled a mere $226 million, and 8.2 million people attended. Similarly, the Broadway season in 1984 saw a gross of $209 million and played to 7.34 million people.[33] In both cases, theater reached more people *on the road* than it did in New York. That the bulk of touring productions is made up of musicals—straight plays almost never go on tour, as they historically have had a hard time finding audiences in large theaters that seat a thousand or more—gives a sense of the reach that musicals possess. Contrary to the misconception that musicals are "dead" or "uncool," Americans are shelling out more money than ever before to go to the theater. With the appearance of TV shows like *Glee* and *Smash* and silver screen adaptations of older works like *Chicago, Les Misérables,* and *Dreamgirls* winning new fans and awards, musicals are still very much a part of our country's pop culture landscape.[34]

And these statistics only speak to professional Broadway companies. Regional, community, stock, amateur, and school productions make up another set of performances that circulate in our society. According to Music Theatre International (MTI), the 1957 musical *West Side Story* is licensed hundreds of times every year to amateur companies.[35] From California to Maine, audiences far away from major metropolises attend this classic show and thus are influenced by the show's racial ideologies. Even if the audience is mainly parents who are cheering on their kids, they too absorb the show's racial politics on a subconscious level.

Live performances of musicals clearly remain ubiquitous in American culture, but they are far from the only ways in which musicals circulate. When *Oklahoma!* premiered in 1943 and was hailed for contributing new features to the musical theater genre, it was also notable for introducing the modern cast album. Though *Oklahoma!* was not the first cast recording—earlier musicals had released 78s featuring song selections, sometimes with and sometimes without original cast members—the phenomenal success of *Oklahoma!* at the Majestic Theatre led Decca Records to record the show with its full original cast and orchestra. Unlike previous selections albums, the songs were presented in the order in which they were performed in the show, thereby creating a virtual theatergoing experience. The resulting cast album with "a full-cast cover shot, with photographs of the individual numbers on the inside left cover, and perhaps a leaflet of lyrics and synopsis, . . . would function not only as a souvenir for theatregoers but as a substitute for those across the country who didn't have access to the show." The cast recording of *Oklahoma!* was an economic windfall for Decca Records and sold "well over a million units at a time when very few *single* discs reached that level: and this was a set of six."[36]

After the success of *Oklahoma!,* other shows soon followed suit, and most musicals, even smaller off-Broadway shows and flops, have been recorded. Thanks to this practice, musicals can circulate far from New York, and theater fans can listen to the same show again and again (as I first did with my cast recording of *42nd Street*). The repeatability of cast recordings allows the social ideologies that shows contain to imprint themselves on their listeners. In turn, these individuals form a unified community across time and space joined by a love for musical theater. In *Place for Us*, the queer theorist D. A. Miller acknowledges the significance of this virtual community for gay men of a certain age who found solace and community by listening to cast recordings and attending Broadway musicals. Though Miller is right to focus attention on this important subgroup of individuals who have become some of the form's most ardent fans, stereotypes aside, Broadway audiences are comprised of more than gay men. Talking with baby boomers, both gay and straight, who grew up during the Golden Age of Broadway often reveals stories of how their childhoods were spent listening to cast albums or going to the theater, so central was the musical to the mainstream culture of the 1940s through the 1960s.

Another important factor in the dissemination of musical theater is, of course, film. Movie musicals have been around since 1927, as one might consider the first "talkie," *The Jazz Singer*, a musical, since it featured its star, Al Jolson, performing several numbers, mainly in blackface. Musicals were ideally suited to showing off the new technological capabilities of sound motion pictures, and frivolous and escapist musicals, many of which marked the years of the Great Depression, became staples of moviegoing. Though these early films included a 1936 film adaptation of the landmark musical *Show Boat*, the majority of early Hollywood musicals were of the standard boy-meets-girl variety with a bevy of attractive chorus girls thrown in for good measure.

With the success of the stage production of *Oklahoma!*, though, movie musicals, like their stage counterparts, entered a Golden Age as well. All the major Rodgers and Hammerstein shows (*Oklahoma!*, *Carousel*, *The King and I*, *South Pacific*, *The Sound of Music*, and even *Flower Drum Song*) went on to have screen adaptations. Other major shows from the forties through the sixties, including *Annie Get Your Gun*, *The Music Man*, *West Side Story*, *Damn Yankees*, *Fiddler on the Roof*, *Cabaret*, and *Kiss Me, Kate*, got decent and in some cases excellent stage-to-screen transfers. Not only were such films hits when released, bringing in new audiences who in some cases had never seen the original stage productions, but in recent years, through cable television, the technology of video recorders and DVDs, and now online websites like YouTube and Netflix, many films are just a click of the remote or a keyword search away. These movies, like cast recordings, circulate in virtually every corner of this country as well as abroad. Thus, musicals have not only propagated their political ideologies here at home, but they have carried their messages overseas, where they serve as seemingly transparent reflections of America.

That racial ideologies become subconsciously pervasive is made evident by Latino scholar Alberto Sandoval-Sánchez's firsthand experience with white reactions to the film of *West Side Story.* He writes:

> The musical film *West Side Story* was frequently imposed upon me as a model of/for my Puerto Rican ethnic identity. Certainly it was a strange and foreign model for a newcomer, but not for the Anglo-Americans who actualized, with my bodily presence, their stereotypes of Latino otherness. Over and over again, to make me feel comfortable in their family rooms and to tell me of their knowledge about Puerto Ricans, they would start their conversations with *West Side Story*: "Al, we loved *West Side Story.*" "Have you seen the movie?" "Did you like it?" On other occasions, some people even sang parodically in my ears: "Alberto, I've just met a guy named Alberto." And, how can I forget those who, upon my arrival, would start tapping flamenco steps and squealing: "I like to be in America!/ Everything free in America."[37]

West Side Story gave people, particularly whites, a representational vocabulary to talk about Latinos. In the ears of white listeners, "America" is "just" a show tune, devoid of racial intent, but cast recordings and films of Broadway musicals have worked to reinforce and construct racialized stereotypes of entire groups of people in just such seemingly innocuous ways.

Who You Calling White?

Before we go any further, I need to discuss the terms *whiteness* and *race* as they play out in this study. The concepts they refer to are not nearly as fixed as some people might think, and much ink has been spilled tracing the fascinating permutations that whiteness and other racial categories underwent over the course of the twentieth century in America. While the focus of this book is not to articulate this genealogy, understanding some key moments in the shift of both concepts, *whiteness* and *race* itself, is helpful. Today, race, despite all the sophisticated arguments that have suggested otherwise, is often still reduced in commonsense fashion to a "simple" matter of skin color. Staying with a standard binary for the moment, white people are those individuals with white skin, while black people are those individuals with black or brown skin. Of course, this doesn't hold for multiple reasons. Skin color is not a clear indication of race, and individuals of mixed-race heritage may exhibit skin color that privileges one part of their background more than another.[38] Then too, this binary is just that, a black-and-white dichotomy that doesn't even begin to address the complicated ways in which other races (Asian, Hispanic, Native American) also circulate in U.S. society and occupy various locations along the white/black divide that structures this country.

Numerous cases of racial passing have attested to the unreliability of skin color as a stable marker of race. These cases, in which an individual of one race "passes" as a member of another race, most commonly a black individual passing as white, highlight the ways in which race is a performance played out for others, as the character Julie does in *Show Boat*, or even as the Jets do in *West Side Story*, aiming to pass as Anglo-Americans despite their ethnic immigrant roots. Sometimes this performance is coerced or imposed, such as when minorities feel they must behave in ways that white society expects of them. All of us are always performing race, even whites who may not see whiteness as a performance because whiteness exists in this country as a normative category. In fact, it is precisely by making whiteness seem like a *nonperformance*, by not drawing attention to itself, that whiteness maintains its position of power in our society.

To say that race is a performance does not mean it is "make believe" or not real. Rather race does not possess any inherent or predetermined value, but instead, as the whiteness scholar David Roediger suggests, it is "produced in social relations over time and is not biological and fixed."[39] The current liberal understanding of race sees it as " 'made' by humans; how humans have assigned people to one race or another has varied dramatically over time and space; and racial categorizations have no intrinsic meaning or validity aside from the particular social circumstances that engender them."[40] Laws, bodies of power, and cultural texts work together to define race at any given moment, both on a legal level and also on a commonsense level, which is to say how the average person understands or perceives race.

Whereas whiteness is often constructed as normative, whites themselves have often manipulated and controlled the racial performances of others. Take, for example, the practice of blackface as employed in nineteenth-century America. This act, which in most cases involved white men applying burnt cork makeup to their faces to perform a highly exaggerated and racist version of black identity, contributed to how white society saw and thought about blacks. Where blackface was a purposeful exaggeration of black identity, made grotesque through the use of makeup, whiteness, in comparison, seemed "normal" and natural. Blackface, whose main period of popularity lasted from the 1830s through the end of the nineteenth century, was not only a major form of entertainment in this country, it was a major antecedent to musical theater. Blackface acts featured songs, jokes, skits, and dancing, all elements that would be utilized by the musical.

Indeed, the two forms passed like ships in the night in 1927, the year that saw both the premiere of the film *The Jazz Singer*, featuring Jewish American actor Al Jolson in blackface, and the premiere of *Show Boat*, which portrayed race in a more equitable fashion, albeit with the major exception of Tess Gardella, a.k.a. Aunt Jemima, performing the role of Queenie in blackface. If blackface, as Eric Lott describes it, is an act of "love and theft," in which whites exhibit an unspoken envy of and fascination with blacks and their culture while stealing and turning a profit from that same culture (theft), then the American musical can be seen as a direct inheritor of this process, but in much subtler terms.[41] Rather than put black bodies or even the blackface facsimiles onstage, the musical creates an all-white world, but one infused with black culture. Ragtime, jazz, and tap dancing, all music and dance staples originally emerging from black culture, are appropriated by whites, especially Jewish creators, and recuperated for mainstream audiences. From George Gershwin's use of jazz and his creation of the black folk opera *Porgy and Bess* to Irving Berlin's take on ragtime and Fred Astaire's tap dancing, black culture had a new face, one that white audiences could feel comfortable watching. While black musicals created by African Americans did exist during the early twentieth century, such now-forgotten shows were segregated from the rest of Broadway and even today are rarely included as part of the larger Broadway canon.

The musicals discussed in this book frequently demonstrate that racial ideologies shift over time, often without great fanfare. Changing understandings of race have brought about profound developments in society: the lessening of societal racism, the opening up of economic equality, and the end of stereotypes. Indeed, the achievements of the civil rights movement can be attributed to the cultural and legal shifts that were part of a process, one that is not yet complete, in which African Americans, in particular, would no longer be treated as secondary citizens.[42]

Seeing the ways in which the category of whiteness itself has been constituted, though, can be difficult, more so than seeing the significant changes that have altered African American identity, life, and legal rights in this country. Rewinding history one hundred years to the moment of mass immigration to the United States from Europe, the Jewish and Italian immigrants who passed through Ellis Island at the turn of the twentieth century, despite the color of their skin, were not "white." Whiteness was a category reserved for individuals of Anglo-Saxon heritage, while Jews, Italians, and the Irish were considered "dark," second-class minorities who often had difficulty finding jobs, getting into schools, and securing housing. While not subjected to the same mistreatment as African Americans, these individuals were still excluded from mainstream whiteness. However, as the twentieth century progressed, the definition of whiteness became more expansive. Those same excluded immigrants, who by midcentury had children of their own and were quickly assimilating into American society, found themselves increasingly embraced by society at large into a new category of whiteness known as "Caucasian."[43]

As for African Americans, Asian Americans, and Latinos, the twentieth century saw a widening of the color line. On one side were whites/Caucasians, and on the other side everyone else. A strange shift, perhaps, but one that can be explained by a desire to embrace those who bear an external phenotypical similarity to oneself. Better to allow non-Anglo European immigrants to assimilate and become white than to provide equal treatment for African Americans or other people of color, who were believed to be inherently inferior.

My genealogy is admittedly oversimplified, but I paint the story with broad strokes to create a basic sense of the racial landscape that informs many musicals. From the whitening of Jews to 1970s ethnic pride, musicals as social products of their time periods are windows into racial identity. Furthermore, seeing that racial categories and concepts change over time emphasizes that race itself is a socially and historically contingent category. Musicals tell the story of these racial shifts, and if there is one predominant theme in the Broadway musical concerning race, it is that "the prospects of becoming American and becoming Caucasian" are "completely intertwined."[44] Given that the musical is deeply invested in American identity and culture, its history cannot be separated out from the story of whiteness in this country.

The Musicals of *The Great White Way*

This book is divided into two parts or "acts," the first looking at shows up through the Golden Age of Broadway, which ended in the 1960s. The second act examines shows from the latter part of the twentieth century through the present. I start where most other books on the musical begin, with Jerome Kern and Oscar Hammerstein II's 1927 *Show Boat*, about a white theatrical troupe that performs up and down the Mississippi River and the black workers who make white privilege possible. My take on the musical, though, is more idiosyncratic. The show usually finds itself entrenched in one of two camps. On one hand, it is typically lauded as the show that revolutionized the musical art form by presenting the audience with a libretto and score of a scope and thematic seriousness that had not been seen before. Such developments would earn the show the title of an "American classic." On the other hand, *Show Boat* has been lamented as a racist text that demeans African Americans by portraying them in stereotypically subservient roles. While these two camps have been construed as mutually exclusive, what both positions overlook is the performance of whiteness itself in grounding the show's racial politics. The white characters in *Show Boat* lead more privileged lives, not because there is anything inherently better about them, but because they can choose the roles they perform in life, while the black characters are not afforded the same luxury. *Show Boat*, which itself is a metamusical about theater, demonstrates the ways in which the musical employs theatrical strategies to allow its characters to construct and perform racial identities, onstage and off.

After *Show Boat*, I look at two midcentury musicals that are about the "Wild West" and Native American identity: *Oklahoma!* (1943) and *Annie Get Your Gun* (1946). Richard Rodgers and Oscar Hammerstein's nationalistic musical about cowboys and ranchers, *Oklahoma!*, never addresses the absence of Native Americans in the musical, despite the fact that the show takes place in Indian Territory. Meanwhile, Irving Berlin and Dorothy and Herbert Fields's *Annie Get Your Gun*, about sharpshooter Annie Oakley and her career in Buffalo Bill's Wild West show, features several Indian characters, most notably Chief Sitting Bull, whose portrayal has been seen as stereotypical if not downright racist. Rather than focus on the Indian representations of the show as simply problematic, which is the typical approach to discussing this musical, I argue that all racial identities including whiteness are consciously performed and speak to the development of new American racial ideologies in the 1940s. *Oklahoma!* and *Annie Get Your Gun*, both products of World War II America, use the mythos of the frontier as a touchstone for American patriotism, cohesive communal identity, and rugged individualism. As for the interplay between white and Indian identities, depending on how the characters in the show (or the shows' creators) wanted to identify and construct their sense of whiteness, they could play the part of cowboys who defended the land against "violent" Indians, or they themselves could align with the Indians as a way to connect to these "First Americans."

Chapter 3 is a comparative analysis of *West Side Story* and *The Music Man*, which both premiered on Broadway in 1957. Despite the creative achievement of *West Side Story*, a then-contemporary retelling of *Romeo and Juliet* set on the streets of New York, it was the overtly white *Music Man*, about a con artist in River City, Iowa, that garnered the Tony Award for Best Musical. While *The Music Man* is a nostalgic throwback to small-town America circa 1912 where people of color are entirely absent, *West Side Story* is about the consolidation and creation of Caucasian identity in the United States in the 1950s within an urban setting. Using archival research, I discuss how *West Side Story* developed from *East Side Story*, the creators' original concept for a musical about Jews and Christians duking it out in the Lower East Side during the holiday of Passover, and the implications this artistic shift had for how we understand Jewish and white identities in the 1950s.

The second act of the book shifts from a text-based study to something more performance-driven. As the twentieth century progresses, the appearance of race in the Broadway musical becomes less about explicit conflict or overt racism and more about the unspoken racial structures that order U.S. society. Indeed, the shows I discuss in the second act are about race, even though they do not explicitly invoke race or whiteness at all. My discussions in the second half of the book focus much more on the normativity of whiteness and trends in casting as opposed to close readings of specific texts. These casting practices, from black productions of white shows to multicultural casting to the return of all-white casting that predominated earlier in the century, are what now shape racial understanding in many of these late twentieth-century works. While the texts of these shows may verbalize very little about race, the performances and the ways the bodies of the actors are utilized divulge a great deal, revealing that racial meaning is sometimes located in the space *between* the text and the performers.

Another thing that occurs in the second part of the book is a shift in the concept of racism itself. In the first part of the twentieth century, racial conflict was heightened and the line between racial categories was more clearly distinguished. At the end of the twentieth century, racism still existed, but how it manifested itself became more subtle. Violent racist acts such as lynchings and the use of derogatory epithets had declined, if not vanished, but were now replaced by *structural* forms of racism that in some ways were more damaging, because they were not only more pervasive but also more difficult to see and therefore to get rid of. By looking at the racial ideologies that impacted these latter shows, we can grasp how race affected work that from a cursory point of view seems to have nothing to do with race.

Chapter 4 is an examination of the phenomenon of black and multiracial productions of white musicals, mainly in the 1970s. These include the Pearl Bailey *Hello, Dolly!* (1967), a mixed-cast production of *The Pajama Game* (1973), an all-black *Guys and Dolls* (1976), *Timbuktu!* (based on *Kismet*) (1978), and David Merrick's next-to-last show, *Oh, Kay!* (1990), an all-black production of an old George and Ira Gershwin musical. Were such shows merely modern-day minstrel shows, or were they at all progressive in offering jobs and new roles to black performers? That these shows emerged mainly during the period of Black Power and ethnic revivalism (late 1960s–1970s) speaks to the uneven ways that the musical genre attempted to address new voices in America. While a great deal of this chapter is about black identity, these productions allow us to get at the heart of what this book is about: the way in which the Broadway musical is a mainly white cultural phenomenon. Black productions of classic shows such as *Hello, Dolly!* and *Guys and Dolls* reveal, inadvertently perhaps, the inherent whiteness of these musicals and challenge us to think about what it means to call a show "universal."

Remaining in the 1970s, we have what was once the longest-running musical: *A Chorus Line* (1975), about a group of dancers auditioning for a Broadway show. While much of the show's success can be attributed to both its strong score by Edward Kleban and Marvin Hamlisch and its fluid direction by Michael Bennett, the show's too-perfect multicultural politics of inclusivity also explains its appeal to audiences of all racial and social backgrounds. *A Chorus Line* suggests that the world operates in color-blind fashion and that race is inconsequential; instead, anyone with talent who works hard, regardless of his or her race, gender, sexuality, ethnicity, social class, or religion, has the potential to get a job, a fanciful white ideology that is quite detached from the workings of the real world. The racial significance of *A Chorus Line* is also considered in light of the history of chorus lines themselves, a theatrical ensemble whose identity is predicated not just on uniformity of costume and movement but also on racial homogeneity.

The final chapter is an examination of two theatrical phenomena that emerged in the 1980s and 1990s and continue today: the creation of new "old" shows and revised musicals (revisals). The new "old" musicals are predicated on white nostalgia and model themselves on the structure of shows from the 1920s and 1930s and/or interpolate classic songs from that era into their scores. Representatives of this category include *42nd Street* (1980) and *The Will Rogers Follies* (1991). These shows, which celebrate the early days of Broadway, emphasize their whiteness both in their casting and their plots, which conspicuously lack people of color and are throwbacks to an all-white period on Broadway. In the case of musical revivals, rather than create new shows that fully represent a truly diversified America, these productions rewrote the librettos of works such as *Annie Get Your Gun* (1999) and *Flower Drum Song* (2001), which have the effect of whitewashing U.S. racial and theatrical history. Both types of shows are a reflection of those decades' newly emergent neoconservative politics, whose racial agenda advocated for a color-blind society that overlooked the nuances of race and seemingly wanted to undo thirty years of civil rights progress.

While not everyone may agree with my analyses of certain shows, I do hope that my readings at least provide a moment of pause and consideration for the genre of musical theater as a whole. So often we simply ignore or write off the musical, but it's an art form that demands our attention and scrutiny. We must continue to make the musical, like whiteness, visible, as it is a significant contributor to this country's rich cultural and social history, especially as matters of race are concerned. This book is a door into that musical history, so that as we sing along to the songs, tap our feet, and clap our hands, we might, for the first time, also open our eyes.

ACT ONE

1927–1957

ACT ONE

1

Only Make Believe

Performing Race in *Show Boat*

It was Anodyne. It was Lethe. It was Escape. It was the Theatre.
—Edna Ferber, *Show Boat*, 1926

The 1927 musical is racist.
—William A. Henry III, *Time*, 1993

Option 1: *Show Boat*, the 1927 musical by Jerome Kern and Oscar Hammerstein II, is a theatrical classic that revolutionized the form, structure, and content of the American musical as we know it. Hammerstein's libretto, based on Edna Ferber's best-selling 1926 novel, charted new territory by addressing the serious themes of alcoholism, miscegenation, race relations, and spousal abandonment, while Kern's music was character-specific and carefully woven into the show's storyline. Many of the songs, including "Can't Help Lovin' Dat Man," "Ol' Man River," and "Bill," quickly became American standards and Broadway classics. Furthermore, *Show Boat* advanced race relations by featuring a racially integrated cast to dramatize the show's concern over the difficult plight of African Americans in the United States. *Show Boat* raised the bar for what the musical could be and the stories it could tell and would forever be known as a watershed moment in American theater.

Option 2: *Show Boat* is a racist musical that demeans and stereotypes African Americans, and Edna Ferber, Oscar Hammerstein II, and Jerome Kern are all bigots for how they have depicted the show's black characters. Whether forced to work on the levee or in the show boat's pantry, the black characters, most notably Joe and Queenie, are given the most subservient jobs and show no character development over the course of the three-hour musical. Forced to speak in a dialect of childish, black-pidgin

English, they are poorly integrated into the plot of *Show Boat* and instead are merely background servants who help the white characters achieve all they can in the decades-spanning work. *Show Boat* is not a "classic" but a travesty of the American stage that should be forgotten and never revived lest it continue to propagate black stereotypes.

And there we have it. The entire critical history of *Show Boat* encapsulated in these two options: classic musical versus racist show. Case closed. Ever since the musical premiered in 1927, these two scenarios have battled for supremacy, achieving nothing more than a stalemate. In fairness, both points of view have merit. *Show Boat did* change the musical art form, and yes, the black characters *are* stereotypes. As the theater scholar Scott McMillin bluntly states, "Ferber wrote badly about black people. If Kern and Hammerstein were to write a racial theme into the show from the beginning, they would have to invent most of it, for Ferber has little beyond routine or ugly stereotypes to call upon for African-Americans."[1] While a love story between two white people drives the plot forward, the musical's real preoccupation is race relations, as exemplified both in the downtrodden lives of African American workers and in the need for certain light-skinned blacks to "pass" as white as a way to transcend the economic and social glass ceiling imposed by a racist society.

Yet *Show Boat* is more than that. It is also a musical about theater and performance itself. *Show Boat*, after all, is about a troupe of actors who perform melodrama up and down the Mississippi River, and many key scenes take place on stages and inside theaters. *Show Boat* isn't only a cutting-edge work, it is also one of the first metatheatrical musicals about show business and life backstage. It reminds us that theater may be what happens on the stage, but all life is a performance of sorts. Such an idea is hardly new. The sociologist Erving Goffman articulated as much in his canonical 1959 text *The Presentation of Self in Everyday Life*:

> When an individual plays a part he implicitly requests his observers to take seriously the impression that is fostered before them. They are asked to believe that the character they see actually possesses the attributes he appears to possess, that the task he performs will have the consequences that are implicitly claimed for it, and that, in general, matters are what they appear to be. In line with this, there is

the popular view that the individual offers his performance and puts on his show "for the benefit of other people."[2]

All of us enter into a kind of contract in which we are both performers *and* the audience to all the other performances that are going on around us.

More significantly, theater plays a key role in how racial identity is shaped in American society. Race is shown to be a performance in *Show Boat*, whether an instance of passing by a light-skinned African American or an act of impersonation by a white character singing black music. Who gets to perform and how is at the heart of what the show is about. Looking at *Show Boat* through the lens of performance itself, however, means that the classic/racist debate must be rethought, as the enactment and performance of race complicate this divide.

As Andrea Most has argued in her groundbreaking work *Making Americans: Jews and the Broadway Musical*, the development of the Broadway musical often accompanied the need for the musical's mainly Jewish American creators to articulate new American identities for themselves.[3] Such performances were typically concerned with how the creators negotiated their Jewishness, but what was equally important was how such individuals constructed their racial identity, which for many American Jews in the early to mid-twentieth century meant becoming part of white America. Although *Show Boat* is not about Jewish identity, Hammerstein reveals, years before performance theory would even be a concept in academia, the ways in which *all* identities, racial and otherwise, are theatrically constructed.[4] But not all performances are alike. *Show Boat*'s white characters have much more agency and freedom within their roles than the black characters. This is one of the musical's lessons: Whites lead more privileged lives, not because there is anything inherently better about them but because they can *choose* the roles they perform, while the black characters are not afforded the same luxury. This idea is further complicated because while it might at times appear that identity is fixed and natural, ultimately the show reveals that everything, including life itself, is a performance.

Show Boat begins in the late 1880s with the Hawks family, led by Cap'n Andy and his wife, Parthy, who run the *Cotton Blossom*, a show boat full of actors that travels the Mississippi River offering theatrical performances. The white troupe is accompanied on board by black workers, namely Queenie, who works in the kitchen, and her husband, Joe. The Hawkses' daughter, the innocent Magnolia, quickly falls in love with Gaylord Ravenal, a vagabond gambler with a good heart who, despite his love for Magnolia, cannot lead an honest life. Magnolia's best friend, Julie LaVerne, the *Cotton Blossom*'s leading lady, is a woman of mixed-race parentage who has been passing as white. When her racial secret is revealed, Julie is forced to leave the *Cotton Blossom* along with her husband, Steve Baker, for committing miscegenation. Magnolia and Gaylord, now in love, take over for Julie and Steve, and the first act ends with their marriage.

Act 2 of *Show Boat* takes a darker turn. Despite an initial windfall of money, Magnolia and Gaylord fall on hard times, and Gaylord abandons Magnolia and their young daughter, Kim. Now alone and without income, Magnolia returns to her performing roots and auditions at the Trocadero, a music hall where, unbeknownst to her, Julie, now an alcoholic, has been performing. Julie, in an effort to help Magnolia, runs off, thereby leaving her job open, which Magnolia quickly secures. Magnolia not only makes a living, she becomes a star, and as time passes, Kim becomes a star in her own right on the Broadway stage. The show has a happy ending of sorts, with Gaylord returning to Magnolia and Kim as the curtain descends.

While so much happens to the white characters in *Show Boat*, the black characters remain virtually unaffected, not afforded the same opportunities for social advancement. They still work the levee and tend the kitchen. Is this a lack of character development or a comment on society? The racist charges—the majority of them leveled at the show at the time of its last Broadway revival in 1994—are hardly out of line. Queenie and Joe, as the theater journalist Robin Breon notes, "represent a more or less defined set of Negro caricatures that had been established by white writers in silent films beginning in the 1920s."[5] Even though Queenie has not been played by an actress in blackface since Tess Gardella, a.k.a. Aunt Jemima, in the original production, "racism is embedded in *Show Boat* and will not disappear with *ad hoc* adjustments like having Queenie or Julie played by black women."[6] Similarly, the literary scholar Leslie Sanders claims that "this isn't a play about 'whites' and 'blacks'; it is a play about some people who are white and about 'blacks.'"[7] Erving Goffman says as much about black performances: "The ignorant, shiftless, happy-go-lucky manner

Tess Gardella, a.k.a. Aunt Jemima, in blackface as Queenie in the original 1927 production of *Show Boat.* *Credit:* Photofest

which Negroes in the southern states sometimes felt obliged to affect during interaction with whites illustrates how a performance can play up ideal values which accord to the performer a lower position than he covertly accepts for himself."[8] In other words, sometimes people, often those who lack power, are coerced into certain acts.

In pointing out that the black characters are performed caricatures, what criticism has overlooked is that the white figures are *also* melodramatic clichés. Parthy is a shrew of a mother; Cap'n Andy, the jolly patriarch; Magnolia, the innocent ingénue; and Gaylord, the dashing leading man. That the black characters *don't* change seems to be at least part of *Show Boat*'s point, revealing the painful limits imposed on African Americans during this time period. This, after all, was 1927, not the age of postmodern deconstruction. The musical in this regard is imperfect. Where a contemporary audience might hope for a more radical dismantling of black racial stereotypes, what *Show Boat* might unintentionally provoke for the contemporary viewer is a reinforcement of the same roles that it is attempting to critique.

The blind spot in *Show Boat* criticism has been to reduce the complaints about race exclusively to analyses of the black characters, while the white characters get a free pass. Such a tactic not only provides just half the story but actually contributes to the notion that white identity is natural, normative, and not worthy of investigation. Hammerstein's libretto and lyrics constantly challenge this notion and examine the complex ways in which the lives of the white and black characters are not just interwoven but framed by a larger sense of theatricality.

While a great deal happens in the plots of both the show and Ferber's novel, the major events, which all touch on the issues of race and performance, can be distilled to the binary of "work and play." *Show Boat* begins, after an epic overture, with what is perhaps the most shocking lyric ever to open a musical. The curtain rises to reveal a chorus of black stevedores working on a dock, singing:

> Niggers all work on de Mississippi,
> Niggers all work while de white folks play.
> Loadin' up boats wid de bales of cotton,
> Gittin' no rest till de Judgment Day!
>
> . . . .
>
> STEVEDORES AND GALS.
> Cotton blossom, cotton blossom,
> Love to see you growin' free.
> When dey pack you on de levee,
> You're a heavy load to me!
> Cotton blossom, cotton blossom,
> Love to see you growin' wild.
> On de levee, you're too heavy
> Fo' dis po' black child.[9]

Hammerstein's decision to open the musical with the word "niggers" is staggering, firmly situating the audience in the world of laboring blacks and foregrounding the issue of race from the show's initial utterance. As

Scott McMillin reminds us, "in 1927 the 'N-word' was remembered in theatre circles from two recent plays by Eugene O'Neill, *The Emperor Jones* and *All God's Chillun Got Wings*."[10] So troubling is this opening chorus that the section has frequently come under revision in subsequent productions. *Show Boat* scholar Miles Kreuger encapsulates the history as follows: "First it was '*Niggers* all work on de Mississippi,' in the 1936 film it was '*Darkies* all work on de Mississippi,' in the 1946 revival it was '*Colored folks* work on de Mississippi,' in *Till the Clouds Roll By* it was '*Here we all* work on de Mississippi,' and by the 1966 revival, it was—*Nobody* works on de Mississippi, because the Negro chorus was omitted altogether from the opening number."[11] Has part of the show's point, namely that blacks *are* degraded, been watered down by the elimination of what is purposely a derogatory term? Does this actually do a disservice to the play's racial message, which reveals an uncomfortable truth, namely, it is blacks who make the comforts of white society possible? To read this opening moment as racist seems to be in direct opposition to what Hammerstein and Kern were trying to articulate about the condition of African Americans. The workers might not have referred to themselves as "niggers," but Hammerstein, imperfect though this moment may be, was clearly aiming to elicit an emotional response in what would have been a predominantly white audience at the time.[12]

Hammerstein, from this opening moment, never turns away from the sobering truth that the toil of blacks (work) enables whites to enjoy a life of luxury (play). The stevedores' initial chorus establishes the thematic of work, but then, as if in a nod to traditional musical comedy, the white chorus of "mincing misses" appears and sings of their superficial flirtations with their "beaux":

> How you love to flatter,
> You rogues, you rogues!
> Oh, goodness gracious,
> They're so flirtatious![13]

As the number progresses, the black and white choruses join together, but with a notable difference in their lyrics. Both groups sing the theme "Cotton Blossom, Cotton Blossom" together, but the stevedores sing:

When dey pack you on de levee,
You're a heavy load to me!

while the beaux and misses sing:

Thrills and laughter,
concert after,
Ev'rybody's sure to go![14]

For the black stevedores, the *Cotton Blossom* is a site of oppression; for the white chorus, it's a place of leisure and entertainment, ignorant of the work that the stevedores do.[15] Hammerstein and Kern provide the white chorus with a traditional opening while imbuing the same song with deeper social meaning for the black chorus. This opening number, like much of *Show Boat*, serves as a metaphor for American, particularly southern, history. The two groups share the same melody, but each sings different words; part of the same moment, but experiencing it from divergent perspectives. Of course, even the name of the show boat, *Cotton Blossom*, is pregnant with contrasting meanings, redolent of cotton picking and slave labor for blacks while evoking a romanticized image of a "genteel" white South.

Shortly after the opening number, the theme of work versus play continues as we meet Gaylord Ravenal, a gambler strolling the docks. He sings:

Who cares if my boat goes upstream,
Or if the gale bids me go with the river's flow?
I drift along with my fancy—
Sometimes I thank my lucky stars my heart is free,
And other times I wonder, where's the mate for me?[16]

Ravenal's life is one of leisure, and his song speaks not only to his class but also to his racial privilege. Ravenal is the embodiment of play. He and Magnolia both identify as "way-farer[s] along the river," and the fact that Hammerstein uses this imagery serves as a significant contrast to the metaphor of the river in "Ol' Man River."[17]

Continuing his stroll along the docks of Natchez, Gaylord meets Magnolia. It is clearly love at first sight, and as the flirtation continues, Magnolia's first impulse is to pretend that the two of them are in a play:

> RAVENAL. . . . are you an actress?
>
> MAGNOLIA. Oh—no—but I'd give anything if I could be.
>
> RAVENAL. Why?
>
> MAGNOLIA. Because you can make believe so many wonderful
> things that never happen in real life.
>
> . . .
>
> RAVENAL. If you like to make believe things, why can't we make
> believe we know each other?
>
> MAGNOLIA. Oh, yes—and we haven't seen each other for seventy-
> five years, and you're my long-lost nephew—There's a scene like
> that in a play called "The Village Drunkard."[18]

Magnolia's world is grounded in the realm of theater; it's all she knows. For her, real life is just an extension of what happens on the stage. This theatrical metaphor established, Ravenal proceeds to sing the famous love duet "Make Believe" to Magnolia:

> Only make believe I love you,
> Only make believe that you love me,
> Others find peace of mind in pretending—
> Couldn't you?
> Couldn't I?
> Couldn't we?[19]

The language that Magnolia and Ravenal employ is steeped in theatrical metaphor. "Make believe" might sound like a child's game, but white adults use it here as a way to engage with the world around them. Indeed, the ability to play or to "make believe" is a luxury that the white characters in the musical possess. Magnolia sings: "The game of just supposing is the sweetest game I know./ Our dreams are more romantic than the world we see." Ravenal answers, "And if the things we dream about don't happen to be so,/ That's just an unimportant technicality."[20] Positioning this song in the context of the opening "Cotton Blossom" chorus is telling. While the black stevedores do not mince words about the reality of their lives, the white characters eagerly assert their desire to play, pretend, and eliminate any fact or event they find disagreeable. "Play," then, registers not only as the opposite of "work" but as an overt embracing of theatricality. As the musical progresses, this investment in "make believe" and "playacting" comes to define the white characters who willfully disengage with racial issues; they can just pretend otherwise.

While all this might seem straightforward, the levels of performance become tricky in *Show Boat.* Two different modes of performance occur within the musical at the same time. First, there are the melodramas that take place on the stage of the *Cotton Blossom,* as performed by the troupe of actors. Often this acting is over the top, as was typical for nineteenth-century melodrama. This "onstage" acting, which takes place on the show boat itself, is meant to be seen as theatrical, thereby creating the illusion that there is a real, or unperformed, world beyond the stage. This leads directly into the second type of performance, which we see in "Make Believe" and throughout *Show Boat:* the characters are in "real life" and yet are still performing for each other and for us. While the characters want to convince us that their behavior is real, insofar as all behavior is essentially performative, this becomes a type of acting as well.

These modes of performance have a great deal in common with another theatrical tradition, one with its own racist history: blackface. Michael Rogin, the author of *Blackface, White Noise,* argues that the burnt cork makeup, while applied in a manner to caricature African Americans, also has the power to consolidate white identity *underneath* the black mask. Speaking of Jack Robin, the title character in *The Jazz Singer,* Rogin writes, "By painting himself black, he washes himself white," and such an act allows the individual in blackface to essentially say, "I am not really black; underneath the burnt cork is a white skin."[21]

Stage acting, the first level of acting described above, has a similar effect. It creates the appearance that there is a difference between real life and the stage, thereby making it seem as if real life is "natural," when it too is a performance. Like blackface, stage acting is the mask that helps consolidate the notion of a "real" identity underneath. The significance of this in *Show Boat* cannot be overestimated. The world in which the musical's characters live is predicated on the idea that black and white identity just "is." Vis-à-vis race, the ability to make things *look* natural serves as a way to validate and rationalize the "inferiority" of blacks and the "superiority" of whites. But as the musical goes on, we learn the opposite: identities are theatrical and constructed, and racial identities that seem fixed are really mutable. Unfortunately, the power to perform as they might like is rarely extended to blacks; rather they are forced to perform in circumscribed roles that whites have defined for them. It is only in the case of Julie, a light-skinned mixed-race woman who can pass as white, where we explicitly see that race *is* performative and, in certain scenarios, racial roles can be altered.

While "Make Believe" firmly introduces the metaphor of theatricality, the song is actually part of a longer sequence that contrasts white theatricality with innate black biological nature. Immediately following the love duet, Joe—he isn't given a last name in the novel or in the play—who has been watching Ravenal and Magnolia, sings "Ol' Man River." The song is the complete opposite of "Make Believe"; it's about life as it really is, not as one would wish or hope it to be. Musically, the work/play dichotomy is teased out by Kern, who "slowed down and inverted the bright, gay notes of the 'Cotton Blossom' song to produce the powerful 'Ol' Man River.'"[22] The songs are mirror images of each other. At one point in "Ol' Man River," a literal echo of "Cotton Blossom" ties the songs together:

> Niggers all work on de Mississippi,
> Niggers all work while de white folks play,
> Pullin' dem boats from de dawn to sunset,
> Gittin' no rest till de Judgment Day![23]

The *Cotton Blossom*, a boat that carries entertainment up and down the Mississippi in the post–Civil War South, resonates with overtones of slavery, taking an equally demanding toll on black workers.

In contrast to the performativity of theater, the river is the show's central symbol of unwavering nature. The river is the antithesis of performance; it serves as the passive audience to white action. It flows and even anthropomorphically sees, but it can only just keep moving, unable to change its course. Joe sings:

Ol' Man River
Dat Ol' Man River
He mus' know sumpin'
But don't say nuthin',
He jes' keeps rollin',
He keeps on rollin' along.
He don' plant taters,
He don' plant cotton,
An' dem dat plants 'em
Is soon forgotten,
But Ol' Man River,
He jes' keeps rollin' along.[24]

Unlike the whites, who can change the direction of their lives, the black workers, like the river, are simply pulled along. The song, while alluding to the difficult lives of the working black underclass, continually returns to the metaphoric qualities of the river itself. The river is silent (it "don't say nuthin'") and refuses to acknowledge the arduous lives that the black stevedores lead, and yet "mus' know sumpin'," a point that highlights the tension between seeing and silence that the black characters themselves embody. The black characters might seem to be peripheral to the action, but they bear witness to everything that happens. The song, in one form or another, is reprised four times over the course of the show and is the principal leitmotif that defines the immutability of black lives.

This association of the black characters with nature, a connection that also appears in "Can't Help Lovin' Dat Man," is a mixed blessing. While it ties the black characters to a truthful, arguably "real" mode of identity, unlike the "make believe" lives of the white characters, this embodiment is also limiting; the black characters are not permitted to deviate from their given roles. They are trapped in stereotypes (for example, being lazy, drinking too much) that are assumed to be true. Clearly, the ability to act and perform gives whites more choices, more agency, something that the mixed-race Julie quickly learns in her decision to pass. To be sure, it's not that the black characters aspire to be like the river. They never express such a sentiment; rather, with both resignation and frustration, they have no choice but to identify with this immutable force of nature. Despite the fact that "Ol' Man River" is written in a low key for Joe, who is a bass/baritone, it always concludes, anthemlike, on a long high note, a seeming indication of black perseverance. The song is a comment on the marginality of the black characters and their being trapped in societal roles they cannot leave, the exact concern that many critics have deemed racist. The connection to the river might be reductive, but conversely such a reading demonstrates by comparison how overtly constructed the lives of the white characters are. The musical becomes a struggle between race as an unwavering biological characteristic and as a performative act that can be learned and impersonated.

Despite this tension, real life and theater become thoroughly confused as the play goes on. In one of Hammerstein's clever lyrics for the love duet "You Are Love" between Ravenal and Magnolia, Ravenal sings:

> I went my way.
> Life was just a joke to tell.
> Like a lonely Punchinello,
> My role was gay.[25]

This skillful pun not only refers to Ravenal's "happy" existence but to the part he is playing, that of "Gay[lord]." Soon thereafter, Ravenal and Magnolia, now the show boat's leading players, are about to be married in real life, and Cap'n Andy is hardly about to let them tie the knot without generating theatrical publicity. As Cap'n Andy tells the curious onlookers who have gathered, "Bein' as how y'all take such an interest in the doin's of show boat folks, I thought you'd like to see the happy couple playin' their own romance off the stage."[26] As if enacting the plot from one of their melodramas, Ravenal and Magnolia's wedding becomes public spectacle.

Show Boat further reveals the seams where real life and performance collide. During a performance of *The Parson's Bride*, a melodrama staged on the *Cotton Blossom*, Frank Schultz, a comedic actor in the troupe, enters the scene as a villain and begins to physically harass Miss Lucy, played by Magnolia. A backwoodsman in the audience, disconcerted by Frank's behavior, suddenly stands up and shouts, "Let 'er go, I tell you."[27] Frank, though scared by the outburst, continues on, causing the backwoodsman to draw a gun, at which point Frank runs offstage and Cap'n

A backwoodsman, confused between real life and the theater, threatens the stage actors in a scene from the original 1927 production of *Show Boat*. *Credit:* Photo by Vandamm Studio © Billy Rose Theatre Division, the New York Public Library for the Performing Arts

Andy is forced to narrate the rest of the scene by himself. The backwoodsman's outbursts are humorous, but they point to a deeper reading about theater. The backwoodsman can't seem to grasp the concept of performance; he doesn't understand the difference between stage acting and "real life." Ferber makes a similar observation in her novel: "[The show boat] penetrated settlements whose backwoods dwellers had never witnessed a theatrical performance in all their lives—simple child-like credulous people to whom the make-believe villainies, heroics, loves, adventures of the drama were so real as sometimes to cause the *Cotton Blossom* troupe actual embarrassment."[28] The ability to grasp the concept of performance is part of what it means to be sophisticated and civilized. In fact, one might even say the "whiteness" of the backwoodsman is called into question, as he is not of the same social class as the other white characters in the show. While we laugh at the backwoodsman, the mistake he makes is perhaps only an inversion of an error that we ourselves have made. He thinks that everything is real, but many of us fail to see that everything is performed.

If we are all actors, then the characters in *Show Boat* seem to be divided into "good" and "bad" performers. Julie tells Magnolia that Steve is a "bad actor," which is perhaps why she loves him.[29] Is Steve's bad acting the reason why he ultimately leaves Julie, because he cannot convincingly play his part? To be a good actor means to play one's part well, to not draw attention to oneself. Julie, after all, is a "good actor," not only because she is one of the strongest members of the *Cotton Blossom's* troupe but because offstage she has, until recently, maintained her ability to pass as white. The potential dangers of stage acting are reinforced by Parthy when she tells Magnolia, "You stick to the pianner young lady—no play-actin' for you."[30] The ostensible fear is that Magnolia will somehow become tainted by acting. Her lily-white racial identity—even her name indicates this purity—is called into question vis-à-vis performance.

In Edna Ferber's novel, this fear materializes when producers think that Magnolia is a "nigger" when she performs Negro spirituals at the Trocadero: "Well, you cer'nly sing like one. Voice and—I don't know—way you sing," says a man at Magnolia's audition.[31] According to the cultural critic M. NourbeSe Philip, the problem with this scene is that "Magnolia is, in fact, a cultural mulatto—culturally miscegenated but biologically 'pure.' It is no wonder the man is distressed, for herein lies the problem for white America—not only how to keep the races separate and prevent this mixing, both cultural and biological, that is so problematic, but how to tell them apart."[32] What *Show Boat* reveals is that the ability to act the part of other races, on- and offstage, is an advantage; it allows Julie to pass (at least initially), and it gets Magnolia a job. But the ability to act has its limitations. Whites and lighter-skinned African Americans can act and control their identities in ways that dark-skinned blacks typically cannot.

Race, acting, and performance all coincide in the show's famous act 1 kitchen pantry scene. Magnolia, Julie, and Queenie, a spectrum of racial identity, chat about love, which serves as a setup for Julie to launch into "Can't Help Lovin' Dat Man," a faux Negro folk song. Queenie, though, becomes suspicious of Julie: "How come y'all know dat song? . . . ah didn't ever hear anybody but colored folks sing dat song—Sounds funny for Miss Julie to know it."[33] This performative moment is the first major clue that Julie might be part black, as she is intimately familiar with this "black-only" piece of culture. As with "Ol' Man River," the content of this song is invested in the imagery of the biological and the natural. Julie sings:

> Fish got to swim, birds got to fly,
> I got to love one man till I die—
> Can't help lovin' dat man of mine.
> Tell me he's lazy, tell me he's slow,
> Tell me I'm crazy (maybe I know)—
> Can't help lovin' dat man of mine.[34]

Like the river that Joe sings about, like animal instinct, love is natural and "just is." As the theater scholar Gerald Mast explains, "Hammerstein relies on natural imagery . . . to suggest that, despite her lover's shiftlessness, the black woman remains faithful to him. The black woman has become Ol' Man River, enduring her 'lazy,' 'slow' mate 'cause she just can't help it. Is this more black stoicism, the female equivalent of Joe's, or a parody of black stoicism, or both simultaneously?"[35] The number builds, with Joe, Queenie, and other members of the black chorus joining in. As the song reaches its conclusion, Magnolia too joins the number, which Hammerstein indicates as "MAGNOLIA gradually starts to do coon shuffle."[36] While the song itself is about immutable nature, the fact that Julie and Magnolia learn the song attests to the fact that race, as manifested in culture, can be performed by anyone and appropriated for social and economic gain. In other words, race transcends biology and skin color and instead is located in (learned) theatrical performance.

When Magnolia does her "hot feet" routine (as amusingly captured in the 1936 film), her white-girl attempts at "shufflin'" are quite funny in comparison to the dancing of the black chorus, revealing that her dance moves are meant to be read as a poor imitation of black culture. As the film scholar Peter Stanfield describes the scene, "Magnolia, now stage front, turns herself 'black' by puffing out her cheeks, sticking out her backside, and sashaying her pelvic region inside her long dress, as a chorus of blacks gather alongside the showboat."[37] The effect of this minstrel-style performance (minus the makeup) is similar to blackface (which Magnolia

Queenie (Hattie McDaniel) looks suspiciously at Julie (Helen Morgan, who also starred in the original 1927 production) as she sings "Can't Help Lovin' Dat Man" in the 1936 film version of *Show Boat. Credit:* Photofest

does do in a number called "Gallivantin' Aroun'," written for the 1936 film but not in the stage production). The theatricality of Magnolia's shufflin' routine, like the black mask, helps to reinforce her "natural" white identity. Magnolia's jerky movements intentionally read as awkward in comparison with the black chorus members. During the number, Magnolia, Queenie, Joe, and the rest of the black chorus "represent various degrees of exaggerated *posing as black*," while "Julie's restraint offers the contrast of *passing as white*."[38]

The connection between race and performance reaches its pinnacle in the miscegenation scene in the middle of the first act when we learn that Julie is part black and that her marriage to Steve, a white man, is considered illegal under the law. What gives the scene its special import is that it takes place in the auditorium of the *Cotton Blossom*, thereby emphasizing the theatricality of the moment. When the scene begins, Julie, Cap'n Andy, Magnolia, and Rubber-Face are in rehearsal. Julie prepares to say her lines at which point the stage directions inform us that "Julie rises and . . . becomes an actress—a totally artificial person."[39] This emphasis on the artificial implies that something else—real life—exists outside of Julie's performance. But the characters in *Show Boat* are like nested Russian dolls; each layer turns out to be just a further level of acting. It's clear that onstage, identities are constructed, but Hammerstein indicates that offstage, identities are equally performed. Of course, this notion has real stakes for Julie, who we know is acting in real life, because she is passing as white. Yet as the film scholar Linda Williams reminds us, "passing is a performance whose success depends on not overacting. Julie has gained the privileges of whiteness . . . by not calling attention to the difference between herself and the role she plays."[40] Julie's "second level" of acting is the opposite of melodrama, a natural type of acting that does not appear to be acting at all.

As the scene unfolds, Steve tells Julie he fears that Sheriff Vallon is going to reveal her mixed-race secret; in response to this news, she faints. Steve decides to enact a plan that the two have discussed implementing should just this scenario occur. Steve takes a knife, cuts Julie's hand, and then licks the blood from her open wound.[41] This grisly, vampirelike act is Steve's attempt to counter the "One Drop Rule," which dictates that an individual with even one drop of black blood in him, regardless of skin color, is considered black. Steve's plan is to take the rule at its most literal; by drinking Julie's blood, Steve will instantly turn black and therefore dispel the charge of miscegenation. What is significant here is that this desperate act must be played out in front of an audience, because the scene is about revealing that, since skin color has failed as a reliable marker of racial identity, race is something that is *performed*.[42] Precisely because blood is something that is not typically seen and cannot be coded as black or white, this overtly theatrical moment is necessary to make blood and race visible, albeit in a farcical manner. The whole act ridicules the "One Drop Rule" and yet reveals serious implications. Does the audience, either we or the one onstage, really believe that Steve is now black? Steve and Julie prove that blood as a stable marker of race is untenable and that more than anything, race is a performance that works as long as the actors and audience believe in what is being dramatized.

Taking their cue from Ferber's novel, Hammerstein and Kern have the scene play out in front of a full audience, thereby turning race into a drama writ large. This entire scene occurs not only before us, *Show Boat's* audience, but in front of an audience of black chorus members, including Joe, who has been watching the whole scene from an upper box, and whom Hammerstein calls a "very thoughtful observer of the drama he has just seen."[43] The black chorus, led by Queenie, provides the musical backdrop to the scene in a haunting song called "Mis'ry's Comin' Aroun'." Queenie sings:

> Mis'ry's comin' aroun',
> De mis'ry's comin' aroun'.
> I knows it's comin' aroun',
> Don't know to who.[44]

The number was cut from the original production but reinstated for the 1994 revival. As the conductor John McGlinn writes, "This dark, brooding piece was deleted after only one performance in Washington, D.C. and is, beyond question, the most grievous loss the score suffered. . . . Kern's affection for it must have been very high—not only did he salvage most of the music for use in the overture (not composed until well after the deletion of the song), but he also insisted that the number be published in the complete vocal score (issued in April, 1928)."[45] Racial tragedy underscores this moment and becomes one of *Show Boat's* major musical motifs.

The theatricality of *Show Boat* is woven into the musical structure of the show itself. The musical is a compendium of musical and theatrical styles from the 1880s up through the date of the show's own premiere in 1927. When *Show Boat* opened on Broadway, operetta was quickly losing its appeal, and the style's connection to an earlier era was purposely employed by Kern and Hammerstein as a way to establish musically the nineteenth-century milieu of the show's first act. "Make Believe" could easily have come from a Sigmund Romberg or Franz Lehar operetta as opposed to a 1920s Broadway musical.[46] Racially speaking, operetta "was defined by whiteness: there were no black-cast operettas. It was a style of performance and set of musical stage conventions reserved for whites, expressing emotions and structures of feeling read by white audiences as the province of white characters only."[47]

As the action in *Show Boat* progresses, the musical styles change as well, most notably through a racialization of music. When Queenie, Julie, and Magnolia perform "Can't Help Lovin' Dat Man," the song is meant to read as authentically "black" by virtue of the lyrics and blues-inspired melody. "Kern builds a history of American theater music into his own historical saga of American musical theater. The 'coon song' ('Can't Help Lovin' Dat Man' and 'Gallivantin' Aroun' ' [added to the 1936 film]), the jaunty two-step ('I Might Fall Back on You'), the cakewalk ('In Dahomey'—a quotation from the first black musical), the sentimental waltz ('After the Ball,' interpolated from *A Trip to Chinatown*) are performed on the stage of the *Cotton Blossom* or on some other in the show, just as they were performed on stages over the years that the show chronicles," writes Gerald Mast.[48]

So far I have suggested that *Show Boat* divides race into two major camps: whites who construct racial identities that are entirely performative and blacks who are not accorded this same freedom and whose identities seem "natural." But in one of the show's now often overlooked moments, even the black actors are allowed to peek out from behind their racialized masks to reveal the fact that they too are performers. The opening of act 2 shifts the action to the Midway Plaisance of the 1893 Chicago World's Fair. It is something of a throwaway sequence in terms of plot advancement and, given the three-hour running time of *Show Boat*, much of the scene was cut from subsequent productions. The scene provides some theatrical voyeurism in the form of the World's Fair exhibits, most notably the Dahomey Village, and was included to make use of the show's black chorus as well as to allow for the necessary costume and set changes that would occur behind the show's traveler curtain while this song was being performed in front.

This scene is based on a real occurrence, and the Dahomey Village was an actual exhibit in the 1893 fair, populated by Africans for the entertainment of white audiences. The historian Barbara Ballard suggests that " 'savage' peoples, such as the Dahomeans, and their artifacts were designed to emphasize the 'ethnic and cultural differences' between them and the fair-goers."[49] Despite the diversity of peoples on display at the real 1893 World's Fair, one group was not allowed their own pavilion: African Americans. This fact was much condemned by the African American community, most notably former slave and abolitionist Frederick Douglass, who wrote a pamphlet with Ida Wells decrying this oversight and injustice, entitled

"The Reason Why the Colored American Is Not in the World's Columbian Exposition."[50] Instead of African Americans being allowed to show the progress they had achieved since Emancipation, "savage" Africans were made to stand in for the African American experience.

In *Show Boat*, Cap'n Andy, who is touring the fairgrounds with Parthy and Magnolia, wants to go into the Dahomey Village, which he says is filled with "wild men. Zulus. Every one of them fellows has a bunch of wives."[51] Ravenal and Magnolia then sing the duet "Why Do I Love You?" The scene ends with the Dahomey Villagers entering to a "tribal" song that begins with the lyrics "Dyunga doe, dyunga doe! Dyunga hungy ung gunga, Hungy ung gunga go!"[52] To these nonsense African words, the white chorus responds with the following and then exits:

> Don't let us stay here,
> For though they may play here,
> They're acting vicious—
> They might get malicious.
> And though I'm not fearful,
> I'll not be a spearful,
> So you'd better show me
> The way from Dahomey![53]

At first glance, the musical seems to be playing into the basest of stereotypes of white fear and black animalism. M. NourbeSe Philip asks of this moment: "How does one reconcile this with the image the media and the producers project of Kern and Hammerstein II, as brave men who took the risk of putting Blacks and whites together on the stage, and with the argument that *Show Boat* was actually a plea for racial justice? Plot, line and sink(her), *Show Boat* is entirely unredeemable as an anti-racist work."[54] Is this really the case? Philip seems to have missed Hammerstein's surprising twist on the Dahomey scene. As the white chorus leaves, the "African" villagers sing:

> In Dahomey,
> Where the Africans play.
> In Dahomey—

Gimme Avenue A.
Back in old New York,
Where your knife an' fork
Gently sink into juicy little chops
What's made of pork.
We are wild folks
When de Ballyhoos bawl,
But we're mild folks
When we're back in the Kraal.
'Cause our home (our little home),
Our home ain't in Dahomey at all!
Oh, take me back today to Avenue A![55]

What's going on here, and just who are these "Dahomeans"?

To answer that, we have to jump back in theater history to 1894, when black theater writers and performers George Walker and Bert Williams found a job performing at San Francisco's Midwinter Exposition. The Exposition was modeled on Chicago's 1893 World Fair with a number of pavilions and ethnic villages, but not nearly as impressive as the Chicago engagement. Like the World's Fair, though, when the Exposition opened on January 1, 1894, it featured a Dahomey Village with one major difference: the real Dahomeans were late in arriving. "Bert and George attended the Exposition as members of the Dahomey Village, called upon to substitute for actual Dahomeans," explains the cultural historian Camille Forbes. It was only "when the forty or so real Africans arrived toward the end of May, [that] the counterfeit Africans promptly left."[56] In 1903, Walker and Williams would take their experiences at the Exposition as very loose inspiration for a musical entitled *In Dahomey*, "the first all-black show to play a major Broadway theatre."[57] Was Hammerstein acknowledging and referencing the contributions of black pioneers Walker and Williams? Difficult to say, but the possibility exists. What's notable is that Hammerstein's "In Dahomey" essentially retells Walker and Williams's experiences at the Exposition: black New Yorkers hired to play the part of Africans. In the process, Hammerstein reveals that the figure of the African "savage" is a performance as well. While perhaps the black New Yorkers who pose as Dahomeans aren't the best answer to stereotypes—they are still characterized by eating "juicy little chops . . . of pork"—Hammerstein makes the point that appearances aren't always what they seem. Indeed, the joke seems to be on us, the audience, for making assumptions about the Dahomean "savages," only to realize that they're just one more example of calculated theatricality.

While some blacks or mixed-race individuals like Julie try to pass as white to improve their social standing, some whites choose to culturally "pass down" for an economic gain of their own. In act 2, the song "Can't Help Lovin' Dat Man" makes a reappearance, but this time in a new context. Steve has left Julie, who has become an alcoholic. Going from one drunken binge to the next, Julie ekes out a living as a torch singer at the Trocadero Music Hall in Chicago. In a random coincidence, Magnolia, recently abandoned by Ravenal and seeking work, enters the music hall hoping to audition as an entertainer, not realizing that Julie is employed there. Asked what her talent is, Magnolia tells Max the booker, "Why— I—I do negro songs . . ."[58] She proceeds to sing a slow version of "Can't Help Lovin' Dat Man" as Julie looks on from the wings. The stage directions indicate that "when MAGNOLIA begins to sing, JULIE enters quietly, passes behind piano—recognizes MAGNOLIA and takes a couple of quick steps up to her, but directly behind her. Stands there during song till next to last line, when she seems to arrive at a decision. She makes a shy hesitant little gesture which is half-throwing a kiss. She disappears quickly and softly through Stage Center."[59] What we essentially see is Julie ceding her place as singer to Magnolia. The staging of the moment, though, reveals something much more complex. Julie stands silently behind Magnolia, figuratively and literally her shadow, in what basically becomes an act of ventriloquism. Appropriating the black song while Julie is silenced in the background, Magnolia demonstrates what M. NourbeSe Philip calls "how to take what you want from Black culture and not be contaminated by it—how to be Black but not lose your whiteness."[60] Whites, then, demonstrate racial maneuvering in a variety of ways in *Show Boat*. Not only do they consciously create theatrical personas that they try to downplay, but they can also take on, when it suits them, the cultural property of nonwhites. When Julie is found missing, the club hires Magnolia to take her place, but only if she'll "rag"—that is, jazz up—the song that she just sang. Ragging represents the white idea of what black music should sound like, and reflects a changing musical style, one that is no longer operetta but jazzy and modern.[61] "Ragging" allowed white audiences to experience their idea of what black culture was and sounded like, yet be dissociated from actual black people.

By the end of *Show Boat*, Magnolia's daughter, Kim, has also become a performer, a star of the Broadway musical. In the final scene, the show's action catches up with the time period of *Show Boat* itself, 1927, and Kim sings "It's Getting Hotter in the North," a jazz-inflected number that radically contrasts with her mother's operetta style.[62] Meanwhile, as he has done throughout the show, Joe sings a final refrain of "Ol' Man River." Musically, the black characters have not changed at all, while the white characters have advanced through a variety of performance styles, sometimes at the expense or through the appropriation of black culture. Julie may be the show's tragic figure because of her miscegenated past, and Joe and Queenie might be reduced to menial roles, but Magnolia and her family, in choosing a theatrical life of artifice, aim to separate themselves from the racial stakes of the play by "making believe" that race has nothing to do with them.

It is impossible to overlook the one-dimensional and stereotypical treatment of the black characters in *Show Boat*, and my reading here hardly has the intention of ignoring the insightful criticism that takes issue with such characterizations. In line with my text-based reading of the show, Todd Decker suggests that the purported racism of *Show Boat* has been partially addressed over the decades by separating the written libretto from the performance of that text. Describing the genealogy of actresses who have played the role of Queenie, Decker writes, "Tensions between text and performance proved central in the effort to adjust Queenie to changing racial sensibilities" and suggests that contemporary actresses, working essentially with the same text and songs, have downplayed Queenie's humor in order to ground the character more in realism than in stereotype.[63] Indeed, inflections and line readings, things that can change radically from one performer to another, can significantly alter characterizations and complicate the layers of meaning that are found on the page.

That said, not fully considering the ways in which whiteness and theatricality work in the musical overlooks the complex way in which race, here and elsewhere, is constructed. While this reading of *Show Boat* may not appease any charges of racism leveled against the show, recontextualizing how the characters are formed and what agency they do or do not have vis-à-vis the theatrical stage will hopefully broaden how we think about this landmark musical. As for the debate over *Show Boat* being a classic or racist work of art, those arguments need to be rethought. Calling *Show Boat* a "classic" places the show in a category that is virtually removed from judgment or criticism. It also positions the musical as a work where whiteness goes uninvestigated, because "classic works" almost always assume whiteness to be normative and natural, not performed. And that in many ways is where the real racism of the show emerges. It's not simply that the black characters are stereotypes, it's that *only* those characters are imbued with race while whiteness is made invisible. By emphasizing theatricality, Hammerstein and Kern have created a musical where everything is performed and nothing is really what it seems.

2

Playing Cowboys and Indians

Forging Whiteness in *Oklahoma!* and *Annie Get Your Gun*

Moving westward, the frontier became more and more American.
—Frederick Jackson Turner, 1893

In the history of America, the western frontier was the site par excellence of heroism and bravery in the national imagination. Valiant cowboys galloped across the prairie, conquered the harsh land, vanquished the bloodthirsty Indians, and built new homes in the great western expanse. Of course, this narrative is only considered "noble" if you're on the winning side of the battle. For Native Americans, the story looks quite different: the frontier in the nineteenth century meant displacement, loss of home, and brutal mass murder. But history is often the story told by the victors, and the experience of the western frontier, a frontier that the U.S. Census Bureau deemed closed by 1890, continued to live on in the twentieth-century imagination in the form of the theatricalized Wild West show in which cowboys and Indians—sometimes real, sometimes just actors—recreated their battles over and over again in a narrative that never varied.

The Broadway musical has not been immune to this history. Early shows including *Rose-Marie* (1924) and *Whoopee!* (1928) offered their own imagined takes on the Wild West and Native Americans, but the most majestic, nostalgic, and nationalistic of the frontier-inspired musicals came in the form of *Oklahoma!* (1943). It's not a coincidence that *Oklahoma!* invokes this mythos, as the musical's creators, Richard Rodgers and Oscar Hammerstein II, were themselves pioneers of a sort, rewriting the book on how to construct a musical. Similarly, just three years later, Irving Berlin and Dorothy and Herbert Fields's *Annie Get Your Gun* (1946) put its own showbiz spin on the Wild West to tell the story of real-life sharpshooter Annie Oakley. Despite stylistic differences between the works—*Oklahoma!* was the more serious of the two, while Berlin's show finds itself more rooted in traditional musical comedy—both shows' plots are intimately tied up with the history of Native Americans. To talk about Indians in *Oklahoma!* may seem out of place, as there is nary a Native American character to be found in the show, while in *Annie Get Your Gun*, stereotyped caricatures of Indians abound. "In the popular imagination," the Native American cultural historian Jace Weaver explains, "real Indians cannot be permitted to survive into the 20th Century. Their very existence serves as a painful reminder of the illegitimacy of white claims to the continent. Indians must therefore be stereotyped, relegated to a fabulous 19th Century, an extinct breed. This is necessary if the myth of the frontier is to survive. In the musical, this is reflected in a form of 'ethnic cleansing,' wherein Natives are either erased entirely from the landscape depicted [*Oklahoma!*] or pushed to the periphery as stereotyped members of a vanishing race [*Annie Get Your Gun*]."[1]

While concerns about Indians are key (even when not explicitly mentioned), these shows are far more engaged with racial identity on a broader level. More to the point, both *Oklahoma!* and *Annie Get Your Gun* are about the creation, negotiation, and consolidation of Caucasian identity as it played out between whites and Native Americans on the western frontier, refracted through the lens of 1940s wartime America. But these shows, despite their similarities, are not the same. Instead, the musical becomes an adult version of playing cowboys and Indians. In *Oklahoma!*, the community of characters embraces the frontier-clearing cowboy who protects against the never seen but always threatening Native Americans; in *Annie Get Your Gun*, the title character identifies with the Indians and preserves her own pseudo-Indian heritage while learning how to become a member of white society.

The appeal to the Wild West mythos for a white audience in the 1940s is not difficult to comprehend. *Oklahoma!* and *Annie Get Your Gun* are products of World War II and used the Wild West as a touchstone for American patriotism, cohesive communal identity, and the rugged American spirit. More importantly, the Wild West story was one in which the racial lines seemed, at least on the surface, clear. Whites were the good guys and Indians were the villains. This simple casting of American racial politics would be rewritten during the Second World War, when Americans would temporarily, or at least superficially, put aside their internal fighting and differences to rally together against Japan and Germany. Even then, hypocrisy remained: Japanese Americans within U.S. borders were viewed as potential traitors and rounded up into internment camps, while African Americans went off to fight (in segregated units) for the United States against Germany's racial genocide, despite not having equal rights at home.

As for the Native Americans, their numbers diminished and displaced to reservations, they served as dual-purpose metaphors in pop culture texts. They could be the enemy, even when absent, allowing white Americans to play the role of the "valiant" cowboy who conquers the frontier and keeps America safe. At other times, though, Native Americans became the symbol of America itself, the "First Americans" as they are sometimes called, the keepers of a noble past and heritage. Playing Indian allowed some Americans, particularly newly arrived immigrants, to feel a connection to a rustic, even primal American past.

Whose Land? The Case of *Oklahoma!*

Every history of the American musical holds a prime place for *Oklahoma!*, and how could it not? While works before it—like *Show Boat* (1927), *Pal Joey* (1940), and *Lady in the Dark* (1941)—had also pushed on the boundaries of the musical's form and content, for most musical historians, there is only Before-*Oklahoma!* and After-*Oklahoma!* The show, which premiered in 1943 with music by Richard Rodgers, book and lyrics by Oscar Hammerstein II, choreography by Agnes de Mille, and direction by Rouben Mamoulian, combined story, music, and dance, creating what forever after would be known as the "integrated musical." Not racially integrated, mind you; that, ironically, was a factor still missing in many "integrated" Broadway musicals of the Golden Age. Rather, "integrated" refers to the ways in which the show's music was directly interwoven into the libretto to both tell and advance the story. This was not some 1920s musical where any love song could be assigned to virtually any character or even any other 1920s show; with Rodgers and Hammerstein, songs became plot- and character-specific, *integrated* into the story being told onstage. This groundbreaking form was a major reason behind the success of *Oklahoma!*, and until the arrival of *My Fair Lady* in 1956, the show would reign on Broadway as the longest-running musical, not a small feat in a period, unlike now, where long runs were the exception and not the rule. Arguably, though, it was not just the work's original and well-crafted structure that explained its appeal. It also helped that *Oklahoma!* tapped into a nostalgic American core that celebrated western expansion. Just as U.S. servicemen were fighting overseas and protecting Americans abroad, the cowboys of *Oklahoma!* were protecting the frontier against an unseen enemy: the Native American—turning *Oklahoma!* into a true celebration of manifest destiny and the nation's original pioneers.

Based on part–Cherokee Indian/Oklahoman playwright Lynn Riggs's drama *Green Grow the Lilacs*, which was first produced by the Theatre Guild in 1931, *Oklahoma!* focuses on the struggles of cowboys and ranchers in Indian Territory just after the turn of the twentieth century.[2] Curly, a cowboy, is in love with Laurey, the daughter of farmers. The two bicker and fight, but it's all just a cover for flirting that barely conceals their true love for each other. Laurey, meanwhile, is pursued by Jud, a violent farmhand who has sexually perverse proclivities—the walls of the smokehouse where he lives are covered in the photos of nude women. Despite Jud's bid for Laurey, Curly gets the girl and the two marry. Jud is killed onstage at the play's conclusion when Curly accidentally stabs him during a fight, a somber plot point that until *Oklahoma!* was basically inconceivable in a musical. Other characters rounding out the show include the gruff but lovable Aunt Eller; Ado Annie and Will Parker, the show's comedic pair, who also fall in love; and Ali Hakim, a Persian (read Jewish) peddler who integrates himself into the pioneer community. The show's principal love plot, though, takes on larger significance, because Curly and Laurey get married at the same moment that Oklahoma becomes a state, which serves as the impetus for the show's rousing title number, thereby tying the micro (love story) and macro (nationhood) plot lines perfectly together.

While on the surface the plot of *Oklahoma!* may appear tame—couples fall in love while a farmhand menaces the community—there is much more at stake on a national, political, and racial level. More specifically, these points all coalesce around the topic of land. Who owns it? White settlers, Native Americans, or the U.S. government? And what should happen on that land? Ranching or farming? These questions weren't unique to the musical. "The history of Oklahoma is a history of movement, possession, and dispossession. It is American history told in fast-forward," says the historian David A. Chang. The 1887 Dawes Act began the process "for dividing up the tribal estate of American Indian peoples in preparation for extinguishing tribal government and extending American citizenship to Indian individuals."[3] Beginning with the Oklahoma Land Run in 1889, whites rushed into the "Unassigned Territories" (Indian Territory) and began settling down. In these land rushes, a complex interplay between race and ownership occurred. Indians were dispossessed of their homeland, whites established their power, and African American settlers looked to make new lives for themselves after the end of slavery.[4] In short, Oklahoma Territory became a battleground where race, color, power, and land all intersected.[5]

From the opening moments of *Oklahoma!*, the land is described in terms that connote expanse and optimism. Bucking musical theater tradition, no dancing girls or chorus open the show. Instead, Curly makes his famous entrance from offstage singing "Oh, What a Beautiful Mornin' ":

> There's a bright, golden haze on the meadow,
> There's a bright, golden haze on the meadow.
> The corn is as high as a elephant's eye
> An' it looks like it's climbin' clear up to the sky.
>
> Oh, what a beautiful mornin',
> Oh, what a beautiful day.
> I got a beautiful feelin'
> Ev'rythin's goin' my way.[6]

The song is a paean to the bounty of the frontier and the promise of the rugged white American spirit that would lay claim to this land. It's hard to imagine Native Americans singing these words in this moment when everything was *not* going their way. Contextualizing the song are Hammerstein's opening stage directions, taken verbatim from Riggs's *Green Grow the Lilacs:* "It is a radiant summer morning several years ago, the kind of morning which, enveloping the shapes of earth—men, cattle in a meadow, blades of the young corn, streams—makes them seem to exist now for the first time, their images giving off a golden emanation that is partly true and partly a trick of the imagination, focusing to keep alive a loveliness that may pass away."[7] The words evoke a pristine, preserved, and untouched landscape that seems too perfect to be real. If anyone had ever owned this land previously, no indication of that is mentioned. The irony is that by the time *Oklahoma!* was produced, the loveliness had long disappeared. The dust bowl had ravaged Oklahoma in the 1930s, as memorably fictionalized by John Steinbeck in *The Grapes of Wrath* (1939). *Oklahoma!* would serve to recuperate the image of and nostalgic feelings for the damaged land that only ten years earlier had been the site of national suffering.

A rather amazing thing about *Oklahoma!* is that despite the musical's frontier setting and the show's thematics about land, farming, and the West, we never see or hear from a single Native American. Even more unusual, part-Cherokee playwright Lynn Riggs never references Native Americans in his play either.[8] *Oklahoma!* is set just after the turn of the century, when the Native Americans had already left Oklahoma Territory.[9] At the same time, Hammerstein is clear to note in the libretto that the action takes place in "Indian Territory (Now Oklahoma)," thereby establishing the land as property that once belonged to Native Americans but has now been occupied by farmers and cowboys. Calling the land "Indian Territory" also creates the perpetual, if invented, "threat" of Native American attack in the white imagination, an unspoken point that subtly works its way through the show. Oddly enough, the only place where Indians do make an appearance of sorts is in a photo of the creators of *Oklahoma!*, decked out in elaborate Native American headdresses and covered in Indian blankets, celebrating the show's fourth anniversary. This captured moment reveals, unintentionally perhaps, the huge absence that permeates the musical.

Despite the omission of Native Americans in *Oklahoma!*, they serve as the unseen force that motivates much of the show's racial politics and plot. For the historian Frederick Jackson Turner, who wrote about the close of the western frontier in his defining 1893 article "The Significance of the Frontier in American History," the frontier is the crucible that produces Americans, and it is the Native American who serves as the crucible's catalyst: "The effect of the Indian frontier as a consolidating agent in our his-

Oscar Hammerstein II (lyricist and librettist), Agnes de Mille (choreographer), Armina Marshall (cofounder of the Theatre Guild), Richard Rodgers (composer), Theresa Helburn (cofounder of the Theatre Guild), and Lawrence Langner (cofounder of the Theatre Guild), costumed as Indians to celebrate the fourth anniversary of *Oklahoma!* on Broadway. *Credit:* Billy Rose Theatre Division, the New York Public Library for the Performing Arts, Astor, Lenox, and Tilden Foundations

tory is important. . . . The Indian was a common danger, demanding united action." The Wild West was "wild" not simply because humans had to conquer the elements but also because the Indian was a constant presence one had to be on guard against. Turner sees the Indian as central to the frontier landscape, a force that had to be overcome to expand even farther west. The twist to this scenario is that once-contentious groups—cowboys and ranchers, native-born Americans and newly arrived immigrants, Jews and Christians—could put aside their differences to combat an even more dangerous enemy: the Indian. It's through this process of joining forces that the "American" is created. In Turner's elegy to the vanishing West, "the frontier is the line of most rapid and effective Americanization. . . . Little by little he [the European colonist] transforms the wilderness, but the outcome is not the old Europe, not simply the development of Germanic germs, any more than the first phenomenon was a case of reversion to the Germanic mark. The fact is, that here is a new product that is American."[10]

For Theodore Roosevelt, who organized the Rough Riders and took them to Cuba to fight against the Spanish in 1898, war became the crucible in which white Americans were created. To him, "the battles of these rural warriors against the savage red man had forged them into a powerful, superior, and freedom-loving race. It also served the indispensable purpose of uniting disparate groups of Europeans into one American people."[11] Of course, missing from these "disparate groups" were Asians and blacks, whom Roosevelt purposely did not include in his regiment. The upshot, as the historian Matthew Frye Jacobson suggests, is that "this western setting, the stage of national expansion, forged 'Caucasians' in opposition to an implacable Indian enemy."[12] Jacobson's choice of the word *stage* is astute here, as this was drama writ large. That a show like *Oklahoma!* would take up this history forty years later is not surprising; the importance of war as a way to forge white identity was quickly becoming *the* national narrative. Responding to the legacy of the Rough Riders, the historian Gary Gerstle argues:

> Over the course of the next fifty years, two more wars, and the conscription of 20 million Americans into the armed forces, this myth of the assimilatory regiment would be reworked and refined until it became the story of the heroic and multiethnic platoon. As the nation that Roosevelt had helped to fashion reached the peak of its power and authority in the 1940s and 1950s, no narrative of nation building was more important than that of how platoons of ethnically, religiously, and sectionally diverse American men had sacrificed their lives for each other, fought valiantly against the enemy, and made their nation the most powerful and wonderful society on earth.[13]

This was the narrative of *Oklahoma!* as well, a narrative of the 1940s told through the lens of the turn-of-the-century frontier.

The consolidation of whiteness and the creation of this new American society are best seen in *Oklahoma!*'s rousing act 2 opening number, "The

Farmer and the Cowman," which takes place at a box social that the whole community has turned out for. Andrew Carnes, Ado Annie's father, sings:

> The farmer and the cowman should be friends,
> Oh, the farmer and the cowman should be friends.
> One man likes to push a plow,
> The other likes to chase a cow,
> But that's no reason why they cain't be friends.

> Territory folks should stick together,
> Territory folks should all be pals.
> Cowboys, dance with the farmers' daughters!
> Farmers, dance with the ranchers' gals![14]

The question is never actually posed in the show, but *why* must territory folks stick together? Is it just to be friends as the chorus indicates, or is there another reason? Despite the differences between cowboys and farmers, they share a common enemy: the Indian. For Theodore Roosevelt, who idolized the early settlers, they "were warriors above all, and their primary task was not placid husbandry but relentless war against the savage Indians who claimed these lands as their own."[15]

The forging of a unified white front is further teased out by Andrea Most, who suggests that Ali Hakim, the Jewish peddler, is able to join the white community by the show's finale, a move that mirrors the larger story of Jewish assimilation in 1940s America. Jud, the show's villain, on the other hand, is not permitted to assimilate and must be killed to preserve the harmony of the community.[16] But this compelling rationale is just part of the story. Ali Hakim can be assimilated into the white community not just because he *isn't* Jud but because he is needed by the white community as an ally to defend against the potential threat of Indian attack should one occur. It's no wonder that *Oklahoma!* was such a success during 1943. As U.S. troops were deployed overseas, Americans of all backgrounds, including some "newly white" individuals (that is to say, Jews) with parents of immigrant backgrounds could prove their American identity and confirm their newfound whiteness by joining the army and fighting against a common enemy in Europe or the Pacific.[17]

While Native Americans do not appear onstage, *Oklahoma!*, inadvertently perhaps, never allows us to forget that the territory in question really belongs to them. Indians are embedded linguistically in every utterance of the word *Oklahoma*, which derives from the Native American Choctaw words *okla* (red) and *humma* (people). The tie between race and land ownership finds full expression in the show's jubilant title number:

AUNT ELLER. They couldn't pick a better time to start in life!
IKE. It ain't too early and it ain't too late.
CURLY. Startin' as a farmer with a brand-new wife—
LAUREY. Soon be livin' in a brand-new state!
ALL. Brand-new state
Gonna treat you great!

. . .

AUNT ELLER. Flowers on the prairie where the June bugs zoom—
IKE. Plen'y of air and plen'y of room—
FRED. Plen'y of room to swing a rope!
AUNT ELLER. Plen'y of heart and plen'y of hope. . . .

Like "Oh, What a Beautiful Mornin'," the lyrics here speak to the openness and seemingly unoccupied status of the land—it's free for the taking—coupled with the excitement of impending statehood. But the irony arrives in the song's chorus:

Oklahoma,
Where the wind comes sweepin' down the plain,
And the wavin' wheat
Can sure smell sweet
When the wind comes right behind the rain.
Oklahoma,
Every night my honey lamb and I
Sit alone and talk
And watch a hawk
Makin' lazy circles in the sky.
We know we belong to the land,
And the land we belong to is grand!

And when we say:
Ee-ee-ow! A-yip-i-o-ee-ay!
We're only sayin'
"You're doin' fine, Oklahoma!
Oklahoma, O.K.!"[18]

The white chorus may believe that they belong to the land, but their chanting of the word *Oklahoma*, which means "Red People," is an unconscious nod to the land's original but now forcibly displaced inhabitants. Were we to substitute "Red People" for "Oklahoma" into the show's refrain, the chorus would end up ironically singing: "Red People! Red People! Red People! Red People! We know we belong to the land,/ And the land we belong to is grand." As the lyric stands, the white chorus/community unintentionally acknowledges the former Indian presence while claiming that *they* are the true landowners. The show's title and the name of the state itself become a palimpsest in which Indians are erased (in many ways literally) but never truly vanish. *Oklahoma!* serves as a perfect example of the ways in which white racial identity shapes the musical as a whole while often appearing invisible to the casual audience member.

Oklahoma! is a show that gets to have its cake and eat it too. The cowboys and farmers are victorious, and they did it all without having to combat a single Indian on- or offstage. If Indians had actually shown up, the logic of the show would call for either their expulsion or their extermination, a truly terrible option to have to witness onstage (or elsewhere, for that matter). Instead, the whites become the victors by default without having to shed a single ounce of blood, with the exception of Jud's death. *Oklahoma!* rewrites history by expunging the painful aspects of frontier history while celebrating the rewards of white American pioneer spirit, features that have helped solidify *Oklahoma!*'s place in the pantheon of beloved American musicals.

Playing Indian: Performing Natur'lly in *Annie Get Your Gun*

Oklahoma! is a show in which Native Americans are physically absent onstage but contextually always present. What happens, though, when Indians make an actual appearance? How does it affect a show's racial politics? That's the question, among others, posed by *Annie Get Your Gun*, which premiered three years after *Oklahoma!* in 1946. The shows have more in common than a similar western setting; they share a link in Rodgers and Hammerstein. The composing duo had been approached by lyricist and book writer Dorothy Fields, who had the inspiration to create a show around Broadway star Ethel Merman based on the life of Annie Oakley. Rodgers and Hammerstein weren't interested in composing the score—they already had other projects on their desk—but were happy to serve as producers. They asked their friend Jerome Kern of *Show Boat* fame if he would take on the project, and Kern agreed. Shortly after signing on, Kern died from a stroke, leaving the producers seeking a replacement. Rodgers called on composer and lyricist Irving Berlin to see if he had any interest, to which his initial response was "I can't write that sort of hillbilly music."[19] Berlin was further worried that he would not be able to create a show that would live up to the new Rodgers and Hammerstein integrated model of musical writing. Ultimately, though, Berlin took on the project and wrote what would become one of his most popular scores.

The libretto of *Annie Get Your Gun* by Dorothy and Herbert Fields is as straightforward as they come, a girl-meets-boy-meets-firearms sort of tale. Annie Oakley, a backwoods sharpshooter, stumbles into the world of impresario Buffalo Bill and is quickly signed to his Wild West show, where she becomes a star. Annie falls in love with Frank Butler, Buffalo Bill's other star shooter, but she is too rough around the edges for him, and her skills as a markswoman constantly upstage Frank, causing him to feel a combination of jealousy and emasculation. As Annie and Frank's romantic entanglements play out, Annie comes under the fatherlike wing of real-life Sioux Indian Chief Sitting Bull, who adopts Annie as his daughter into his tribe, dramatized in the racially contentious song "I'm an Indian Too." Sitting Bull teaches Annie how to finally hook Frank at the show's conclusion: purposely lose a shooting match so Frank will think he's the best shot.

If the actual western frontier serves as the "stage" for *Oklahoma!*, for *Annie Get Your Gun*, the stage is the Wild West show as produced by Buffalo Bill, an entertainment that has come under repeated historical scrutiny and criticism. On one hand, Wild West shows defined the stereotype of the violent Indian savage. "The wild west exhibition presented," writes the scholar William Brasmer, "in truth, an incorrect picture of western life and dealt with the frontier character as a stereotype melodramatic figure from a border drama or yellow-back novel. The Indian was presented as a freak to be exhibited or as a silent combatant in a shoot-out in which the Indian always lost."[20] On the other hand, there was an often unseen upside to the Wild West show: it provided better employment and opportunity to Native Americans than could be found on the reservations. Sarah Blackstone, a historian of the Wild West show, says that producers like Buffalo Bill "paid a regular wage, fed the Native Americans well, and most importantly let them relive moments of glory and re-enact some of their old customs."[21] Despite the fact that Indians in Wild West shows had to conform to and perform certain stereotypes, the Wild West show prided itself on its authenticity. Unlike the musicals of the 1920s and 1930s, in which Native Americans are basically parodied figures, "in this most American of educations [the Wild West show], the authenticity—ethnic and otherwise—of the performers was stressed above all."[22]

What makes a discussion of the Native American characters in *Annie Get Your Gun* difficult is that "the Indian as stage performer" and "the Indian as real-life individual" are conflated, making it hard for the audience to tell the two apart. The stage Indian is foregrounded from the moment the curtain goes up revealing a painted drop that, according to the stage directions, shows "a stage coach being attacked by a band of Indians. . . . Terror-stricken women passengers, clutching babies, kneel to plead for mercy from a towering brave. The driver is about to be hit on the head with a tomahawk. On a hill in the distance we see the comforting figure of Buffalo Bill mounted on a chestnut stallion."[23] From this initial tableau, the musical opens with the number "Buffalo Bill," in which Charlie, Buffalo Bill's manager and promoter, drums up business by telling the townspeople about the show that has just pulled into town.

> CHARLIE. What is it all about you ask? It's Indians!
> CROWD. Indians?
> CHARLIE. Indians!
> CROWD. Indians?
> CHARLIE. Very notable, cut-your-throatable Indians!
> CROWD. Indians?
> CHARLIE. Just when they've taken ev'ryone by force,

Who makes an entrance on a big white horse?
Who starts a-shootin' 'til
There's no one left to kill?
VOICE. General Grant?
CHARLIE. No! Colonel Buff'lo Bill![24]

Native Americans are depicted by Charlie in stereotypical terms, but we're meant to read this performance as just that, a performance. After the number ends, Indians are seen serving as stagehands, carrying a box of Frank Butler's guns in anticipation of a shooting match.[25] The "threat" is quickly dispersed, and nowhere in the show do the Indians come off as violent. In other words, it's the milieu of the Wild West show that creates the stereotypes, but the creators of *Annie Get Your Gun* seem cognizant of the fact that they are purposely engaging the stereotypes in order to defuse them. While it's true that the Native American characters in the show are not three-dimensional and have a penchant for causing trouble (they start a cooking fire in a train at one point and dismantle the train seats), Annie Oakley consistently runs to their defense.[26] Childlike though they may be, they are often depicted in a sympathetic manner whereas white characters like Dolly Tate are shown to be truly unlikable.

But looking at the show's racial elements only from the perspective of the Native Americans misses a lot of what the musical is about. What can we say about the racial identity of the show's eponymous character? Like Natty Bumppo—James Fenimore Cooper's European character who identifies with the Native Americans and goes by the Indian moniker Leatherstocking in works like *The Last of the Mohicans* (1826)—Annie is an "off-white" figure whose behavior reads more as stereotypically Native American than Caucasian: her speech is unpolished and full of backwoods dialect, she is basically illiterate, and she is followed by her four younger, unparented, bedraggled siblings. In terms of her appearance, photos from the original Broadway production show Annie in a green buckskin dress with fringes that recall Indian garb, with a leather belt and bag. She is the epitome of the rustic outdoors. Annie might be officially adopted into Sitting Bull's tribe during "I'm an Indian Too," but her unsophisticated costuming at the top of the show quickly establishes her connection to nature.

In her opening number, Annie views her rusticity as an advantage. Her

Ethel Merman as Annie Oakley, shown here in her buckskin, Native American–inspired garb, designed by Lucinda Ballard. *Credit:* Photofest

folksy upbringing informs her entire philosophy of life, as she sings in "Doin' What Comes Natur'lly."

> ANNIE. Folks are dumb where I come from;
> They ain't had any learnin'.
> Still they're happy as can be
> Doin' what comes natur'lly.
> KIDS. Doin' what comes natur'lly.
> ANNIE. Folks like us could never fuss
> With schools and books and learnin'.
> Still we've gone from A to Z
> Doin' what comes natur'lly.[27]

The song is a celebration of all that is unlearned and natural, and Annie's life, like that of her family, is the antithesis of performance, free from the ills of modern society.[28]

In addition to connecting Annie with rural life, *Annie Get Your Gun* presents us with a nostalgic vision of the West, but one that differs from that of *Oklahoma!* This nostalgia is evident in "Let's Go West Again," a song cut from both the stage and the film versions of *Annie Get Your Gun*.[29] Sung by Annie during the act 2 opening as she and Buffalo Bill's troupe sail from Europe to New York, the song romanticizes manifest destiny.

> ANNIE. Let's go west again—
> I won't rest again
> Till we're west again
> You and I.
> Let's go back where the skies are seldom gray,
> Where the sun goes the end of ev'ry day—
> Let's return again,
> How I yearn again
> To return again,
> You and I.
> Don't forget there was someone who knew best
> Said "Go west, young man, go west."[30]

Although Annie and company are traveling to New York, which is not the frontier, their journey is nevertheless an evocation of that prairie mythos. The song serves as a love song to Frank Butler as well as to the frontier itself, and Annie expresses a longing for a time and place that no longer exist. Wild West shows, on the other hand, fill this gap and become a site of wistfulness where whites can reproduce again and again the birth of their country in contrast to the staged death of the Native Americans.

In contrast to nature, which "just is," white behavior is revealed to be a complex construction that is epitomized by the motif of show business and performance that runs through the musical. Indeed, the show's best-known song is "There's No Business like Show Business," which in the years since its debut has become an anthem of Broadway itself. And sure enough, Annie proves that she is a quick study and learns how to perform when the situation calls for her to do so. If she is going to win Frank Butler's heart, she must be what he wants her to be: white. As Andrea Most reminds us, Annie "has been raised, significantly, in Darke County, and indeed she lives 'in the dark.' Numerous connotations of darkness apply. She is illiterate and uneducated; she is associated with primitive 'dark' races; and she has never been exposed to the bright lights of the theater."[31] Frank sings that the girl he marries will be "as soft and as pink as a nursery" and "will wear satins and laces and smell of cologne."[32] His dream girl is the embodiment of femininity, but it's more than that. Annie tells Frank, "All I wanna be is a pink and white woman like the kind ye said ye liked," to which Frank responds, "You're gettin' pinker and whiter every day!"[33] Annie's transformation into a refined woman requires her further whitening, a desire that is realized in Annie's costumes as the show progresses and symbolized by her multiple references to the upper-class women who wear "white gloves." After hearing how Frank has been surrounded by society ladies, Annie asks, "Those long white gloves ye wuz talkin' about . . . Is there any particular pair he likes?"[34] The 1950 film version of *Annie Get Your Gun* provides a further gloss on the process of Annie's whitening. Betty Hutton, the film's Annie, transforms from bumpkin to polished performer by scrubbing her face via a montage of shots in which her face literally becomes whiter and whiter. Annie is not simply dirty; rather she must scrub her face clean of racial darkness. By the time that Annie has become a star in Buffalo Bill's show, her arrival into the white world of show business is made complete by her outfit: she is attired in a white dress, white bolero, white gauntlet gloves, and a white hat.[35]

While Annie's ability to perform and one might even say "pass" as white improves, her core identity as a country hick remains unchanged. In act 2, Annie shows up at a fancy dress ball in a last-ditch effort to win back Frank, who has left Buffalo Bill's troupe. Now garbed in a ball gown, she endeavors to become like the other white society women, but her attempt at total integration is marred by a faulty performance on her part. Annie introduces herself to the other "white gloves" at the party with a script of set introductions she has learned.

LADY GUEST. Charmed!
ANNIE. Chanted!
LADY GUEST. Enchanted!
ANNIE. Charmed!
LADY GUEST. Charmed!

ANNIE. Chanted!

LADY GUEST. Enchanted!

ANNIE. Charmed!

MRS. POTTER-PORTER. Delighted!

ANNIE. (*Ignoring her extended hand*) Oh no, you gotta be charmed
or chanted![36]

This funny bit of stage business reveals Annie's desire to correctly play her
part, but it ends up backfiring. Not knowing what else to do when Mrs.
Potter-Porter is "delighted," Annie sticks to the script, which limits her
ability to fully assimilate into upper-class society. Furthermore, nothing
in Annie's behavior leads us to believe that she would ever be mistaken
for an actual society matron; the seams of her performance constantly
show, and underneath the fancy gown is a redneck. At the same time, the
scripted greetings reveal just what an artificial performance (as opposed
to Annie's "natural" persona) the construction of white identity is. *Annie
Get Your Gun* may be a show about performance and show business, but it
constantly critiques performance as much as celebrates it.

This scene continues with Sitting Bull telling Annie that she needs to
sell the expensive medals she wears proudly on her chest in order to seal a
merger with Pawnee Bill's troupe, which now includes Frank Butler. While
Annie initially doesn't want to sell the medals, getting Frank back is worth
it, and she reflects on the meaning of true wealth in the song "I Got the
Sun in the Morning," which reestablishes her connection with nature.

ANNIE. Got no diamond, got no pearl,
Still I think I'm a lucky girl—
I got the sun in the morning
And the moon at night.
Got no mansion, got no yacht,
Still I'm happy with what I've got—
I got the sun in the morning
And the moon at night.
Sunshine
Gives me a lovely day,
Moonshine

> Gives me the Milky Way,
> Got no checkbooks, got no banks,
> Still I'd like to express my thanks—
> I got the sun in the morning
> And the moon at night,
> And with the sun in the morning
> And the moon in the evening,
> I'm all right.[37]

Like the Native Americans who have been dispossessed of their lands and own very little, Annie is fine with her impending lack of material possessions. Annie's personality is consciously split: she holds to her native/natural roots but is able to perform as white when called on to do so.

In this case, there is perhaps another reading to tease out of *Annie Get Your Gun*. Annie embodies characteristics similar to those of the immigrant, particularly the Jewish immigrant, as summed up by Peter Antelyes in his study of Jewish redface: "In short, they [Jewish immigrants] played cowboys and Indians like everyone else. Like everyone else, they sometimes figured themselves as cowboys and hence as white, Christian Americans, as opposed to dark, savage others; and sometimes they figured themselves as Indians and hence as original Americans, as opposed to jaded, corrupt, lapsed Americans."[38] In reading this thread into *Annie Get Your Gun*, my point is not to turn the musical into a crypto-Jewish show or claim that Annie Oakley or Ethel Merman, who played her, should be read as Jewish, but rather to note that the narrative is an inherently American story; it's the story of twentieth-century American immigration and assimilation. The immigrant comes to society with "backward" ways and is given a choice: give up her old customs and assimilate or hold on to her past. Or, better yet, do both: maintain traditions at home while presenting an assimilated outward appearance.

Berlin himself was a Russian Jewish immigrant who came to the United States in 1893 with his family at the age of five. Born Israel Baline, Berlin had aspirations to enter show business and as a young man soon established himself as a mainstay of Tin Pan Alley in the early twentieth century. Berlin, one might argue, shared a great deal in common with his 1946 stage creation. Both he and Oakley had humble rural beginnings, and both found ways to assimilate into white society. But a major difference remains.

Whereas Berlin seemed happy to essentially throw off all vestiges of his personality that would mark him as Jewish—fellow composer Jerome Kern famously stated, "Irving Berlin has no place in American music. He is American music"—Annie Oakley holds on to her backwoods roots.[39] True, Annie has not immigrated, but her story parallels that of other assimilationist texts. Like the Jewish American who was trying to figure out the conundrum of being Jewish in America, Annie could embrace her natural identity while exhibiting an outer performed American identity.

Comparing *Annie Get Your Gun* to the narrative of Jewish immigration might seem a stretch if not for a significant connection. Early twentieth-century vaudeville, with its penchant for ethnic humor, fancifully engaged the Jewish-Indian connection, including songs such as "I'm a Yiddish Cowboy (Tough Guy Levi)" and "Big Chief Dynamite."[40] More specifically, in 1910, a then unknown Jewish comedian by the name of Fanny Brice made her debut in the Ziegfeld Follies singing "Goodbye, Becky Cohen." The composer of the song? None other than Irving Berlin, writing what was also his first song for the Follies.[41] The spin on this song was that Berlin told Brice to perform it with a heavy Yiddish accent; the result was a tremendous success, which contributed to the period's ongoing craze for ethnic songs.[42] Jumping ahead to 1921, Brice introduced another song penned by a onetime Berlin collaborator, lyricist Blanche Merrill, who shared Berlin's penchant for ethnic material. Entitled "I'm an Indian," this song played up the Jewish–Native American connection. The parallels to Berlin's 1946 number are noteworthy, and I quote both in full for comparison:

"I'M AN INDIAN" (1921)
Lyrics by Blanche Merrill, Music by Leo Edwards

Look at me I'm what you call an Indian
That's something that I never was before
But one day I met Big Chief Chickamahooga
And right away he grabb'd me for a squaw
He wrapp'd me up in blankets
Put feathers in my head
Between the blankets and the feathers
I feel just like a bed

And now oi oi my people
How can I tell them how
Their little Rosie Rosenstein
Is a terrible Indian now, O!

Chorus:
Look at me, O look at me
I'm an Indian, I'm an Indian
Down at the feet is the moccasins for the shoes
Up in the back is a little fat papoose
Up in the head is the feathers from a goose
It's a goose, it's a goose, but I'm an Indian
I pal around with Hunting Bear
Laughing Foot and Standing Hair
Such people I never saw before
They do a war dance all around
While I take a skip too around the ground
Oi, oi, oi, oi, I'm a terrible squaw.[43]

"I'M AN INDIAN TOO" (1946)
Music and lyrics by Irving Berlin

Like the Seminole,
Navajo, Kickapoo,
Like those Indians,
I'm an Indian too.
A Sioux–ooh-ooh—
A Sioux.
Just like Battle Ax,
Hatchet Face, Eagle Nose,
Like those Indians,
I'm an Indian too,
A Sioux—ooh-ooh—
A Sioux.
Some Indian summer's day
Without a sound

I may hide away
With Big Chief Hole in the Ground.
And I'll have totem poles,
Tomahawks, pipes of peace,
Which will go to prove
I'm an Indian too,
A Sioux—ooh-ooh—
A Sioux.

With my chief in his teepee
We'll raise an Indian family,
And I'll be busy night and day
Looking like a flour sack,
With two papooses on my back
And three papooses on the way.

Like the Chippewa,
Iroquois, Omaha,
Like those Indians,
I'm an Indian too,
A Sioux—ooh-ooh—
A Sioux.
Just like Rising Moon,
Falling Pants, Running Nose,
Like those Indians,
I'm an Indian too,
A Sioux—ooh-ooh—
A Sioux.
Some Indian summer's day
Without a care
I may run away
With Big Chief Son of a Bear.
And I'll wear moccasins,
Wampum beads, feather hats,
Which will go to prove
I'm an Indian too,

A Sioux—ooh-ooh—
A Sioux.[44]

On the surface, both songs are quite similar. One reviewer of the Berlin musical even notes that "in 'I'm an Indian' Miss Merman reminds one of that notable musicomedienne, Miss Brice—who once sang a song about 'Whoops, I'm an Indian squaw.' "[45] Both songs invoke stereotypical Indian images from moccasins to papooses and use made-up Indian character names. For both Annie Oakley and Brice's character, Rosie Rosenstein, being an Indian is about performance. By wearing feathers and beads, they can play Indian. But is there a difference between *playing* an Indian and truly *being* an Indian? In "I'm an Indian," Rosie Rosenstein pulls off a "bad" performance. She dresses up like an Indian, but Brice sang the song with a strong Yiddish inflection, emphasizing the fact that Rosie Rosenstein remains a Jew and makes a "terrible squaw."

As opposed to the outright humor of Brice's song, the "I'm an Indian Too" sequence begins with a serious-sounding Ceremonial Chant that sets the scene's tone. What is missing here, though, is the significant opening verse to the song that was included in the number's published version.

> ANNIE. Since I was a child of three,
> They've had the Indian sign on me.
> They'd sit and watch me as I grew;
> I would dream how nice 'twould be
> To have an Indian family—
> And now my dreams have all come true.[46]

This verse provides some interesting backstory and reveals that for Annie, becoming an Indian is the achievement of a lifelong dream. Following this logic, being adopted into the Sioux tribe is simply a full acceptance and confirmation of what Annie *always already was*, a Native American.

The original staging of "I'm an Indian Too" as choreographed by Helen Tamiris was also constructed in earnest. Tamiris's notes for the Indian Dance indicate that the dancers should wear "Full Pow-Wow Regalia" and attempt to be legitimate in reproducing traditional Native American dances. Tamiris writes, "Find some authentic Indian themes, present them

Annie Oakley (Ethel Merman), outfitted as an Indian, poses with Chief Sitting Bull (Harry Bellaver), who adopts her into the Sioux tribe. *Credit:* Photofest

to Irving Berlin—to be used along with Tom Toms."[47] For many critics, the dance was the choreographic high point of the show. It was only when "Miss Merman is inducted into the tribe" that the dance "quickly shifts to farce."[48] And that in many ways is the point. The song is never meant to parody Indians; rather Annie is the odd woman out who is thrown by the unfamiliar ceremony. It's not the dance that is comical, it's Annie (and Merman) who is funny. The song has a sort of split personality that mirrors Berlin's life; it is a legit Broadway number with its roots in the world of ethnic vaudeville comedy writing.

What then are we to make of the Native American characters here and the charges of racism or stereotyping that have dogged the show? "I'm an Indian Too" begins with an invocation of real Native American tribes: the Seminole, the Navajo, and the Kickapoo, but it then shifts to a humorous comparison, again combining the serious with the vaudevillian. Annie sings, "Just like Battle Ax, Hatchet Face, Eagle Nose,/ Like those Indians, I'm an Indian too." Annie compares herself to what are essentially stage Indians, performed caricatures. While the Native Americans who performed in the Wild West show were real Native Americans (that is, Seminoles, Sioux, etc.), the personalities they had to play were Indian caricatures. "Annie makes it clear from her song," writes Andrea Most, "that she realizes Sitting Bull is making her not a *real*—that is, racial—Indian, but rather a theatrical *acted* version of an Indian ('*like* an Indian')."[49] But here's the rub. Just as Annie is doing an act here, *so too were the Native Americans* forced to perform as stage versions of themselves. What both parties learn, Annie in *Annie Get Your Gun* and the Native Americans in Wild West shows, is that performing a stereotype—or performing in general, for that matter—was a strategy to assimilate and be part of society, to not remain on the margins, or in this case, in the woods. What these acts do not diminish, though, is the fact that Annie and the Native Americans, in spite of what roles they may perform for others, have not lost connection with their roots. They preserve, to continue borrowing for a moment from Jewish culture, *dos pintele yid*, the little spark of Jewishness retained by the assimilating Jew who changes his outward appearance but holds on to an essence that still makes him Jewish. In "I'm an Indian Too" Annie Oakley doesn't become a real Indian, because at her core, she was already an Indian to begin with.

Performative behavior drives the characters in *Annie Get Your Gun*, especially Annie, but to say that *everything* becomes performance overlooks the idea that there may be something we could call a core identity behind the performance. Even if we were to accept the belief, as most performance studies scholars propose, that all identities are a performance of one sort or another, this does not negate a reading in which multiple performances can exist simultaneously. "I'm an Indian Too" must be read both as serious *and* as parodic, because that is the lesson of *Annie Get Your Gun*: to be a success, one must embrace both nature and performance, to be like the immigrant who could retain his roots but also assimilate.

This layering of performance on top of real identity is perhaps best witnessed in the show's final scene when Sitting Bull instructs Annie on how to win back Frank. Handing her a gun whose sights are purposely misaligned, Sitting Bull tells Annie, "You get man with this gun." Annie realizes if she fakes being second best, she'll get Frank, but deep down she knows she's still a champion. With over-the-top dramatics as she misses one shot after another, Annie exclaims, "I cain't! I cain't! I quit! I give up! I concede this match to Frank Butler! The greatest sharpshooter in the world!"[50] Frank believes that he's actually won and reunites with Annie. So while this performance of Annie's unsuccessful shooting tricks Frank, *we* know that the real Annie hasn't given up.

Does *Annie Get Your Gun* ever redeem the Native American figures from caricature? Not really. The show is, and will always be, a product of 1946, and therefore defined by that era's cultural and racial context. Do we never revive the show again and condemn it to oblivion, or do we close our eyes and look the other way at a number like "I'm an Indian Too"? Or do we do what the recent Broadway revival of *Annie Get Your Gun* did and just cut the song, excising anything that's deemed racist or problematic? I don't think there's one simple answer, but I think we can at least try to look at the show on its own terms and make sense of it and what it might have to say about race at that particular moment in time.

Oklahoma! and *Annie Get Your Gun* reveal competing strategies for how Americans used the Wild West as a device to create new patriotic and nationalistic identities. Sometimes they played cowboys (and ranchers), as in *Oklahoma!*; other times they were Indians, as in *Annie Get Your Gun*. But both offered ways to negotiate whiteness, sometimes looking to truly assimilate into a larger white community, and in other cases simply performing whiteness when suitable as a way to join a community but not lose one's roots in the process. Any way you look at it, though, Indians got the short end of the performance stick, while whites (or immigrants who wanted to become white) could use the figure of the Indian, whether noble, caricatured, or even vanished, as a tool to consolidate their own white identity. This discussion of whiteness is not meant to lessen the difficulties of representation that actual Native Americans have had to endure either in Wild West shows or in nostalgic frontier-based Broadway musicals, but rather to point out that race is a category that affects everyone, whites included, regardless of whether or not they see themselves implicated in the discussion.

3

Trouble in New York City

The Racial Politics of *West Side Story* and *The Music Man*

If America looked to some like a land of liberty and sunshine, for others it was
a world of McCarthyite paranoia, deep racial tension, and hysteria in the face of
rock and roll, comic books, and teen delinquency.
—Philip J. Deloria, *Playing Indian*

Think quick. Which of the following shows won the Tony Award for Best
Musical in 1958? *Jamaica*; *The Music Man*; *New Girl in Town*; *Oh, Captain!*;
or *West Side Story*? If you guessed the groundbreaking dance musical *West
Side Story*, you'd be wrong. More than fifty years after it opened in 1957,
most people are still surprised to learn that the Jerome Robbins–Leonard
Bernstein–Stephen Sondheim–Arthur Laurents show lost the Best Musical distinction to rival *The Music Man*. Not that *The Music Man* was poor
fare by any means. Meredith Willson pulled off the impressive hat trick of
writing the book, music, and lyrics for the show, creating what has become
one of the American theater's most beloved musical chestnuts. But how is
it possible that the revolutionary *West Side Story*, created by four theatrical
innovators, all working at the top of their game, lost to Willson's corn-fed
show? Critics, fans, and scholars have tried to argue that *West Side Story*
was simply too theatrically sophisticated or too thematically gritty for its
time. With its gang violence and extensive use of dance, *West Side Story*
was unlike anything that audiences had seen before. Many of the original reviews for *West Side Story* were mixed to positive, but nothing like
the ecstatic across-the-board raves that *The Music Man* garnered. By the
early 1960s, though, as return engagements and revivals of *West Side Story*
appeared and the 1961 movie adaptation swept the Oscars, the show was
deemed a "classic" in the canon of musical theater.

While critics are right to argue that part of *West Side Story*'s slow rise to fame was due to its being too ahead of its time, what they have yet to consider is both shows' racial politics. *West Side Story* is obviously about race, as its story centers on two rival racialized gangs: the "white" Jets and the Puerto Rican Sharks. But what about *The Music Man* and its ostensible lack of racial politics? Both shows reflect a particular moment in U.S. racial history in which whiteness is recalibrated to incorporate not just Anglo-Saxons but "white" individuals from a variety of ethnic backgrounds including Italians, Jews, Poles, and other once-marginalized white ethnics to form a new group: Caucasians. *West Side Story* and, on the flip side, *The Music Man* exhibit a new ambivalence about whiteness in the late 1950s that complicates how we view the shows' receptions in the world of Broadway musicals.

What also ties the shows together is the connection between race and place. *West Side Story* is a musical of the "big city" and its ensuing racial tensions, while *The Music Man* is a nostalgic embrace of homogeneous small-town life. But considering that both shows debuted on Broadway at the same time compels us to consider how these disparate scenarios actually dialogue with each other and are comments on the late-1950s world in which they were produced, both responding to tensions and fears about race, but in completely different ways.

West Side Story might be one of America's most famous musicals, but its almost ten-year genesis is not well known by even the show's most ardent aficionados. The musical is a modern-day retelling of Shakespeare's *Romeo and Juliet*, now set in the streets of late-1950s New York. The Montagues and the Capulets have been replaced by the Jets, a gang of native-born Americans and the scions of immigrant parents, and the Sharks, a gang of Puerto Rican immigrants. Romeo has become Tony (of the Jets), and Juliet is Maria, recently arrived from Puerto Rico. The action proceeds quite quickly: Tony and Maria fall in love almost immediately at a neighborhood dance, and their ominous fate is sealed by the next day. While many of the characters in *West Side Story* have their Shakespearean counterparts, book writer Arthur Laurents took a few significant liberties with the text. Where Romeo dies by drinking poison, Laurents eschews poison (considered too esoteric and unbelievable a plot device for the 1950s) and instead has Tony die by gunshot. Maria, rather than die with her lover (as

Juliet does by stabbing herself), remains alive at the show's conclusion and delivers the final searing monologue about the power of hate. Of course, *West Side Story* also deviates from Shakespeare in that the rivalry that has developed between the two gangs is not simply the residue of some "ancient grudge" but is continually fueled by social and racial tensions.

But for all these changes, what is perhaps most interesting is that this was not the show that was initially imagined by the creators at all. *West Side Story* is a musical with a fascinating history, a genesis that speaks to the work's racial underpinnings as well as to the lives of the show's Jewish creators themselves. While this history might seem merely anecdotal, tracing the show's development provides insight into the musical's ultimate handling of racial themes that complicates how many critics and audiences have traditionally interpreted what seems like a clear-cut story of racialized gang violence set to music.

The history of *West Side Story* begins with Jerome Robbins, a dancer and choreographer who was quickly making a name for himself in the world of both classical dance and theater. Born Jerome Rabinowitz, the son of Polish immigrants, he began dancing as an alternative to working in his father's corset company. By the late 1930s and early 1940s, Robbins earned his credentials as a dancer and burgeoning choreographer. It was his 1944 collaboration with Leonard Bernstein, though, a ballet called *Fancy Free*, that put Robbins on the map. The success of that piece led to a full-length musical based on the ballet later that year, entitled *On the Town* (1944) with music by Bernstein and lyrics by Betty Comden and Adolph Green, about three sailors on leave in New York City. *On the Town* positioned Robbins as a force in the dance world and established a strong connection with Bernstein.

West Side Story had its genesis when an actor friend who was performing the role of Romeo asked Robbins for advice on how he should approach his character. A lightbulb went on, dim at first. Make *Romeo and Juliet* contemporary. The idea sat in Robbins's head until 1949, according to Bernstein, when "Jerry called up and gave us [Bernstein and Laurents] this idea. . . . It was an East Side version of *Romeo and Juliet*, involving as the feuding parties Catholics and Jews at the Passover-Easter season with feelings in the streets running very high, with a certain amount of slugging and bloodletting. It seemed to match the Romeo story very well, except that this was not a family feud, *but religion-oriented.*" Arthur Laurents picks up on Bernstein's narrative: "My reaction was, it was *Abie's Irish Rose,* and that's why we didn't go ahead with it."[1] Laurents writes in *West Side Story's* 1957 Playbill: "*East Side Story* was the original title of *West Side Story.* . . . The locale was to be literally the lower East Side of New York: specifically, Allen Street for Juliet and the Capulets, Mulberry Street for Romeo and the Montagues."[2]

What caused the show to change from *East Side Story* to *West Side Story?* A fair amount of time elapsed between Jerry Robbins's original idea in 1949 and the Broadway premiere in 1957. Various drafts involving Jews and Catholics were written and discarded. Broadway pros Betty Comden and Adolph Green were originally going to provide the lyrics but were unavailable in Hollywood working on a film; instead, newcomer Stephen Sondheim was brought on in 1955 and actually co-wrote the lyrics *with* Leonard Bernstein, another little-known fact.[3]

Early on, the idea of doing a show that would focus on the issue of religious and ethnic tolerance inspired Bernstein, Laurents, and Robbins (Sondheim would enter the project after the transition to *West Side Story* had already occurred), but something wasn't working. Following World War II, Jewish identity was in flux. Jews were no longer entirely marginalized, and yet anti-Semitism lingered, a fact evident in the success of the 1947 film *Gentleman's Agreement,* which pointed a finger at America's ongoing subtle hatred for Jews. At midcentury, according to the racial scholar Matthew Frye Jacobson, "ethnic revision of race stopped at the color line, universalizing *whiteness* by lessening the presumed difference separating 'Hebrews,' 'Celts,' and 'Anglo-Saxons,' but deepening the separation between any of these former white races and people of color, especially blacks."[4] Yet even at this early moment, a conflation of racial issues and religious ones seemed to be occurring. What exactly were Jews? A race? A religion? A people? A culture? All of the above? It was hard to say.

One possible answer to this ambiguity of categories can be found in the Library of Congress, which has Bernstein's own annotated copy of *Romeo and Juliet,* presumably marked up after Robbins pitched Bernstein his idea. Library of Congress senior music specialist Mark Horowitz explains that "in the inside cover of the book, Lenny has penciled a scene breakdown. Act one begins with scene 'I. Street Scene—pushcarts–enter R—or Mulberry St. Festival—or Easter=Passover.' Scene three is 'Balcony Scene'; Scene five is 'Bridal Scene' and the act ends with scene six 'Street Fight.' Act two includes this cryptic description of scene two: 'Sex—Plan to escape to Mexico'; and the act ends with scene four's 'Romeo's death with Tante' and scene five 'Juliet's death.'" From the allusion to Passover as well as what we know about earlier instantiations of the musical, it's clear that Shakespeare would be given a Jewish makeover. Yet perhaps the most interesting annotation is the one that appears on the top of the first page of dialogue, where Bernstein has written, "An out and out plea for racial tolerance." Assuming that this annotation was made early on in the process, what does this mean for how we understand Jews and race? Does this apparently simple notation not offer, at least in theory, the possibility for us to read Jews, at this moment, as a distinct and even visible group of people? Bernstein's call isn't for religious but *racial* tolerance. "Throughout the text he makes various notes in the margins for staging or casting ideas," Horowitz observes, "and the occasional song ideas, including one he describes as 'Song on racism' and titles 'It's the Jews'—a song he ultimately wrote for another project."[5] While much remains lost about the meaning of the annotated text, at least parts of it seem to provide clues for how we understand a shifting sense of Jewish racial/ethnic identity in post–World War II America.

What, though, did *East Side Story* look like? Several drafts were penned, and traces of the early incarnation live on in theatrical archives. In one manuscript, simply titled "Rough Outline: 'Romeo,'" Romeo is Italian and the Capulets are Jewish. Laurents's script takes its cue rather directly from the Bard. The play opens with a fight involving Mercutio, Benvolio, and Romeo. Romeo has been following Rosalind, much as in Shakespeare's original, and the script informs us that "Mercutio and the others kid him [Romeo]. He ought to know better than to 'chase a Jew babe.' 'They don't put out.' But 'Rosalind ain't orthodox' etc."[6]

Not much changes in Laurents's script from Shakespeare, except for the ethnic and religious backgrounds of the characters. In act 1, scene 4 of the draft, Shakespeare's balcony scene is reset on a fire escape, and Laurents writes that "the difference in religion should not matter to either of them and Juliet here explains she is a cousin come to visit the Capulets for the

Passover holidays with her Tante." Act 2, meanwhile, opens with a seder at the Capulets':

> Scene One: A tenement is revealed and we are looking into one of the upper apartments: the Capulets'. *To music*, a seder is in progress The Cpaulet [*sic*] family, Julet [*sic*], Tante, other cousins (how many?) are all there. They have come to the Four Questions. Tybalt, the only child, should ask these but he is not home. Loafing with that gang, his mother says irritably, and a cousin asks the questions. The seder (*sung in English*) continues and the background slowly is lighted.

Outside, a cop chases Romeo. The seder continues, and "they have reached the last of the ten plagues: the death of the first born (Tybalt)," who was killed by Romeo. The scene even involves the search for the "hidden Matzoth."[7]

Can we even imagine a show in which Jews would be looking for the *afikomen* ("hidden Matzoth")? Broadway's most Jewish musical, *Fiddler on the Roof* (1964), was still a few years away. While this *East Side Story* had the potential to be game-changing by putting Jewishness onstage so nakedly, the show's racial politics were fiercely dated. Jews and Catholics might have had some latent animosity, but they were hardly murdering each other on the streets of New York in the late 1940s or early 1950s.

Another early undated script by Laurents, set in what seems to be early twentieth-century New York, highlights the Jewish thematics even more. Dorrie and her Tante, Jewish immigrants who have just arrived in America, are walking in the streets of the Lower East Side.

> Scene Two
> (The curtains open on a blaze of light, color, music, movement. People dance and mill about the street which is festooned with lights and winds between the front of a tenement, downstage right, and facades of shops opposite. We can see part of a candy-drugstore and/or its sign: DOC'S; possibly something of SIRON-SKY'S BRIDAL SHOPPE; a sign with the symbols for kosher;

PIZZERIA, etc. One or two floats with the Virgin; a couple of pushcarts or stalls selling religious figures, souvenirs, penny candy, etc.

Tonio, a delivery boy for Doc, appears. Then Dorrie shows up with Tante. People have been dancing in the street. Dorrie ends up in Tonio's arms and they dance together. Joshua (her brother?) tears them apart.

JOSHUA. Stick to our side of the street.
TANTE. *(Coming up):* What's such a rumpus. *(Looking at Tonio)* A shaneh boychik.
JOSHUA. A wop!
TANTE. *(Shrugging, to Dorrie):* Still shaneh.

The Italians and Jews exchange words, but police officer Shrank shows up, trying to find out what is going on and what happened to A-rab, a Jew who has been beaten up in the first scene.

COP. Kid got four teeth knocked out, Lieutenant.
SHRANK. Well, he can shake his head Yes or No. Was he the one? *(No answer)* You dumb little matzoth ball, this is for your own protection.
SHRANK. O.K. You Jews clear out. This ain't your party. Get!
COP. *(Edging the Jews)* Go on. *(The Jews start off toward the tenement side. Tante leads Dorrie with a shrug)*
TANTE. Nu, in the old country, they rode horses.[8]

The animosity between the two groups feels like a holdover from a previous generation; by the late forties Jews weren't immigrating to the Lower East Side, they were leaving it. While *Fiddler on the Roof* would highlight the violence between Jews and their neighbors, this draft's turn-of-the-century setting clearly marked such violence as part of the legacy of eastern European pogroms and not the current experience of Jews, who by the late fifties were enjoying a veritable open-arms welcome in the United States. It's no wonder this project died. As Bernstein himself recalls, "I had a strong feeling of staleness of the East Side situation and I didn't like the too-angry, too-bitchy, too-vulgar tone of it. We talked and slowly the project fizzled out."[9]

What's interesting about this history of *East Side Story* is that even as the Jewish/Catholic plot line changed to the "American"/Puerto Rican story, Laurents and the creators hung on to a bit of Jewish particularity. In another version of the script, also called "Romeo," but in which the gangs are now Puerto Rican and "American," act 1, scene 6 takes place in a drugstore where "Doc (possibly a Jew) tries vainly to stop the rumble."[10] What does it mean that Doc is now the sole Jewish character in the show? Was it the Jewish creators' own attempt to mark their commitment both to Jewish difference and social justice by making the play's moral arbiter one of their own? In another undated script, Tony tells Doc that he's in love, and Doc responds with the Yiddish-inflected "So soon, boychik? So soon?"[11] By the time the show reaches its finalized form, though, Doc has lost all religious and ethnic coloring, and his response to Tony's proclamation of love is a simple "How do you know?"[12] In the finalized show, the Jewish element is entirely erased, and yet, at least in rehearsal, a trace of Jewishness remained. Jerome Robbins, in trying to get the cast members to internalize the show's gang animosities, turned to a particularly vibrant metaphor. According to Laurents, "Puerto Rican immigrants versus Polish Americans wasn't something they could identify with so he divided them into Jews and Nazis in a concentration camp."[13] This technique, along with forcing the cast members of the opposing gangs not to eat lunch together or associate with each other outside of rehearsal, was meant to heighten the tension and create a palpable sense of Method-acting-infused animosity.

What, though, was the turning point that took the show away from its Jewish/Catholic roots? Arthur Laurents was at least partially correct; there was something very *Abie's Irish Rose* about the whole initial project, but is there more to the story than that? Was the underlying issue related to Bernstein's comments that the original concept was based on religious/racial politics—a concern that perhaps the creators themselves could not fully articulate? As work continued at a haphazard pace on the musical—all the creators had competing projects that often drew their attention away—they realized early on that something wasn't working. Bernstein and Laurents "recognized that the East Side wasn't what it used to be: there had been an influx of Latin Americans, and the Jewish-Catholic ghettoes were not now the exclusive zones of gang rivalry."[14] In other words, the idea of an *East* Side story was dated not simply because the project bore resemblances to *Abie's Irish Rose* but because the racial and ethnic landscape of America, particularly the country's *white* landscape, was quickly changing as the team was writing.[15]

Arthur Laurents recounts the moment in which the key to *West Side Story*'s puzzle appeared. While lounging at the pool of the Beverly Hills Hotel and talking about all things theatrical, he and Bernstein began to discuss that morning's headline in the Los Angeles papers: "More Mayhem from Chicano Gangs." Conversation soon turned to the possibility of using Latin music in the show, and the pieces began to come together in their heads. Laurents, though, had no knowledge of Chicanos in L.A.: "New York and Harlem I knew firsthand, and Puerto Ricans and Negroes and immigrants who had become Americans. And however it turned out, the show wouldn't be *Abie's Irish Rose*. It would have Latin passion, immigrant anger, shared resentment. The potential was there, this could well be a 'Romeo' to excite all of us. We called Jerry."[16] Bernstein recalls a similar moment in a fictionalized journal entry he wrote for the show's Broadway playbill: "We're fired again by the *Romeo* notion; only now we have abandoned the whole Jewish-Catholic premise as not very fresh, and have come up with what I think is going to be it: two teen-age gangs, one the warring Puerto Ricans, the other self-styled 'Americans.' Suddenly it all springs to life. I hear rhythms and pulses, and—most of all—I can sort of feel the form."[17] With this new direction established, Robbins quickly delved into sociological research, collecting newspaper articles concerning gang murders in 1955.[18]

Following this change in the project's focus, Arthur Laurents emphasized the topicality of the new show in a letter to Bernstein and Robbins:

> I don't know whether you've been so busy that you've missed all the juvenile gang war news. Not only is it all over the papers everyday, but it is going to be all over the movie screens. Arthur Miller, or so I read, is doing an original drama on the subject for movies.[19]
>
> By accident, then, we have hit on an idea which is suddenly extremely topical, timely, and just plain hot. For this reason, I hope we

can get to serious work on it as early as we planned. . . . I don't know if it's possible but with all this splurge of interest in the subject, I think we would be missing a big opportunity if we didn't capitalize on it.

Incidentally, I hope you noticed I didn't say "East Side Story." This was because of our mutual feeling that the locale should not be specific or definitely placed in any specific city.[20]

In October 1955, Robbins wrote to Laurents of his frustration at still not being able to move ahead with "Romeo," as he called the show. In a postscript to the letter, he urged, "By the way, get a copy of Jo Sinclair's book 'The Changelings.' It's about the undercurrent background of gangwar on a street which is inhabited mostly by Jewish people but is slowly being taken over by Negroes. Somewhat apropos."[21] Laurents did get Sinclair's book, but he didn't like it; still, it's significant that the book was on their radar.[22] In *The Changelings* (1955), Jo Sinclair tells the story of Judy Vincent, a young Jewish tomboy who leads a gang and becomes friends with a black girl in town. Like some of Sinclair's other work, the book emphasizes the similarities between Jews and African Americans. This was hardly the politics of *West Side Story*, where the emphasis seemed to be about highlighting racial difference, but Sinclair's book is also about white racial identity where Jews are no longer the minority; blacks are.

Work continued on the show, but the team found themselves confronting another problem: producers who didn't see the commercial viability of a musical about gangs.[23] This clearly wasn't musical comedy as they knew it. Cheryl Crawford, who had found success as a producer with *Porgy and Bess, Brigadoon*, and several plays by Tennessee Williams, had gotten behind the creative team, but as time progressed, she became more and more disenchanted with the work. As if playing the part of the racial theorist, even Crawford wanted to know "why the poor in New York were now predominantly Puerto Rican or black and not Jewish any longer."[24] Laurents would later claim that Crawford wanted the creators to "delineat[e] how middle-class Wasp [*sic*] had given way to immigrant Jews to poor Negroes to motley mix. Set that to music."[25] Crawford wrote to Laurents:

It occurs to me that the basic truth of this environment is that the street was once respectable middle class. Then the owners were able to move on to better places, poorer people moved in. . . . They made enough money to move on and Negroes moved in. As some of them did better financially, they moved out and Puerto Ricans came in. To each successive wave these houses were better than what they had before. I don't see this handled in a documentary fashion but this step up movement, with the weaker or unfortunate left behind is a symbol which an audience can grasp and appreciate of our particular kind of social progress.[26]

The team, though, wasn't writing a show about how the gangs came to be or what led to changes in racial identity; rather the rivalry, as in Shakespeare's text, was constructed as if age-old. It didn't help that Laurents was writing a pseudo-realist libretto that, though grounded in the gang violence of the day, contained a purposely made-up language spoken by the Jets. The show seemed to be both too realist and not realist enough. "Six weeks before rehearsals were due to begin," Keith Garebian explains in his history of the show, "[Cheryl Crawford] met with the collaborators in her office. Her tone was more angry than agonized, and she insisted that the libretto explain why the gang members were the way they were. She rejected contentions that the play was a poetic fantasy rather than a sociological document."[27] Crawford wanted a work that would explicitly name the social and racial problems the creators were grappling with. She gave the team an ultimatum: rewrite the show or she would walk. The collaborators beat her to the punch and marched out of her office. Laurents and Sondheim made some calls, and over the next few days the team found producer support in the form of Roger Stevens, Hal Prince, and Robert Griffith, who would keep the creators' vision intact.

While street violence was continuing in New York, and Bernstein, Laurents, Sondheim, and Robbins were bringing their dance drama to Broadway, another musical was also trekking to the Great White Way. Trying out in Philadelphia (as did *West Side Story*), *The Music Man* was probably about as far away from the thematics of *West Side Story* as you could get. Written by a first-time Broadway composer, lyricist, and book writer, Meredith Willson, *The Music Man* tells the story of a con artist, Harold Hill, who comes to River City, Iowa, in 1912. Hill passes himself off as a bandleader to swindle the good-natured townspeople out of their money by having them buy instruments and band uniforms for the town's kids. The catch is that Hill knows nothing about bands or music. Feisty librarian Marian Paroo catches on to Harold's wily ways and sets out to take him down, but in classic musical comedy fashion, the two fall in love. Despite an attempt to run him out of town, Hill finds himself surprisingly vindicated when his fictitious ploy to get the boys in the band to play music just by thinking about it ("the think system") actually turns out to work. Love reigns, the townspeople rejoice, and the band marches off. All in all, a tidy ending to what is pure Americana.

When I would tell friends that I was planning to include *The Music Man* in my book about race and the Broadway musical, many of them expressed sheer confusion. "The show doesn't have anything to do with race," they would say. Their belief is paradoxically 100 percent correct *and* incorrect. *The Music Man* never explicitly brings up racial issues, but that fact alone speaks volumes about the politics of the day. What does it mean for a show to turn so fiercely away from the topic of race when it was a subject that was extremely present in New York and elsewhere around the country? *The Music Man* falls into a category of shows that seem not to be about race simply because there are no people of color present, but whiteness, once again, rears its (not so invisible) head, and *The Music Man* comes to embody an artificial and imaginary homogeneous America as only musical comedy can do. While 1957 America had a slew of issues to contend with—from the Cold War to the death of Joseph McCarthy, whose Communist witch hunts plagued America in 1954—the citizens of the fictitious River City were living in contented bliss. And they weren't alone. On October 4, 1957, *Leave It to Beaver*, which celebrated suburban white America, hit the TV airwaves, joining 1954's *Father Knows Best*. Donna Reed, the world's most perfect suburban housewife, would become a TV icon just a year later in September 1958. Not a gang in sight.

Like the suburban America portrayed in 1950s television, "River City isn't in any trouble," Marcellus Washburn, an old friend of Harold Hill's and a River City resident, says. "Then I'll have to create some" is Harold's reply, a setup that leads into the song "Ya Got Trouble," where Hill enumerates the "evils" of gambling and smoking facing the town's youth. These evils, so Hill claims, will send the youth out of the pool halls and— God forbid!—into the "Dance at the Arm'ry" where they'll hear "RAG-

Harold Hill (Robert Preston, who also starred in the role on Broadway) performs "Seventy-six Trombones" and stirs up trouble in small-town 1912 River City, Iowa, in the 1962 movie version of *The Music Man*. *Credit:* Photofest

TIME/ Shameless music that'll/ Grab your son and/ Your daughter with the/ Arms of a jungle/ Animal instinct/ MASS-steria!"[28] Ragtime—code for African Americans?—will ensnare the youth and bring out their savageness. A subtle racial aside, but one that is used as a scare tactic for small-town white America. The cleverly constructed song connects one evil to another until finally the town's youth seem beyond redemption, that is, unless they buy into Hill's scheme and join his band.

While some have argued that Willson's show is a satire of small-town life, in the end, the musical is a glorification of Americana.[29] *The Music Man* virtually spews red-white-and-blue patriotism, layering on one all-American motif after another. The show is set in Iowa, as corn-fed a state as you can get, in a town where only white people live. Iowa is a state that, like Oklahoma, was built from what was once Indian Territory, and Native Americans were forcibly removed from Iowa, but their presence remains in *The Music Man*. The mayor's wife, Eulalie Mackecknie Shinn, performs an Indian-inspired dance at the town's Fourth of July celebration. Mayor Shinn informs the townspeople that "the Wa Tan Ye girls of the local wigwam of Heeawatha will present a spectacle my wife— (Catching himself HE looks at notes again) —in which my wife . . . will take a leading part."[30] The girls and Eulalie then appear: "Each wears a feather in a head-band and they are doing an Indian war dance step. EULALIE precedes them in full Indian head-dress, carrying a tom-tom which she beats to MARIAN'S Indian rhythm." Eulalie then says she will "count to twenty in the Indian tongue! Een teen tuther feather fip!"[31] As if unable to stop their fetishizing of Native Americans, the show's barbershop quartet appears at the top of act 2, for reasons never explained, "dressed in Indian regalia."[32] What these Indian motifs recall is that once the "threat" of actual Native Americans is removed from the picture, white Americans can play as cowboys and Indians in a sort of patriotic nativist redface routine. That this Indian act occurs during the Fourth of July ties nativism, manifest destiny, and patriotism together in a tidy package.

The action of *The Music Man* begins on July 4, 1912, presenting lots of opportunities for the show's designers to create a theatrical patriotic fantasy. Classic American iconography is even invoked when the "Iowa Stubborn" number stops for a moment to frame a farmer and his wife in a tableau of Grant Wood's *American Gothic*.[33] Musically, the show pays tribute to patriotic musical traditions: barbershop quartets and marching band music in the style of John Philip Sousa, with whom Willson himself performed, predominate.[34] In her own scholarly analysis of *The Music Man*'s engagement with whiteness, Carol Oja reads the show's barbershop quartet, played by an actual quartet known as the Buffalo Bills, as a symbol of whiteness. Oja relates that the history of barbershop quartets is tied to segregation and claims that "in the 1950s, barbershop was emphatically coded as white, and its tie to *The Music Man* ran deep."[35] The quartet, like bands in general with their identical outfits, becomes a symbol of racial homogeneity and supports the show's overwhelming picture of whiteness.

The Music Man and *West Side Story* engage race in very different ways, but both are centered on the evolving concept of whiteness. Despite the fact that the authors of *West Side Story* did not delve into the sociology of race, there were many societal changes that affected racial ideologies in the 1950s and influenced the show's creation. During *West Side Story*'s D.C. tryout, Strom Thurmond "launched a filibuster in the Senate that lasted over 24 hours . . . to thwart passage of the Civil Rights Act of 1957, the first in a string of legislative initiatives that led eventually to the historic Voting Rights Act of 1965." The day before *West Side Story* opened on Broadway, "President Eisenhower sent federal troops to force the admittance of nine African American students" at Little Rock Central High School.[36]

These changing racial ideas were being documented in the social theory of the time. In the late 1950s and early 1960s, sociologists Nathan Glazer and Daniel Patrick Moynihan were researching and writing their popular text *Beyond the Melting Pot* (1963), a study of the social and economic success of various racial and ethnic groups in New York City, including Negroes, Puerto Ricans, Jews, Italians, and the Irish. As this list makes clear, Glazer and Moynihan combine race and ethnicity, marking the book's immediate historical context at an interstitial moment in which white ethnics were becoming Caucasians. Glazer and Moynihan are not entirely ignorant of the ways in which whiteness articulates itself: "It was reasonable to believe that a new American type would emerge, a new nationality in which it would be a matter of indifference whether a man was of Anglo-Saxon or German or Italian or Jewish origin."[37] Of course, the indifference would be because of the ability of these new immigrants to become white via assimilation. The book attempts to be progressive in its racial views, but its overarching impact strengthens the sense of difference between whites and people of color. The book constitutes Jews as a perfect model minority, while Puerto Ricans and Negroes are deemed lacking in certain character traits. The idea was to consider each of these groups equally, but by not considering the effect that race and skin color had on people's social opportunities, the book overlooks the particular challenges facing people of color.

These elisions very much inform *West Side Story*. The creators of the musical "were pretending that Puerto Ricans were no different from the Jews, Italians, Poles, and so on who had come before them—no different, in fact, from the 'white ethnics' who had been so popular in the gangster movies of the 1930s."[38] Despite the ways in which Glazer and Moynihan shy away from discussing race, they cannot help but be drawn into its organizing effects, now focused around skin color. Their introduction concludes with the following: "The body of the book describes five major groups of the city. There is no great significance to the order in which they are arranged. We begin, as the visitor might, *with what immediately strikes the eye,* and proceed from there."[39] The chapter that follows is on "The Negroes," so what strikes the authors' eyes, despite their insistence to the contrary, is indeed race as constructed by skin color.

West Side Story works hard to play up the issue of color. In an undated letter to Robbins, Laurents writes that his friend the American ballerina Nora Kaye "thinks the Puerto Rican change is good, although she was dubious before. She thinks, however, that Tonio should not be Italian but Irish or Anglo-Saxon: contrast between light and dark." This prompts Laurents to write in the margin of the letter, "Just had an idea: Tonio could be a Polak. Color is thus [?] blond-family immigrants—can be cursed as 'Polak' instead of 'wop.' Only his name would have to be changed!—??"[40] While I hate to place too much emphasis on this moment, this seems to be one of the clearest instances in the genesis of *West Side Story* that illustrates the shift from race to ethnicity with a new emphasis on skin color. By the time we reach some of the 1957 drafts, the emphasis on color is apparent: Bernardo "might dance with two girls, but both would be dark-skinned," one script states. Anita is also marked as being "dark-skinned," while the script is clear to note that at least one of the Jets is a "blond."[41] This highlighting of color serves as one of the main points of contention for Frances Negrón-Muntaner, who finds *West Side Story* to be essentially the apotheosis of cultural texts that portray Puerto Ricans negatively. Regarding the show's film version, Negrón-Muntaner writes, "The three most obvious signs of racialization efforts are the use of 'brownface' for Bernardo, the always shifting, asinine accent deployed by most Puerto Rican characters, and the unnaturally blonde hair of the Jets. Without these three devices, most actors would simply look and sound like what they technically are: 'Americans.' "[42] Negrón-Muntaner's feelings are valid, but ironically, she wasn't alone. Laurents concurs, "The movie, I thought, and still think, was appalling. . . . *West Side Story* begins, and you see all these boys, with dyed hair and color-coordinated sneakers, doing tour jetés down a New York street. Not in this life. And then, when the so-called Puerto Ricans came on, made up to look like day-glo characters for some caricature of what they think Hispanics are—it was really disgraceful."[43]

So, if dyed hair and Day-Glo colors don't define race, what does? Instead of Jews and Catholics, we have the "white" Jets and the Puerto Rican Sharks. At first glance, this racial distinction seems fairly straightforward, but the show's racial complexity is based on the confusion around the Jets' racial makeup. Are they Americans? Whites? Anglos? Ethnic immigrants? Keith Garebian calls the Jets "white, urban-American street youths," while Walter Kerr in his *New York Times* review of the 1980 revival is clear to put quotation marks around "white" to refer to the Jets.[44] In his 1957 review, the *New Yorker*'s theater critic Wolcott Gibbs marks Maria as Puerto Rican and Tony as a Polish American. He goes on to note that "there has always been bitter feeling between the Sharks, who are Puerto Ricans, and the Jets, who consider themselves 'Americans,' however various and obscure their origins."[45] As late as 2007, Rachel Rubin and Jeffrey Melnick use the following terms to describe the Jets in the space of one critical essay: "Anglo Jets," "willing Anglos-in-training," "white," "Euro-Americans," "Anglo-Americans," and "mixed-white."[46]

But despite this confusion for audiences and critics, Laurents was quite explicit in the libretto's opening stage directions, in which we are told that "the Sharks are Puerto Ricans, the Jets an anthology of what is called 'American.'"[47] Here and in an article he wrote before the show's premiere, Laurents maintains his quotation marks around "American," terming the Jets "a polymorphous self-styled 'American' gang."[48] While there is seemingly no confusion over the Sharks' identity, the Jets, we learn, are actually a hodgepodge of individuals. Laurents draws our attention to the Jets' ostensibly fraught racial status by putting "American" in quotes and continues to drive home their tenuous white status over the course of the musical.

Only Tony is singled out with a Polish ethnic background, but it's clear that none of the Jets come from what we might term Anglo-Saxon stock. In a moment of gang antagonism, Pepe (of the Sharks) shouts "Micks!" and Indio shouts "Wop!"[49] It's not clear who of the Jets is of what lineage, but obviously there are Irish and Italians in their midst. In an early draft of the show, Tony (then called Tonio) was marked as Italian, prompting Bernardo to call him "Wop."[50] Presumably making Tony Polish helped to whiten him even more, as Laurents indicated in his letter to Robbins.[51] In this game of urban manifest destiny, the Jets work to secure their own place in the shifting American racial landscape. They might not have the

The Jets, "an anthology of what is called 'American,'" are shown here in a still from the original Broadway production. *Credit:* Photofest

social standing of blue-blooded Anglos, but in comparison with the dark-skinned Puerto Ricans (and African Americans, who don't even figure into the picture), they're way ahead. By the 1950s, "a complex system of races," Matthew Frye Jacobson writes, "had given way to a strict scheme of black and white, which itself implied an absence of race on the white side and a presence of race on the black. The 'ethnic' experience of European immigrant assimilation and mobility, meanwhile, became the standard against which blacks were measured—and found wanting."[52]

Why does Laurents put the term *American* in scare quotes? What is it that he is questioning? The Jets were born in America, true, but their racial status is a bit fraught. The fact that they are an "anthology" of individuals, coming from various backgrounds, speaks to a defining mythology of America: the melting pot of immigrants. It might seem that the Jets' whiteness solidifies their Americanness, but as the musical itself makes clear, the Sharks are also American citizens.[53] Do the quotation marks around the word *American*, then, call the bond between American identity and whiteness into question?

Is the musical not merely calling for an end to prejudice at its conclusion, but rather questioning the divisions between minorities from the get-go? The show repeatedly challenges and plays with the notion that being "American" is directly tied to being white. Yet this very whiteness, the "whiteness" of the Jets, is suspect and conditional, suspended in quotation marks.

This tension over whiteness has infused the show since day one and continues to do so today. Even current criticism that aims to address the show's purported racism and stereotyping of the Puerto Rican characters tends to misread the actual subtle racial makeup of the musical. Alberto Sandoval-Sánchez, in his rather excoriating "A Puerto Rican Reading of the America of *West Side Story*," views the characters as divided into two camps, the Puerto Ricans and the Anglo-Americans: "Although the Jets constitute an anthology of 'Americans,' the gang is made up solely of the children of white European immigrants. Their actions and values embody the ideological apparatus of the Anglo-American national subjectivity— that is, the ideological program and ways of doing of the 'all-American boy.'" But Sandoval-Sánchez's observation is a misreading, as Laurents has not said that the gang is "all-American"; rather, they are "what is called 'American,'" which seems, paradoxical though it may be, both an asser- tion and questioning of their Americanness at the same time. Sandoval- Sánchez further remarks that the Jets "emblematized the ideology of the all-American boy, a totally white identity that does not leave room for any other ethnoracial groups in the gang." The Jets do aim to be seen as white, but these guys are hardly the boys next door, unless the "all-American boy" carries a switchblade. Sandoval-Sánchez glosses over the musical's complex and drawn-out creation process to claim that "the writers moved comfortably from Jews and Italians, to Chicanos, to blacks, and finally to Puerto Ricans. They were simply searching for a confrontation between peoples of color and Caucasian Anglo-Americans."[54] That the Jets have become Caucasian, no doubt, but Anglo-Americans, absolutely not.

Meanwhile, *The Music Man* was dealing with its own issues with white- ness on a more subtle level. On the surface, the conflicts in *The Music Man* seem rather straightforward. Mayor Shinn mistrusts Hill, as does librar- ian Marian Paroo, but there are also smaller skirmishes that undergird the main plotline and cast a racialized shadow on the town's rosy homogene- ity. The gossipy women in River City, led by the mayor's wife, are much disturbed by Marian. She provides their children with "scandalous" books to read—Chaucer, Rabelais, and Balzac—and they imply that she has had some sort of illicit relationship with Old Miser Madison, after whom the town's library was named. But what is left unspoken is a characteristic of the Paroos that makes them stand out from almost every other townsperson: they are Irish. Marian's mother, known simply as Mrs. Paroo, is based, says Willson, on "a wonderful German lady named Mrs. Buehler" who "used to help Mama clean house on Saturdays."[55] Originally played by Irish actress Pert Kelton, Mrs. Paroo speaks with a pronounced Irish accent throughout the show. If the Irish didn't face the same prejudice as people of color, they did face a fair share of prejudice and stereotyping up into the 1960s. From feelings of anti-Catholic sentiment, which would remain at least until the election of John F. Kennedy as president, to concerns over the political machine Tammany Hall, Anglo-Americans had some concerns and fears about their Irish neighbors. Governor Al Smith, a Democrat from New York, lost the presidential election in 1928 largely because he faced Irish Catholic prejudice. While it is true that the characters in *The Music Man* never explicitly make an issue of the Paroos' Irishness, one can't help but consider that it might add to their general "off-white" minority status. Their Irishness allows Willson to highlight the family's outsider position in the town, especially Marian's shunning by the townswomen. But Irish identity is not so inassimilable; once the River City women welcome Marian into their midst, she quickly becomes part of the community.

The Paroos aren't the only ones in River City facing prejudice. A minor plotline involves a romantic relationship between the mayor's daughter Zaneeta and Tommy Djilas (pronounced "gee-less"), a young hooligan who is always playing pranks. When we first meet Tommy during the Fourth of July celebration, the stage directions tell us he is wearing "obviously 'poor' clothes," clearly a sign of his social status. We don't know much about Tommy's family except that "his father is one a'them day laborers south a'town," as Mayor Shinn dismissively says.[56] Djilas is a Yugoslavian name, and given Tommy's questionable background, Mayor Shinn doesn't want his daughter running around with such a boy. Might Tommy be the sort of racial threat that could damage the moral fiber of the town? The play never explicitly says, but it would explain why Tommy is so looked down upon. By the end of the play, though, Djilas has become part of the homogeneous uniformed band, revealing that white assimilation is only a musical number and costume change away.

These concerns about whiteness and ethnicity are directly connected to the issue of place and location in the musicals. In *West Side Story*, this translated to the physical space of the streets of New York. A concern for many Americans in this time period was: who are my neighbors and does it matter if they look like me? Laurents highlights this in *West Side Story*'s opening stage directions: "The action begins with the Jets in possession of the area: owning, enjoying, loving their 'home.'"[57] *West Side Story* becomes an allegory of sorts, the streets of New York representing the larger American landscape that was coming to terms with changing racial ideologies on a national level.

The conflict over race and place was most felt in the show's oft-rewritten opening scene. Most of *West Side Story* remained fairly constant during rewrites and out-of-town tryouts, but the creators strove to find the right tone to open their musical. While the musical would ultimately begin with its famous danced prologue, two songs were tried out in this scene in addition to the "Jet Song." The first, "This Turf Is Ours," written out of town for the Washington, D.C., pre-Broadway stop, was meant to replace the "Jet Song" but was considered "too harsh" by the creators.[58] The lyrics of "This Turf Is Ours" reflect the Jets' bracing xenophobia:

> This turf is ours!
> Drew a big white line
> With a "keep out" sign,
> And they crossed it.

> This turf is ours!
> Gotta hold our ground
> Or we'll turn around
> And we've lost it!

> We're stakin' a claim,
> The boundaries are set out!
> The foreigners came—
> Well, now they're gonna get out!

We know the score,
We fought before—
And this is war!

So let 'em leave us alone
And get a turf of their own.
This turf is ours![59]

The song leaves little to the imagination, and the Jets' antipathy for the Sharks could hardly be made any clearer.

Another song, "Mix!," didn't fare much better. Stephen Sondheim writes that the song, sung by the Jets and intended as an ending for the first scene, "pleased nobody but Lenny [Bernstein]," and so it too was ultimately relegated to the trunk of cut songs:

Mix!
Make a mess of 'em!
Pay the Puerto Ricans back,
Make a mess of 'em!
If you let us take a crack,
There'll be less of 'em,
There'll be less of 'em.
. . .
Spics!
Every one of 'em's chicken, chicken!
Fix 'em!
Give the suckers a lickin'!
If those brown little bums are lookin'
for kicks,
Every brown little greasy son-of-a—
Puerto Rican
Gets a kisser full of bricks![60]

The anger leaps off the page and the song was, in addition to having lyrics difficult to understand, deemed too harsh for an opening number.

The song that finally took the place of both these numbers is the famous

"Jet Song." While less directly explicit about "place," the song plays up, using the metaphor of gang bonding, the racial cohesiveness of the Jets. Riff, the leader of the Jets, sings:

> When you're a Jet,
> You're a Jet all the way
> From your first cigarette
> To your last dyin' day.
>
> When you're a Jet,
> If the spit hits the fan,
> You got brothers around,
> You're a family man.
>
> You're never alone,
> You're never disconnected.
> You're home with your own—
> When company's expected,
> You're well protected!
>
> Then you are set
> With a capital J,
> Which you'll never forget
> Till they cart you away.
> When you're a Jet,
> You stay
> A Jet![61]

The song speaks to the love that the gang members feel for each other and the pride they have in being Jets. It's an anthem of gang bonding, but it's also the song that comes closest to articulating a sense of the Jets' racial identity, because the unspoken glue that makes a Jet a "Jet" is whiteness. After all, there isn't much else that distinguishes them from the Sharks. Indeed, to emphasize this idea, the visual differences between the two gangs were highlighted in the costume design by Irene Sharaff—deep purples, pinks, and oranges for the Sharks and lighter colors for the Jets: "The colours were ingenious choices, seeming to suit the gang-members' physical appearances. Even though the Puerto Ricans were on the defensive, their outfits gave them an aggressive quality, and their girls, less uniform and more exotic, had brilliant colours, in startling contrast to the Jets' girls who wore pastels and seemed homogeneous."[62] Laurents's stage directions inform us that during the famous scene at the dance, "the line between the two gangs is sharply defined by the colors they wear."[63] While the film version used hair dye and makeup to point up racial difference, the show's costumes were meant to theatrically heighten and stand in for differences in skin color.

The emphasis on color was not only evident in costuming but woven into the libretto. In a 1957 draft, Officer Schrank is given a great deal of rabid, racist dialogue:

> You know, Doc, down in Jewtown, a guy was making a pretty good livin' outa his drugstore until the kids began usin' it as a hangout. . . . Look: you know I know you're gonna rumble. *Regular white Americans don't rub with coons otherwise.* Where's it gonna be, that's all I wanna know? The park? The river? . . . C'mon I'm on your side! I'll even keep the coast clear for ya.[64]

Schrank emphasizes the whiteness of the Jets, juxtaposing them with "coons." By the final version of the show, the line has become "I know regular Americans don't rub with the gold-teeth otherwise." "Regular" has become synonymous with "white," and it was probably considered redundant to place the two terms together. Whiteness has become so normative in this case that the word itself is erased and made invisible, with "regular Americans" now substituting for "white people." Schrank's role in the musical is significant, and as the embodiment of official power, he reveals the racism that exists on an official level and makes the point that prejudice is not simply a concern for the hoodlums. "I'm for *you*. . . . I wanna help ya get rid of them!" he tells the Jets.[65] Schrank might not like the gang, but he clearly states which side he is on.

While the Jets are silent about their newfound racial superiority, the Puerto Rican characters are more than attuned to the nuances of racial politics. When Chino, a member of the Sharks, tries to defend Maria's dancing with Tony, Bernardo, Maria's brother, responds, "With an '*American.*' Who is really a Polack." Anita, Bernardo's girlfriend, chimes in: "Ai! Here comes the whole commercial! . . . The mother of Tony was born in Poland; the father still goes to night school. Tony was born in America, so that makes him an American. But us? Foreigners!"[66] Anita's logic is only partially correct. Tony's "native" identity does make him an American, but the fact that the "Polack" has become white has solidified Tony's and the Jets' American status. This dialogue between Bernardo and Anita leads into the famous number "America," yet there is little discussion of race in this iconic song; rather "America" is a mini-treatise on nationality, discussing the pros and cons of Puerto Rico versus America. Regarding the genesis of the song, Bernstein wrote to Robbins:

> Steve and I have been talking about a song for Anita and a group of girls (Puerto Ricans), light and almost pastoral in character, and kind of P-Rican-Cuban music of the interior, not urban. It would deal in a charming and not nasty way with trying to be American: dressing a certain way, fixing their hair a certain way, etc., until they all wind up looking 200 percent Spic.[67]

Only with the movie version of *West Side Story* in 1961 were the lyrics punched up to be more direct. According to *West Side Story* screenwriter Ernest Lehman, "the number 'America' on the stage was purely about conditions in Puerto Rico. These were Puerto Ricans, transplanted to New York, singing about conditions in Puerto Rico. I thought it would be much more appropriate if the number were about the conditions the Puerto Ricans encountered in America."[68] Sondheim's new lyrics in the song contained the following exchange that hammer home the show's racial politics:

> Life can be bright in America,
> If you can fight in America.
> Life is all right in America,
> If you're all-white in America.[69]

References to white identity are woven throughout the text. When Anita tries to get a message to Doc to let him know that Maria is going to meet Tony later that night, members of the Jets give her a hard time and accost her. "Will you let me pass?" she asks as she tries to maneuver past the gang who blocks her way. Snowboy twists her question with racial insight and responds, "She's too dark to pass."[70] The Jets, of course, are passing too, as newly minted white folk whose own racial identities are also suspect.

West Side Story and The Music Man both imagine what could be termed utopic visions for dealing with the race/space conundrum. For The Music Man, utopia is a nostalgic return to small-town America. Such a world might not exist anymore, but in the time of Leave It to Beaver, artistically reconceiving it was a way to avoid dealing with the "problem" of the racially changing city. After all, just two years later in 1959, Lorraine Hansberry's play A Raisin in the Sun would engage the thematic of "white flight" from an African American perspective, revealing the difficulties that blacks would go through to secure decent housing.

West Side Story is hardly nostalgic about some lost white past; rather, Tony and Maria envision a world where race doesn't exist at all, let alone racial violence. This desire surfaces as soon as they see each other for the first time at the neighborhood dance. Laurents writes: "The lights fade on the others, who disappear into the haze of the background as a delicate cha-cha begins and Tony and Maria slowly walk forward to meet each other. Slowly, as though in a dream, they drift into the steps of the dance, always looking at each other, completely lost in each other; unaware of anyone, any place, any time, anything but one another." Tony and Maria enter a fantasy space where nothing exists except the two of them. Freed of physical space itself, they are also liberated from the racial categories in which they are forced to live. Tony and Maria flirt via dancing, only to be interrupted by Bernardo, who asks, "Couldn't you see he's one of them?" Maria replies, "No; I saw only him." What should Maria have "seen"? It has to have been more than his clothes. Race here is something that for Bernardo and others (if not the creators) is grounded in skin color. As Tony and Maria's love blossoms in the scenes that follow, Maria tells Tony, "I see you," and he responds, "See only me."[71] The lovers have been imbued with magical color-blind glasses in which individual identity and love triumph over skin color.

That West Side Story is a musical about the intersection of place and race is emphasized in the staging and set design of the production. Oliver Smith, the musical's original set designer, invented some revolutionary stage magic for West Side Story. Jerome Robbins asked Smith early on in the design process, "Where's your close-in on one so we can work in one while you're changing the sets behind?" "Well, we're not going to do that," was Smith's answer.[72] Smith instead designed the show—full of brick walls, chain fencing, and dark urban alleyways—to allow for seamless transitions, part of its revolutionary theatricality. Sets not only "dissolved" from one locale to another; at times they entirely disappeared. While Laurents set most of the show in either late-night exteriors or dark interiors, the show also contains moments in which the characters and story leave the world as we know it altogether. If the gritty streets of New York City become an allegory for the racial politics of the United States, the creators of *West Side Story* provide the audience with their own utopian space, free of racial tensions. In the duet "Tonight," when Maria and Tony sing of how their love knows no boundaries—"I saw you and the world went away"—the Broadway set literally disappeared. Laurents's stage directions indicate: "And now the buildings, the world fade away, leaving them suspended in space."[73] Only as the song ends does the set return.

All these elements, visual, musical, lyrical, and choreographic, come together in the song "Somewhere," which occurs in act 2 after Tony has returned to Maria, having just killed her brother, Bernardo. Tony and Maria, despite this tragedy, vow their undying love for each other. "We'll find some place where nothing can get to us; not one of them, not anything," Tony tells Maria.[74] As in "Tonight," Stephen Sondheim's lyrics serve as much for technical cues as they do to express emotion.

> TONY. I'll take you away, take you far far away out of here,
> Far far away till the walls and the streets disappear,
> Somewhere there must be a place we can feel we're free,
> Somewhere there's got to be some place for you and for me.

As if playing the part of the stage manager who says "go!" to cue the set, Tony's words cause "the walls of the apartment [to] begin to move off, and the city walls surrounding them begin to close in on them. Then the apartment itself goes, and the two lovers begin to run, battering against the walls of the city, beginning to break through as chaotic figures of the gangs, of violence, flail around them. But they do break through, and suddenly—they are in a world of space and air and sun. . . . Their clothes are soft pastel versions of what they have worn before." The city has disappeared, and the characters find themselves in a place where identities, racial, ethnic, national, and otherwise, have lost all meaning. Gone are their stark, racially defining costumes. A woman sings offstage: "There's a place for us/ Somewhere a place for us." Where this place is, we don't know. It exists nowhere and not in the present, only in a fantasy world devoid of race that is the complete antithesis of New York's grimy streets. The song turns into the "Somewhere" ballet, one of Robbins's choreographic highlights, and the Sharks and the Jets dance together in harmony. Suddenly, though, "there is a dead stop. The harsh shadows, the fire escapes of the real, tenement world cloud the sky, and the figures of Riff and Bernardo slowly walk on. The dream becomes a nightmare: as the city returns, there are brief re-enactments of the knife fight, of the deaths." The emphasis on utopia alters our larger reading of the musical. While harmony between the two gangs would be ideal, the creators imagine a place where race itself, at least temporarily, becomes irrelevant.

Despite the fact that *West Side Story* aims to be positive by imagining a racial utopia, it was *The Music Man* that won the critics' hearts. When *The Music Man* first tried out in Philadelphia, some critics were relieved that the show wasn't going to take audiences into *West Side Story* territory. "For those theatergoers who think twice about going to a modern musical these days, fearing the New York showmakers are going to offer them the Black Hole of Calcutta or perhaps Murder, Incorporated, in song and dance guise," wrote critic Wayne Robinson, " 'The Music Man' offers no stabbings, no gang fights, and nothing more violent than Onna White's dancers behaving outrageously in a public library as if they thought they were working up a Broadway stage number, complete with handsprings." Robinson goes on to claim, " 'The Music Man' is for people who hate modern musicals."[75] Brooks Atkinson of the *New York Times* felt the show was "as American as apple pie and a Fourth of July oration."[76] John Chapman, a week after writing a rave of *The Music Man*, wrote a second piece for the *Sunday News* comparing the different types of musical theater then in vogue:

Our musical theatre in its quest for realism, has tended toward the smudgy and even the tragic. We have faced the problems of scarlet women, unborn bastards and hoodlum rumbles. . . .

Perhaps, with the enormous success of "The Music Man," we have begun a return to an age of innocence. The problems of global life and strife are enough to keep us occupied during thinking hours, and the right kind of musical comedy offers the perfect state of mind in which to hide. "The Music Man" is a fond backward glance at the kind of life that once we led in the small towns of the nation before World War I. It is spotless, sentimental, and joyously funny.[77]

And this is from a critic who actually enjoyed *West Side Story*. The show may be backward-looking, but one wonders if it isn't a bit of wish fulfillment as well—the hope that America could return to such simpler and whiter times.

Two shows at the same moment in history. One running away from racial conflict, the other diving headfirst into the fray. *West Side Story* reflects the racial ideology of its period, but in ways that are uneven. On a surface level, the show's themes predate that famous plea for racial tolerance made in the late twentieth century by Rodney King, "Can we all get along?" And yet *West Side Story* is more subversive and complex than many people give it credit for being. By putting the Americanness of the Jets in quotation marks, the show actually reveals *not* that we should all just get along but that we should question the creation of ethnic, racial, and national categories in the first place. Just who *is* an American, and what makes someone an American? In a seemingly paradoxical move, while it does make a case for a new unified Caucasian whiteness, the show *also* calls that whiteness into question. Sure, the Puerto Ricans are suspect figures, but suddenly so too are the Jets, who are no more blue-blooded than the Sharks. Perhaps the musical's Jewish American creators, reflecting on their own status in society, desired a newfound mainstream Caucasian whiteness and yet questioned a racial system that also divides groups. Wouldn't it all be better, they ask, if there were a "Somewhere" where race didn't exist?

West Side Story's Jewish origins are more than a footnote in the annals of musical theater history. Rather, the never-completed *East Side Story* is both a window into the racial history of the time and a key to further unlocking the meaning and significance of *West Side Story* itself. The history of *West Side Story* reveals not only the genesis of a major musical but the transformation of racial categories over a ten-year period.

ACT TWO

1967–2012

4

Carbon Copies
Black and Interracial Productions of White Musicals

What's playing at the Broadway?
I'll tell you what's playing at the Broadway.
A revival of a classic musical, so in tune with current trends
That it puts white characters into blackface from
Miss Adelaide to Nicely-Nicely.
That's what's playing at the Broadway.
—Charles Michener, *Newsweek*, August 2, 1976

The 1940s, 1950s, and 1960s were the Golden Age of the Broadway musical. It was a period of intense creative production that gave birth to hit shows like *Guys and Dolls, Gypsy, Funny Girl, My Fair Lady, Fiddler on the Roof*, and *Mame*. Influenced by the theatrical innovations first established by Rodgers and Hammerstein in 1943 with *Oklahoma!*, Golden Age shows exhibited a maturity of musical form and subject matter that some argue has not been seen since this defining era. The productions of this period were populated with stars like Ethel Merman, Mary Martin, Alfred Drake, and Julie Andrews and written by some of the most famous composers and lyricists, including Frank Loesser, Jule Styne, Jerry Herman, Alan Jay Lerner and Frederick Loewe, and Jerry Bock and Sheldon Harnick. All of these individuals, performers and creators alike, were working at the peak of their careers, and the Broadway musical in this moment occupied a prime place in American culture that it would never fully occupy again.

As the 1960s came to an end, so too did the Golden Age. Rock and roll had exploded during the decade, and the music of Broadway, once associated with a sound that was primarily orchestral, began to take on the musical influences of this new age. This shift would be best embodied by *Hair* (1967), by Galt MacDermot, James Rado, and Gerome Ragni, which spoke to the issues of the day—Vietnam, free love, and youth culture—through a rock idiom that was as far away from *Oklahoma!* as you could get.

But the sound of Broadway wasn't the only thing that was changing. The United States itself was also experiencing racial growing pains as a robust and vocal civil rights movement was aiming to bring true equality to the country's African American population. *Brown v. Board of Education* ended racial segregation in schools in 1954; President Lyndon B. Johnson signed the Civil Rights Act in 1964 banning discrimination in schools, the workplace, and other public venues; and the Voting Rights Act of 1965 removed many voting restrictions that negatively impacted African Americans. The Broadway musical, which had been a mainly white-populated art form up until this moment, was not immune to these changes and finally began to see actors of color as part of its makeup, not just in supporting roles but as protagonists as well. A handful of original musicals such as Rodgers and Hammerstein's *Flower Drum Song* (1958), featuring an all-Asian cast, and *Hallelujah, Baby!* (1967), a musical about African American lives in the twentieth century (written by a white creative team including Jule Styne, Betty Comden, Adolph Green, and Arthur Laurents), did grace the boards, but another theatrical phenomenon also came into prominence at the end of the 1960s: black productions of white musicals.

In 1967, an all-black version of the 1964 hit *Hello, Dolly!* starring singer/actress Pearl Bailey became a hot ticket in New York. This production set off a decade's worth of black versions of white shows and was unusual in that nothing was done musically, lyrically, or textually to explain the shift of the actors from white to black. What it revealed, however, was the way in which the supposed normativity of whiteness was made visible when nonwhite performers played roles assumed to be the domain of white actors.

The 1967 all-black production of *Hello, Dolly!* was not the first Broadway musical to recast what was considered to be a "white show." The producer Billy Rose had pulled off a similar feat in 1939 with *The Hot Mikado*, a black, swing-inflected production of Gilbert and Sullivan's 1885 operetta *The Mikado*, a show set in Japan but performed by white actors. In December 1943, nine months after *Oklahoma!* premiered, Oscar Hammerstein II opened *Carmen Jones*, an all-black version of Bizet's opera *Carmen* for which he had written a new libretto and lyrics. Now set in Chicago during World War II with Carmen working in a parachute factory, *Carmen Jones* preserved Bizet's original score, but Hammerstein's new lyrics were written in faux Negro speech, similar to the dialect that he crafted for the black characters in *Show Boat*.

Following in the spirit of the Pearl Bailey *Hello, Dolly!*, a number of originally all-white shows were recast with all-black or, in the case of *The Pajama Game*, interracial companies in the 1970s. Given the forward-thinking racial politics of the decade, such a move hardly seems racially progressive despite the productions' ability to bring black actors to Broadway. The impact of the civil rights movement may have been more than present, but one might say this was the theater's lingering version of "separate, but equal." Were these productions a type of reverse minstrel show? Critics, actors, and audiences were divided on the matter, and the fact that these productions existed at all reveals multiple ambivalences about performance and representation at a key moment in our country's racial history.

While multiple all-black productions of white shows appeared, the decade marked a milestone of new forays into black musical theater as well, some of them quite invigorating, others capitalizing on the trend started by the Bailey *Hello, Dolly!* The political effects of Black Power created a new space where black culture, including black culture intended for a mainstream (a.k.a. white) audience, could actually be commercial. Broadway was hardly immune to this new development, and the seventies witnessed exciting new musicals and revues that focused on the black experience in America.[1] *Purlie*, based on Ossie Davis's play *Purlie Victorious*, opened in 1970 and featured the talented young singer Melba Moore in what would be a breakthrough Tony Award–winning performance. With a tuneful score by Gary Geld and Peter Udell, *Purlie* was a decidedly moral tale in which downtrodden black folk get their revenge on Ol' Cap'n, a Colonel Sanders–type patriarch who wants to keep his black sharecropping tenants poor, overworked, and in a state of prolonged financial servitude.

Another original musical was *Raisin*, based on the Pulitzer Prize–winning Lorraine Hansberry play *A Raisin in the Sun*. *Raisin* won the Tony for Best Musical in 1974, beating out the snappy 1940s-set Sherman Brothers show *Over Here!*, featuring two of the Andrews Sisters, and Cy Coleman's brassy, if troubled, *Seesaw*. The decade also saw multiple black revues, including *Bubbling Brown Sugar* (1976), *Ain't Misbehavin'* (1978), and *Eubie!* (1978), which all celebrated the contributions of twentieth-century black composers and performers from Fats Waller to Eubie Blake. Perhaps the most famous original black show, though, was *The Wiz* (1975) by Charlie Smalls and William F. Brown. While many people think of it as an all-black version of *The Wizard of Oz*, it is an entirely original musical that looks at L. Frank Baum's famous children's story through an African American lens. *The Wiz* was a commercial hit, running for four years and nabbing the Tony Award for Best Musical.

While these original shows gave voice and needed stage time to African Americans, black productions of white musicals engendered various debates in the white and black theatrical press, which questioned their inherent value and purpose. Many critics asked: is nontraditional casting acceptable insofar as theater is a representational art form, or does ignoring race do a disservice to the work by failing to recognize the importance of its specific historical and social, and therefore racial, context? It is limiting, of course, to say that only people of a certain race can play certain parts, but to ignore race, particularly in shows that feature white milieus, reinforces the notion that whiteness is raceless, invisible, and normative. While restricting the casting options available to actors of color is not desirable, pretending that race does not exist at all, that it has not shaped the course of U.S. history, is equally problematic. Yes, to some extent, theater is "make believe," but that doesn't mean it is devoid of context. As Angela Pao explains, "Nontraditionally cast productions of Broadway musicals have in fact provided some of the most widely publicized reminders of how unhappy audience members can become when the customary foundations of realism are rocked, even when those foundations support an imaginary universe that corresponds only intermittently to any lived or historical reality."[2] What many of these black productions revealed was a strong ambivalence, particularly on the part of white audiences and black artists.

In the late sixties and seventies, as racial lines in the country continued to change, theatergoers opened up their minds as to the types of representations they would pay to see onstage, but rather than truly support the creation and production of *new* black theater (which did exist off-Broadway and off-off-Broadway), the compromise was going to see tried and trusted white vehicles (*Hello, Dolly!; Guys and Dolls; The Pajama Game*) reinterpreted by black actors. Black artists, too, approached the situation with uneasiness. These productions provided black actors, directors, and designers with new opportunities for work, even if it was not always on the terms or about the subject matter that they wanted. Many of these artists would have preferred to have the funds to produce new work that spoke directly to the black experience, but they saw black productions of white shows as an important way station on the road to producing their own theater.

Theater, by its nature, is a representational art form, one that inherently requires some suspension of disbelief. If this is the case, why is race, or more precisely skin color, a category that some individuals cannot look past? Theater, unless we are watching a kitchen sink drama, is inherently *not* realistic. Sets are often representational and suggestive of locales, people may be dressed in ways that they would not be in everyday life, and in the musical, people burst into song and dance. Since our sense of reality is already altered, to play with race through color-blind casting should not be such an issue. Shakespearean theater, as we may recall, initially involved male actors playing female roles, while the practice of blackface was employed outside of minstrel shows for plays like *Othello* that required the presence of black characters. The notion of what is considered "normal" or acceptable casting practices continues to change over time. With the rise of realism, audiences began to expect that what they were witnessing onstage would directly reflect the real world. As Richard Schechner writes, "The naturalistic bias [of theater] trains spectators to desire a neat fit of who the performer is to what the performer represents."[3] Race, and more precisely skin color, remains a category that exerts its seeming immutability in the face of theatrical "make believe."

As the racial theorists Michael Omi and Howard Winant have argued, "There is a continuous temptation to think of race as an *essence*, as something fixed, concrete, and objective. And there is also an opposite temptation: to imagine race as a mere *illusion*, a purely ideological construct which some ideal non-racist social order would eliminate."[4] Race, of course, is both and neither of these things. We live in a world where race is quite real and has very tangible effects on everyone in society. Even when scholars argue that race is "nothing more" than skin color, that racial differences do not really exist, the fact that race still exerts a powerful force over us cannot be easily dismissed. So even within the theatrical world, where the "realistic" is constantly questioned and everything onstage is put in quotation marks, race may be the one issue that feels real, permanent, and immutable.

This chapter is an exploration into these thorny issues of casting and representation and looks at a handful of black and interracial productions of white musicals— *Hello, Dolly!* (1967), *The Pajama Game* (1973), *Guys and Dolls* (1976), *Timbuktu!* (1978), and *Oh, Kay!* (1990)—as examples of this phenomenon. While to some, these shows might appear as anomalies in the history of the American musical, they illustrate, via relief, just how white the Broadway musical genre really is. They bring up difficult questions about nontraditional casting and urge us to read race into shows that appear raceless and universal at first glance, revealing that whiteness too has a specific and contextualized history.

Hello, Dolly!—1967

Among some musical theater lovers runs an unanswered, if slightly obscure, question: just what is the ethnic and racial background of that most meddlesome matchmaker Dolly Gallagher Levi? The 1964 smash hit *Hello, Dolly!* was just one in a long line of adaptations of the same source material—the musical is based on Thornton Wilder's play *The Match-maker* (1955), itself based on the 1842 German farce *Einen Jux will es sich Machen* by Johann Nestroy, which was based on a yet earlier play, John Oxenford's 1835 English original *A Day Well Spent*—but none of the versions provides any real answer to Dolly's origins. The little we know about the character in Wilder's play is that she was once married to the Jewish-sounding Ephraim Levi, but Dolly's own maiden name, Gallagher, leads us to believe that she has Irish roots. The musical version, which won an outstanding ten Tony Awards, with music and lyrics by Jerry Herman and a book (based heavily on Wilder's play) by Michael Stewart, did little to significantly enhance or rethink Wilder's work. In fact, the success of the musical rested mainly on its catchy score and a long line of female stars in the larger-than-life title role, including Carol Channing, Ginger Rogers, Mary Martin, Martha Raye, and Ethel Merman.

The plot of *Hello, Dolly!* is farcical. A widowed matchmaker, Dolly, has her sights set on Horace Vandergelder, a rich merchant in turn-of-the-century Yonkers, New York, who wants her to set him up with a respectable woman of means. Meanwhile three pairs of secondary characters—Cornelius Hackl and Irene Malloy, Barnaby Tucker and Minnie Faye, and Ambrose Kemper and Ermengarde Vandergelder—experience their own misadventures in New York while falling in love. Of course, all ends well for the couples, and Dolly too gets her wish and makes the ultimate match with the gruff but still lovable Horace.

As first portrayed by Carol Channing (and the many revivals thereafter in which she starred), Dolly's ethnicity might have best been described as "wacky." Yes, we saw Dolly as white, but there wasn't much, aside from "Gallagher Levi," to hint at a deeper story. Though Barbra Streisand's 1969 film version of *Hello, Dolly!* edged toward a Jewish interpretation due to Streisand's own background and vocal inflections, the movie hardly clarifies the issue of Dolly's ethnic past. Most recently, in a 2006 production at the Paper Mill Playhouse in New Jersey, Tovah Feldshuh, often typecast in Jewish roles from Yentl to Golda Meir, decided to run with Dolly's maiden name of Gallagher and settled on a thick Irish accent for her character:

> Seeking to avoid invidious comparisons with Carol Channing, her most celebrated—and most possessive—predecessor in the role, the enterprising Tovah Feldshuh has traced the roots of Dolly Gallagher Levi back to an imagined homeland in Ireland, locating the character's feisty spirit in an early life of want in the days of the potato famine. Speaking—and even singing—in a brogue as thick as the shtick it must serve, Ms. Feldshuh places her own stamp on one of the musical theater's most celebrated female roles.[5]

An overcompensating choice? Perhaps, but still plausible given the little we know about Dolly.

A third possibility was thrown into the mix in 1967 when original *Dolly!* producer David Merrick, one of Broadway's most inventive, loathed, and powerful theatrical titans, had the idea to reinvigorate *Dolly!*, then in its fourth year on Broadway, by casting African American singer and actress Pearl Bailey in the title role. But this would be no simple replacement; rather Merrick recast the entire production with black performers,

Pearl Bailey as Dolly Gallagher Levi and
Cab Calloway as Horace Vandergelder in
the 1967 production of *Hello, Dolly!*
Credit: Photofest

from the legendary Cab Calloway as Dolly's love interest, Horace Vandergelder, down to the very last chorus boy at Harmonia Gardens. Was
this a plausible version of 1890s Yonkers, New York, and if not, did it even
matter? What did it mean to turn a musical from white to black without
changing a word of dialogue or a single song lyric? Was this progressive
racial politics at its best or cultural segregation at its worst? Merrick hardly
seemed to be making a racial statement; he was all about making a buck,
and as far as the critic John Chapman was concerned "putting a Negro
company into this old musical [was] a brilliant stroke of showmanship."[6]
Merrick inserted fresh life and audience interest into a show with waning
box office appeal and propelled it to become, at least for one moment in
Broadway musical history, the longest-running musical of all time.

David Merrick's idea to recast the immensely popular *Hello, Dolly!* with
Pearl Bailey was both inspired and, from the get-go, controversial. From
Actors' Equity to theater critics to Bailey herself, everyone had a perspec-
tive on the racial implications of this production to share. As one blurb in

the *Philadelphia Tribune* reported just a week before the all-black *Dolly!* was scheduled to open on Broadway:

> Hollywood people are talking about: The fact that producer DAVID MERRICK is having some non-headline headaches and meetings with militant civil rights advocates regarding his PEARL BAILEY–CAB CALLOWAY version of "Hello, Dolly!" It seems that some people—black and white—think the all-Negro show is a throwback to the Cotton Club–type shows of the thirties and has set the civil rights movement back 30 years.[7]

Was the production essentially a type of blackface? Was it reinforcing segregation? Did race even matter at all? The answers were all over the place.

From the very beginning, there was skepticism. Ragni Lantz related in *Ebony* magazine, "When it was first announced that David Merrick was planning an all-Negro version of *Hello, Dolly!,* many people questioned his motives. Most were the so-called white liberals who felt this would be a relapse to the all-Negro shows of an earlier, less-enlightened era. Cynics contended it was just a gimmick to attract people who had already seen the show, and the Women's National Democratic Club voted down a proposal to engage the show for a benefit because the cast was 'segregated.'"[8] Whites were just as concerned about this casting stunt as were blacks, fearing to be perceived as condoning racism.

If critics were unanimous about one thing, it's that Pearl Bailey was a wonder in the role, perhaps even besting original star Carol Channing.[9] Kudos went to co-star Cab Calloway as well as to the supporting cast, including Calloway's own daughter Chris, who played Minnie Fay. There was no question that this was a top-notch production, restaged by Lucia Victor from Gower Champion's original incarnation. Audiences were extremely enthusiastic about the show—the pre-Broadway engagement of this company in Washington, D.C., set a new box office record at the National Theatre—and the critics were effusive.[10] So tremendous was the response that Bailey commanded the cover of *Life* magazine on December 8, 1967, with the headline "Well, Hello Pearl!" One of the greatest raves came from the African American sports legend Jackie Robinson, who in 1947 broke the color line by becoming the first black baseball player in the Major Leagues. In a piece he wrote for the *New York Amsterdam News* entitled "'Hello, Dolly!' Something Else," Robinson gushed over the Bailey production:

> "Dolly," as you know, is all Negro cast. It wasn't too long ago that some people would have regarded this fact as a step backward. But "Dolly" is a long leap forward. It is such a beautiful company with its combination of colors from fair, through yellow, tan, brown and black. The quality and creativity of the costuming enhances the picture....
>
> What a marvellous thing it would be if "Hello Dolly" could play the streets, not only in the ghettos, but in all kinds of neighborhoods in New York, Chicago, Los Angeles, Detroit, Newark, South Carolina— and yes, even in Jackson, Mississippi. Or maybe, especially there.[11]

High praise, indeed, from a racial pioneer.

A look at the critical responses to the show, though, reveals a cross-section of opinions about race itself. For Richard P. Cooke of the *Wall Street Journal*, the issue was almost moot, and he simply mentioned that *Hello, Dolly!* now boasted an "all-Negro cast."[12] Jesse H. Walker of the *New York Amsterdam News*, New York's black newspaper of record, wrote that "'Hello, Dolly' is still a hit, albeit an ethnic show this time around."[13] Strange that the mere casting of black performers in the musical without any alteration to the script or score made the work "ethnic," but such was Walker's impression. Clive Barnes at the *New York Times* engaged the issue more directly, although he came out in defense of the production: "My sensitive white liberal conscience was offended at the idea of a nonintegrated Negro show. It sounded too much like 'Blackbirds of 1967,' all too patronizing for words. But believe me, from the first to the last I was overwhelmed. Maybe Black Power is what some of the other musicals need."[14] An endorsement like that could only help the show, and probably more than a few white audience members looked to Barnes's review for permission to enjoy the new *Dolly!* and not feel that they were perpetrating segregation.

Frederick O'Neal, the president of Actors' Equity at the time, expressed major reservations when the Bailey casting news was announced: "This seems to be a favor in reverse. It's very difficult for our policy to get through to producers—casting should be done according to ability."

O'Neal's stance, expressed more than a decade before affirmative action would become standard policy, makes a case for color-blind casting (that is, ability before race), but he goes on to claim that "having an all-Negro cast—or an all-Jewish or all-Chinese one, for that matter—is not the idea at all. Of course, Negroes need the work they will get in the new production of 'Hello, Dolly!' But we are sacrificing our principles for a few bucks."[15] What principles is O'Neal referring to? If it's casting exclusively for talent, why was Actors' Equity not helping to promote more integrated casts on Broadway by 1967? Clearly O'Neal was upset by the notion of reverse favoritism, but he didn't seem or want to acknowledge the glass ceiling and even outright racism that actors of color face in the casting process. If he believed that an integrated version of *Hello, Dolly!* would have made more sense, he never said as much. More importantly, given O'Neal's thoughts about talent, would Bailey, superstar that she was, have even been considered to open the musical, based on talent alone, when it premiered in 1964, or was such a premise simply unthinkable because of the show's milieu, which, historically speaking, was white?

This question of verisimilitude was a big concern: is the version of black life depicted onstage in this production authentic and/or representative of the black experience? Jack Crowder, the production's Cornelius Hackl, asked: "Why is there so much discussion any time Negroes work? . . . Every character is valid as a slice of black society in early New York. Isn't it unrealistic for people to be asked to believe that all Negroes do nothing but crusade and protest?"[16] Crowder's question might not be wrong, but the likelihood that such a genteel cross-section of the black community existed in Yonkers in the 1890s is unlikely. "Pearl Bailey's 'Hello, Dolly!' would have made much more sense," wrote Mel Gussow, "if the production had not been all black. We kept wondering what all those blacks were doing in Yonkers at the time. Yet a black Dolly Levi is imaginable, if she has the force of personality of a Pearl Bailey."[17] The ability to inhabit roles that departed from the stereotypes of maids, criminals, or porters, regardless of how realistic this other reality was, was deemed a plus by the black acting community, even if such casting didn't seem to make a whole lot of sense.

Discussing the sequence "Main Street" from the 1949 movie version of *On the Town*, which theatrically imagines small-town America, Richard Dyer asks, "But down how many main streets in how many small US towns can we imagine a black couple strolling with such unwary joy? This is not to demand that the musical be realistic, but rather to suggest how even the utopian imagination has its boundaries of plausibility. 'Main Street' works because it feels psychically right to imagine whites, but only whites, so at ease in the heartland of the United States."[18] Dyer's observation is more than apt for the Pearl Bailey *Hello, Dolly!* and encourages us to question our assumptions about locale, time period, and audience and the ways in which whiteness becomes so normative that it goes unquestioned.

For some critics and audience members, the fact that the show didn't draw attention to race in either the libretto or songs was interpreted to mean that race didn't matter at all. That was hardly the case; it was just that no changes were made to the production to explain or reflect the casting choice. The upshot of this was reflected by *Life* magazine's Tom Prideaux: "It happened overnight. One day it was *Hello, Dolly* just as usual on Broadway. At the next showing, in the same theater, the arresting changeover to an all-Negro cast had taken place—presto!—like a magician's act."[19] How odd this announcement reads. It would seem that white experience and black experience are interchangeable, and that race is nothing more than some sort of magical sleight of hand. Others chose to read theater as a space where the American dream truly did prevail: "At any rate, 'Hello, Dolly,' headed by Miss Bailey, is a magical evening in the musical theater. The fact it is a *so-called* white show played by Negroes has nothing to do with it, other than to prove that color makes no difference but that talent does."[20] But if that were the case, why was the show not integrated rather than left to operate in a segregated black-only universe?

David Merrick's own take on the production was more frank but hardly without its problems. Pearl Bailey recounted that in trying to convince her to do the show, Merrick said, " 'Think of it this way, Pearl. It's just like moving a colored family into an elegant white neighborhood and everybody stands up and cheers.' And I said now I'm happy, because I live in just such a neighborhood (in North Ridge, Calif.)." Merrick's statement reflects unequal social standing between blacks and whites; whites have money and live in nice neighborhoods, blacks don't. Less a value judgment than an observation about the connection between race and economics, Merrick's metaphor might have been perceptive in describing white/black relations in America, but it was hardly accurate in describing his black production of *Hello, Dolly!* It wasn't lower-class blacks moving into a better neighborhood; rather somehow, magically (?), these blacks were already well-to-do. As for Bailey's happiness at Merrick's idea, it seems a little far-fetched. Bailey made this statement less than ten years after the premiere of Lorraine Hansberry's moving 1959 drama *A Raisin in the Sun* about the difficulties of a black family's moving into a white neighborhood, so it's unlikely that every "elegant white neighborhood" was eager for black residents. Despite Bailey's repeated desire to quell any negative criticism about the show reinforcing segregation, she offered the most perceptive observation on the situation: "I ask them why didn't they raise this question (of all one race) five years ago when Carol Channing created the role with an *all-white* cast. I tell them wherever I am *I* am integrated."[21] More than any critic, Bailey acknowledged the unquestioned normative white nature of the American musical and of *Hello, Dolly!* in particular.

A major problem with the production, though, was not merely that the casting seemed to reinforce segregation but that race itself became a sort of elephant in the room. As one caption in a story about the show put it, "Though cast is all-Negro, each character is presented merely as an authentic member of society in early New York, with no racial references."[22] To pretend that race does not matter might be utopic, but such thinking is merely wishful. The late sixties were a time of intense protest due to both the war in Vietnam and the country's own racial tensions at home. The all-black *Hello, Dolly!* falls squarely between the assassinations of Malcolm X (1965) and Martin Luther King Jr. (1968). At such a moment of unrest, how do we contextualize this frothy piece of entertainment? Perhaps even in 1967, there was "a feeling the producers had eschewed a black and white cast in order to avoid dealing with the issue of having an actor of one race playing a character romantically pursuing a character played by an actor of a different race."[23] It had only been a few months earlier, in June, when the Supreme Court in the case of *Loving v. Virginia* overturned antimiscegenation laws with a unanimous decision. Unspoken or not, the era was pregnant with racial tensions and overtones that could not be ignored.

Perhaps, for that moment, an all-black production of *Hello, Dolly!* made the most sense for changing whites' perceptions of blacks. The show is fangless, regardless of who inhabits the roles, and in contrast to the outspoken black activists of the time period, the Pearl Bailey *Hello, Dolly!* provided an image of black America in which blacks were just like whites *because in the logic of this production they essentially were white*. With the lines, songs, costumes, and staging unchanged, race really did become nothing more than skin color, since all historical context was removed from the picture. It was, perhaps, an inverted minstrel show with blacks now playing the part of whites.

In 1975, just five years after the original Broadway production of *Dolly!* had closed, the show returned to the Big Apple following a lengthy U.S. tour, with Pearl Bailey once again in the lead. Finding a home at the Minskoff Theatre for two weeks, the production received mixed to poor notices, with critics commenting that it looked shoddy. Hobe Morrison for *Variety* opined that "while Dolly may be back where she belongs, as the song lyrics say, she's not looking great, fellahs—in fact, the show adds up to an animated disaster. The visibly low-budget physical production has apparently been cleaned up for Broadway, but the performance is ragged and the company, including the self-indulgent star, seemed tired."[24] Bailey received the highest praise from these pans, but the critics noted that she herself was not taking the show very seriously, often ad-libbing, breaking the fourth wall, and going out of character. In terms of casting, however, this production was different: it was integrated. "It isn't the segregated, modern day minstrel show that Pearl Bailey's original 'Hello, Dolly!' was," wrote Martin Gottfried. "This is a fully integrated company rather than that one whose main identity was not the show, or even the star, but the fact that everyone in it was black. Could a black actor work only in an all-black show? And what in the world did 'Dolly' have to do with a completely black setting? This Bailey version is admirably interracial."[25]

Bailey's 1975 production quickly disappeared and seemed a halfhearted attempt to relive the magic of the 1967 version while correcting its segregationist bent. In many ways the damage was already done, as the Pearl Bailey *Hello, Dolly!* launched a series of imitators that capitalized on this nontraditional casting experiment.

The Pajama Game—1973

In 1973, the 1954 musical *The Pajama Game*, which focuses on the goings-on, romantic and otherwise, at a pajama factory, got a major Broadway revival. With a treasure chest of classic songs by Richard Adler and Jerry Ross including "Steam Heat," "Hey, There," and "Hernando's Hideaway," the show's plot centers on Sid Sorokin, the new factory manager, who falls in love with union organizer Babe Williams, despite their differing politics. *The Pajama Game*, if never the most widely celebrated musical, was an audience favorite. George Abbott, who directed the original production, took on directing duties again at the sprightly age of eighty-six, and Zoya Leporska re-created a young Bob Fosse's choreography. For this production, white actor Hal Linden played the musical's hero, shop foreman Sid Sorokin, but in a bit of radical casting for its time, Linden's leading lady was black singer/actress Barbara McNair as Babe Williams. The cast also had star power in the figure of Cab Calloway, who took on the character of Hines, who keeps track of the pajama factory's time efficiency. Calloway was joined again by his daughter Chris as well as some other black *Dolly!* cast members.

While this wasn't an all-black production but an interracial one, the way in which the show itself engaged with racial representation was awkward, to say the least, and it wasn't exactly clear why this casting choice was made. "Its interracial casting . . . seemed more a commercial exploitation than a sensible idea," wrote Martin Gottfried.[26] Douglas Watt claimed that "since only passing reference to the fact is made in the new edition, there's probably little reason to report that it [*The Pajama Game*] has come back with a mixed cast of blacks and whites. In addition to being entirely appropriate [in what way, Watt never explains], it serves to stress the point that 'The Pajama Game' is meant to be taken as an up-to-date musical and not just another exercise in nostalgia." Watt's assertion is interesting. Does casting a show with black actors or an integrated cast automatically make it "modern"? That didn't seem to work with *Dolly!*, and *The Pajama Game* is a show that is clearly set in the 1950s; neither the setting nor the costumes of the show were updated to represent the era of the revival. Rather than contextualize the subtleties of race in any specific time period, Watt read for the universal: "Labor-management disputes and their attendant strike threats, which form the show's primary concern, are as common as ever, and I doubt that pajama factories look much different today than they did in 1954."[27] Maybe, but 1954 was the year of *Brown v. Board of Education*, so arguably the idea of integration was felt much differently in '54 than in '73.

If anything, one of the key complaints brought against the show—there were seven favorable reviews and ten mixed to negative reviews—was that the libretto itself felt dated. The "book . . . has worn very badly. A young factory manager falls in love with a young union activist. Today the factory manager is Polish [as opposed to "white"] and the union activist is black—yet it doesn't really work. The story is not silly enough to be taken seriously as a musical. It either needs less conviction or, preferably, a great deal more," wrote Clive Barnes.[28] Perhaps this, combined with the general lack of reimagination that went into the production, contributed to its brief 65-performance run, much shorter than the original's 1,063 performances. For most of the critics, much of the pleasure found in the revival derived from the pleasant memories that many of them still had for the 1954 original.

While the black actors were added into *Hello, Dolly!* without a single book change, *The Pajama Game*'s libretto was tweaked, although not always in ways that were clear or helpful to address the shift in casting. Martin Gottfried felt that the interracial casting "has added a depth to its story—as a matter of fact, this 'Pajama Game' makes more sense on racial matters than most of the recent plays that mean to. Yet, the script has been only barely changed to acknowledge the black-white romance (the girl says, 'It wouldn't work . . . there's a little thing called racial prejudice,' and the guy replies, 'You mean you won't go out with us Polacks?')."[29]

Walter Kerr best captured the new awkwardness created by the cross-racial casting in his *New York Times* review:

There is, I think, one moment in the revival that creates a sharp silence in the auditorium that may mean something. Ethnically, the evening is now a black-and-white mix, which it might always well have been, and Miss McNair is black and beautiful while Mr. Linden is white and mustached. Mr. Linden has summoned Miss McNair to his office, most officially, and once the lady has seated herself primly for a possible dressing-down, he has—with a splendid bluntness— asked for a date. She refuses and he damn well wants to know why. She asks him if he's never heard of racial prejudice. That's the silence. What's interesting about it is that the audience was not expecting her line and did not want her line. It would seem that, in the theater at least, we are past asking questions like that.[30]

Kerr's observation is puzzling. Is it that the audience was really past addressing the issue of race (which doesn't seem to be the case), or that in this context, the asking of the question is out of place? In other words, the question is necessary to address the producers' decision as to why they cast the show interracially, but out of place because the issue was awkwardly shoehorned into a show that was never explicitly about race in the first place. Perhaps it would have been better if, in true color-blind fashion, the casting choices in this production weren't acknowledged at all.

While reading the reviews of the 1973 *Pajama Game* reveals that there wasn't much new or exciting to provide the box office boost for this revival, clearly the idea—or should we say gimmick—to integrate the cast didn't really make the musical any more socially relevant. If anything, the cross-racial casting concept, executed in such a halfhearted style, only served to confuse the already complicated topic of race, rather than provide any new or productive insights into the matter.

Guys and Dolls—1976

Unbothered by the critical drubbing of the 1975 Pearl Bailey *Hello, Dolly!* or the lackluster incarnation of *The Pajama Game*, the next fully realized all-black musical production came in the form of a revival of *Guys and Dolls* in 1976. The show was produced by Moe Septee, a Jewish, Philadelphia-based concert promoter turned Broadway producer, who also produced the black revue *Bubbling Brown Sugar* that same year. *Guys and Dolls*, which premiered in 1950, is considered by many to be one of the most perfect examples of Golden Age Broadway musicals. Based on the stories of Damon Runyon, with a book by Jo Swerling and Abe Burrows, and featuring a score by Frank Loesser, *Guys and Dolls* follows two couples. Sarah Brown, an uptight worker in the Save-a-Soul Mission, and gambler Sky Masterson are the show's romantic leads, who fall in love despite coming from very different worlds. The show really belongs, though, to the comedic pair: Nathan Detroit and Miss Adelaide. Engaged for fourteen years, Nathan can't make the commitment to marry Adelaide, a dancer at the Hot Box Revue who suffers from an ongoing psychosomatic cold. The show is filled with one hit number after another, including "If I Were a Bell," "Fugue for Tinhorns," "A Bushel and a Peck," "Miss Adelaide's Lament," and "Sit Down, You're Rockin' the Boat." Running for a respectable 239

Robert Guillaume as Nathan Detroit and Norma Donaldson as Miss Adelaide in the 1976 Broadway revival of *Guys and Dolls. Credit:* Photofest

performances and even receiving its own cast album, the 1976 revival featured Robert Guillaume as Nathan Detroit, Norma Donaldson as Miss Adelaide, Ernestine Jackson as Sarah Brown, and James Randolph as Sky Masterson.

For some individuals, the idea to do an all-black production of *Guys and Dolls* was, by 1976, problematic to say the least. Martin Gottfried put it most directly:

> The blackness of the actor is being used as a theatrical motif. It is a condescending exotica attitude that was supposed to have passed with minstrel shows and "Carmen Jones." . . .
>
> All-black versions of white shows also make as much sense as all-white versions of black shows. Material that was specifically written for one milieu is recklessly stretched to fit another or, as is more commonly the case, is simply ignored.[31]

Gottfried hit the nail on the head: white shows have a context and milieu just as much as black shows do. While it was the hope of *Guys and Dolls* director/choreographer Billy Wilson that one day there would be black producers with their own financial resources to produce on Broadway, he and others saw all-black productions as a necessary stopgap measure to develop black audiences and establish theatrical credibility.[32] Robert Guillaume, the show's Nathan Detroit, provocatively suggested that "an all-black cast is only important to white people. That colors their interpretation."[33] Insofar as the musical genre has been the domain of white people, once the face or color of that domain changes, white audiences are caught off guard.

At first glance, an all-black production of *Guys and Dolls* may have seemed more plausible than other shows. Based on Damon Runyon's stories of gangsters and their "dolls" and subtitled "A Musical Fable," *Guys and Dolls* is set not in a real New York but in a fictional, romanticized New York. That said, the production's creators, critics, and presumably audience members didn't seem to be clear about *where* the 1976 production took place. As Howard Kissel noted, "Perhaps because no one made a firm decision about whether the show is still set in Times Square or further uptown, the sets have absolutely no flavor. One wonders if the show might have had more energy, more vitality if it had been revised to reflect black reality; but who would have the nerve to revise such a wonderfully crafted book or so gorgeous a score?"[34] Here, of course, the problem of *Guys and Dolls* being a "classic" rears its ugly head, limiting just how much change the producers, designers, or directors can inflict on the property before audience members revolt at the notion that their prized work has been infelicitously damaged beyond recognizability.

For many, the fact that *Guys and Dolls* seems devoid of racial specificity does not mean that the show is without ethnic markers. Frank Loesser, the show's Jewish composer and lyricist, sprinkled his lyrics with Yiddishisms. This point did not go unnoticed by critics, most notably Martin Gottfried, who took exception to the all-black production. Gottfried felt that *Guys and Dolls* is "very white and very Jewish" and that "the songs, the jokes, and the dialogue that create the show's very nature are Jewish through and through. Even as one tends to adjust to any show as it proceeds this one again and again reminds you of the inconsistency between the white material and the black company."[35] Charles Michener was blunt about this production; it was essentially blackface: "This 'Guys and Dolls' has acquired a black cast but, for the most part, the cast is just a cast—a darker shade of make-up uneasily applied over white characters."[36]

Interestingly enough, it was the black cast who was most energized about the production and other black shows of the period (*The Wiz*, *Bubbling Brown Sugar*, and *Me and Bessie* were also running at the time). They saw the show as a source of jobs for black actors as well as a way to stretch themselves theatrically and not be restricted to playing stereotypes and supporting roles. James Randolph (Sky Masterson) felt that "it's a positive thing for all people—Black and white—because at last they are getting to see some authenticity of the Black Experience against the caricatures they have conjured up in their minds in terms of what they think we ought to be."[37] An interesting statement given that it's unlikely that the show's creators intended to write about the "authentic" black experience.

And there were rewards for the audience as well, particularly in how the show helped develop audiences of color. As Norma Donaldson (Miss Adelaide) put it, "The black audiences at 'Guys and Dolls' enjoy our production because it relates to a part of their life experience, and whites like it because it's pure entertainment. . . . For me, it's Harlem, that beautiful place that existed when I grew up there 15 years ago. Gambling, women, nightclubs, that whole street thing. Our 'Hot Box' now is the Cotton Club then."[38] The issue of "context" seems mutable. For whites the show (like most Broadway musicals) is "just" entertainment; for blacks it becomes a social document.

People saw in the show what they wanted to see, but the production's problem with the Jewish content did not go without comment. The *Variety* review of the Philadelphia out-of-town tryout asked, "How do they rationalize a black Nathan who says 'nu?' and 'all right already'?"[39] This was a problem that needed to be solved, and so most of the Yiddishisms were excised as the show made its way from out of town to Broadway. When *Guys and Dolls* was still previewing in Washington, D.C., the reviewer Jacqueline Trescott found the work "colorless," because "cheesecake and strudel asides have not been axed for ones extolling sweet potato pie or spare ribs."[40] By the Broadway opening, though, the cheesecake *did* change. It became "famous apple pie and strawberry shortcake."[41]

For the critic John Beaufort, the modification in language in the 1976 production was less about diction and more about intention: "The change from white New Yorkese to Afro-American is not so much a matter of altered accent and idiom. It is rather the replacement of one kind of big-city sharpness for another."[42] The production's director and choreographer, Billy Wilson, had no question that the show's original context was Jewish. Wilson claimed, "It was like taking chicken soup and making it a little more gumbo." Some language was updated to reflect a black worldview, and Wilson said that "now and then, we injected phrases in their place that were more relative to the black way of speaking, like when Nathan Detroit puts down Benny Southstreet by saying, 'Oh, you jive turkey.' That was not in the original."[43] While Nathan Detroit and Miss Adelaide seemed Jewish to John Simon, Simon's bigger problem with the show was with Sky and Sarah: "There is no easy way of suggesting the social abyss between Sky and Sarah. Of course, there are rich black girls today with every solidly middle-class privilege. But such girls would not be in the Salvation Army—especially if the time were 1950."[44] As with *Hello, Dolly!* or *The Pajama Game*, the show's historical time period called certain casting choices into question. It's not just that black casts don't seem to fit into a white social milieu; rather, the basic historical facts of black segregation and prejudice in this country at specific moments directly counter the worlds of these all-black shows, where such racial realities are entirely absent.

For Wilson, the idea of an all-black *Guys and Dolls* resonated with the experience of life in Harlem: nightclubs, gamblers, and women. The show's eleven o'clock number, "Sit Down, You're Rockin' the Boat," which was essentially written as a gospel number in its original 1950 incarnation, really came into its own in this new production as many critics felt that it was this song, as performed by Ken Page as Nicely-Nicely Johnson, that most fit with the show's all-black environment. Other numbers were given a "black" musical makeover as well. Angela Pao explains that "the musical arrangements were altered by Danny Holgate to incorporate jazz and swing orchestrations and rhythms from rock and disco music."[45] The overture now sounded like something out of Motown, while "If I Were a Bell" and "I've Never Been in Love Before" had a bouncy groove. This just gave Martin Gottfried more to complain about: "Only [the orchestrators] Danny Holgate and Horace Ott knew what they were doing in resetting the famous songs to beguine, samba and two-step rhythms, fitted out with bland, big band voicings. If this was an attempt to fit Loesser's score with a soul sound, it was like putting mayonnaise on a corned beef sandwich and calling it all-American."[46]

But if it seemed the show was torn between being read as authentically black and authentically Jewish, Abe Burrows, the original director and book writer, had another take: "It was never a 'white' idiom to begin with. We're doing the Damon Runyon idiom—the idiom of Broadway. Remember, the original poster said: A Musical Fable of Broadway."[47] Brendan Gill of the *New Yorker* agreed: "Damon Runyon's Noo Yawk is a never-never land peopled with symbolic cutouts bearing preposterous names (Nicely-Nicely, Harry the Horse, Nathan Detroit, and the like); he makes of our city something as fanciful as Wodehouse's Edwardian English countryside. . . . These hoods and gamblers are the murderous scum of the earth, yes, but they are also as little dangerous as Winnie-the-Pooh."[48] Burrows's embracing of a Ruyonesque New York is accurate insofar as *Guys and Dolls* is not an attempt to create a realistic portrait of the Big Apple, but this would hardly mean that Broadway is raceless or color-blind.

The 1976 production seemed to want to have it both ways: tying into the black experience as a way to develop a new African American audience but also to capitalize on the show's classic status. As Brendan Gill further wrote, " 'Guys and Dolls' is a classic American musical comedy—if one gives extra points for indigenous subject matter, it is arguably *the* classic American musical comedy."[49] Indeed, on the marquee outside the Broadway Theatre, the show was deemed "America's Favorite Musical." Critics could find whatever they wanted to in this production; it could speak to the "black experience" or, as Jessica Harris claimed in the *New York Amsterdam News*, " 'Guys and Dolls' is not a Black production in the sense of 'The Wiz' or 'Me and Bessie.' It is simply a damned good production of 'Guys and Dolls' with a cast of Black performers."[50] Ernest Leogrande of the *Daily News* thought that having an all-black cast was merely "incidental": "This could be an all-Asian cast and the factor of importance still would be only: Do they have the talent to make the show work all over again?"[51] The success of the production seemed to be dependent on the race of the reviewer, with black writers embracing the work as a liberating example of color-blind casting and whites lamenting the incongruity of African American actors into a show that was white and Jewish at its core.

Oddly enough, as if following the 1975 version of *Hello, Dolly!*, for the fiftieth anniversary of *Guys and Dolls* in 2000, the show went on a national tour featuring the black actor Maurice Hines as Nathan Detroit. This time, though, the cast was integrated and included white, black, and Latino performers. "It's a big mix of all the races, just like the city," remarked Hines.[52] Perhaps because the show was fully integrated, there was less of a disconnect, as the multiple races made *Guys and Dolls* closer to both the real New York *and* its fictional Runyonesque counterpart. The 1976 production was caught in theatrical and racial limbo: black in body, if not always in spirit; still a (white) classic, but now able partially to reflect the experiences of African Americans in the 1970s.

Timbuktu!—1978

The 1976 revival of *Guys and Dolls*, despite whatever issues might have existed with the production, at least had a wonderful score, a tight book, and an intrinsic charm to keep it on track. The same, though, could not be said of the middling *Kismet*, an unusual Broadway property even when it first appeared in 1953. While the show had a decent run of 583 performances, it was not particularly edgy or original. As a matter of fact, *Kismet's* composer and lyricist team, Robert Wright and George Forrest, "borrowed" the themes and melodies of classical composer Alexander Borodin to form the musical basis of their show. The plot of *Kismet* focuses on Hadji, a poet who manages to become an emir, and his daughter, Marsinah, who falls in love with the Caliph. The show was based on a romantic, Arabian-inspired play of the same name, written by Edward Knoblock in 1911. *Kismet*, set in an imaginary world of Arabian Nights, was basically an excuse for romantic Orientalism and pretty music.

Why this play, as opposed to any other work in the musical theater canon, was deemed worthy of revival in the form of the all-black *Timbuktu!* in 1978 is not clear. There was little that seemed to be relevant to the African American experience, but one surmises that the original *Kismet* book writer, Luther Davis, who helped to produce and rewrite *Kismet* for its *Timbuktu!* incarnation, smelled "cash cow" along the lines of earlier all-black productions in the 1970s. For *Timbuktu!* the world of Arabia shifted to Africa in 1361, turning an Oriental fantasy into an African one. Geoffrey Holder, who also helmed *The Wiz*, took on the responsibilities not only of

Melba Moore and Eartha Kitt in *Timbuktu!*, based on the musical *Kismet*. *Credit:* Photofest

director and choreographer but also of costume designer. The musical was led by a powerhouse cast, most notably the legendary Eartha Kitt, who returned to Broadway for the first time in twenty years to play the Wazir's wife, and Melba Moore of *Purlie* fame, who played Marsinah.

Unlike other all-black productions of the 1970s, *Timbuktu!* didn't seem to generate much comment about the show's racial politics. Perhaps reviewers were over the whole issue, or maybe they just didn't care, given that the musical wasn't thought to be particularly good. Eartha Kitt got raves for stealing the show, and many critics liked Holder's costumes (which others found garish and over-the-top), but the general consensus was that *Timbuktu!* was dull, poorly miked and sung, and just lackluster. As Hobe Morrison wrote, "Aside from its black cast and brightly colorful scenery and costumes, 'Timbuktu' lacks exciting or memorable qualities, so its appeal is likely to be mostly the large and growing Negro showgoing public."[53] *Kismet* underwent some transformation on its road to becoming *Timbuktu!* The book was revised, some songs were cut and others added, and African folk music was interwoven into the Borodin-inspired score.

Writing in the *New York Amsterdam News*, Barbara Lewis queried whether this show would be just another "'blackface' production—like 'Hello, Dolly,' 'The Wiz' and 'Guys and Dolls.'" In response William Marshall, who played Hadji in out-of-town tryouts, conceded that Broadway wasn't called the "'great white way' for nothing" but commented that "this play will do a great deal to encourage our Black writers who have the richest heritage of any people on earth. 'Timbuktu' is preparing the white theatre world to let them know the richness of our culture. Everything takes time. We're just coming around the bend."[54] Similarly, the librettist, Luther Davis, saw the work as celebrating African heritage: "Some of my black friends felt that 'Roots' did not tell the whole story of African history. That dealt with peasants and country people. Timbuktu is a turn-on name for people who study black history. It says, 'Yes, we had kings and queens and armies and wicked wazirs.' Timbuktu was a fabulous city. In my mind, this is an African, rather than a black musical."[55]

Rather than try to make the black experience more relevant to the audience, *Timbuktu!* simply emphasized the exoticism of a fantastical African past. "*Timbuktu!* seemed a great opportunity to show that 'black' doesn't have to mean gospel singing, 'strutting' or ghettoes," wrote Davis in the *Timbuktu!* program.[56] For Henry Weil in the *New York Tribune*, the problem with *Timbuktu!* was that it suffered from a clash of contexts and styles: "'Kismet' is traditional Broadway musical comedy in form and concept, and whenever Holder successfully establishes an Afro-ethnic tone, it is promptly disrupted by the predictable mechanics of plot followed by musical comedy turn. 'Timbuktu!' doesn't go far enough in transplanting 'Kismet.' The Malian impetus is there—sets, costumes, jungle drums—but the songs and plot refuse imperturbably to budge from Times Square."[57]

Timbuktu! would be the last major all-black production of a white musical in the 1970s. The musical seemed to confirm a feeling that had nagged all of these black productions: namely, casting a show with black actors was not a good enough reason for producing the work. Only if musicals were produced in ways that fully and appropriately served the material would the show succeed.[58] An all-black replacement cast of the Cy Coleman musical *I Love My Wife* would wrap up the decade in 1979, but by then, it seemed as if audiences were tired of the whole deal.

Oh, Kay!—1990

While black productions of white shows were mainly a product of the 1970s, history tends to repeat itself, and so perhaps it is not surprising that this phenomenon made a final reappearance in 1990 under the eye of David Merrick, the force behind the Pearl Bailey *Hello, Dolly!* The first major revival in over sixty years of George and Ira Gershwin's *Oh, Kay!*, this production, his eighty-eighth, would be Merrick's next-to-last Broadway offering. Adapted from a flimsy 1926 Gershwin boy-meets-girl show about bootleggers on Long Island, it was reset in 1920s Harlem to provide a new context for the all-black cast. The 1990 production, which first had a run at the Goodspeed Opera House in Connecticut, was directed by Dan Siretta, to much critical drubbing. Starring a young Brian Mitchell (sans the Stokes), who would go on to star in *Ragtime, Kiss Me, Kate,* and *Man of La Mancha,* the show was a silly romp and a frenetic throwback to early musical theater that featured the well-known tunes "Do, Do, Do," "Fidgety Feet," "Clap Yo' Hands," and "Someone to Watch Over Me." Several Gershwin songs that weren't in the original production were added as a way to further enhance the "classic" status of the musical.

Other than shifting the setting to Harlem, very few significant changes were made, leaving some critics to consider this, once again, a production in blackface. Frank Rich, who cited the Pearl Bailey *Hello, Dolly!* as an early example of nontraditional casting, wrote off *Oh, Kay!* as "a minstrel show" with "eye-popping gags and stereotypes that are less redolent of the Cotton Club than of 'Amos 'n' Andy'."[59] What *Oh, Kay!* revealed, as did many of the other all-black productions, was that simply casting a show with black performers often exposed a rift between lived black experience, as myriad and diverse as it could be, and theatrical representation. *Oh, Kay!* was clearly a last-gasp effort by Merrick to capitalize on a previous success, but it was especially evident by 1990 that no one was falling for what was really no more than a theatrical stunt. As David Richards wrote in the *New York Times,* "The production is black only to the extent that it employs a black cast. In no significant way does it reflect a black sensibility or illuminate, however passingly, the black world in which it is presumably taking place. If you were to close your eyes, the notion of color probably wouldn't even occur to you."[60] What's interesting is that even as late as this production, the African American press continued to support this theatrical tactic. Abiola Sinclair for the *New York Amsterdam News* gave the show a rave review, failing to see the production as potentially objectionable.[61] After it played for two months to mixed to good reviews but little spark at the box office, Merrick decided to close the production down in January for the winter, but with the intention to open again in the spring at a new theater to remain a viable contender for the Tony Awards. This plan never came to pass, and the show remained permanently closed, thus finally ending an unusual chapter in Broadway musical theater history.

Musical Anomalies or Lessons in Nontraditional Casting?

At least one important revelation emerged out of the conversations around these productions, even if the critics themselves did not fully see it or grasp it. In questioning the plausibility of black productions of white shows, these critics revealed that race, even when not the show's central thematic, was still a determining factor within many works. The danger here is reading white shows as *universal* in theme, time, or place as opposed to being culturally and historically specific. As Toni Morrison argues in her assessment of white American literature, "A criticism that needs to insist that literature is not only 'universal' but also 'race-free' risks lobotomizing that literature, and diminishes both the art and the artist."[62] By reading race back into white shows, we can make a case for casting certain shows with white actors by claiming that it is necessary to do service to that particular worldview. While it's true that such shows make up a disproportionate part of the Broadway musical canon, by viewing them as reflecting a *particular* experience and not *all* experience, we can begin to rethink how whiteness works in musical theater, if not in society at large.

Perhaps the challenge of color-blind casting was best encapsulated by Bob Weiner writing about the all-black *Guys and Dolls*. Weiner disliked the show and asked, "Can you imagine white performers doing *Lost in the Stars*, *Porgy and Bess* or *Cabin in the Sky?* This is what this version of G&D is like."[63] Personally, I can't imagine white productions of any of those shows because each is firmly grounded in contexts that deal specifically with black lives and experience. To cast against that, while not impossible, I suppose, seems to defeat the purpose of what those shows are trying to communicate and reflect. Weiner recognizes that white shows too are about race, even when they seem not to be. The question remains: in shows that are not *explicitly* about race or race relations, can only actors of a certain race play those parts? Or for that matter, are shows only "explicitly" about race when people of color are involved? Where do we draw the line (if it is to be drawn at all) between color-blind casting and respecting the historical and social context of a show? It would seem to be particularly conservative to follow the latter option, but to completely throw race out the window does not seem to be the solution either. Despite a friend of mine telling me that her high school produced an all-white version of *Show Boat*, that's not a production I particularly want to see, amateur or otherwise.

Shows like *Show Boat* or *Flower Drum Song* are clearly about specific racial or ethnic groups. Not to cast them with individuals who fit the racial or ethnic backgrounds that the show indicates does a disservice to the integrity and meaning of the work (besides taking still more opportunities away from actors of color). William H. Sun evokes this in his description of a Chinese production of August Wilson's *Fences*, which he calls "a failure of a universalist approach that is hypothetically based on a color-blind mind-set, which does not yet exist either in the actors or in audiences."[64] Wilson's work has specificity, but so too do many white works, and yet those works are often seen as universal in nature.

The issue on the table here is quite complicated, even more than proponents of color-blind casting make it out to be. Nontraditional casting advocates feel that casting practices need to be opened up to give nonwhite actors more opportunities. The reasons for this are manifold. Most obviously, if nontraditional casting practices are not embraced, actors of color will have fewer roles available to them, thereby decreasing the chance that such individuals will find work. And if they do find work, the roles they are typically offered range from minor supporting roles at best to stereotypes at worst.

But the argument for nontraditional casting falls apart because nontraditional casting only seems to work in one direction. No one ever suggests or approves of white actors performing a black drama. There are no white productions of *Fences*, *Purlie*, or *A Raisin in the Sun*. The "why" might appear self-evident, but a double standard about race remains. To say that *Flower Drum Song* or *Cabin in the Sky* is marked by race but *Hello, Dolly!* is not fails to acknowledge the ways in which race works. When people talk about color-blind casting, the discussion is almost always predicated on a white European model where the goal is to incorporate racial and ethnic minorities into a white worldview, rather than take a more aggressive approach to casting and truly cast across categories and base casting choices exclusively on talent.

The main thing overlooked in the entire discussion of color-blind or nontraditional casting is whiteness itself, because so many fail to recognize it as the normalizing force it is in society and theater. Clinton Turner Davis in his open letter on nontraditional casting rightly argues that "the end of racism needs to become the white man's burden."[65] Davis signals that only by engaging with whiteness, by marking it, can change occur. Instead what persists is policies that try to incorporate actors of color but leave whiteness itself untouched. Ironically, August Wilson's own trenchant stance *against* color-blind casting, which he expounds upon in "The Ground on Which I Stand," acknowledges the specificity (and not the universality) of whiteness: "To mount an all-black production of *Death of a Salesman* or any other play conceived for white actors as an investigation of the human condition through the specifics of white culture is to deny us our own humanity, our own history, and the need to make our own investigations from the cultural ground on which we stand as black Americans."[66] Wilson's concern is with self-defined black representations, but in articulating the problem the way he does, he emphasizes that whiteness too has a cultural specificity and history. Wilson's stance against color-blind casting escalated into a fierce debate on paper and in person with the theater critic and producer Robert Brustein, who asked, "Are black actors now to perform only black parts written by black playwrights?"[67] Other nonwhite artists agree with Wilson, arguing that color-blind casting in which actors of color play white roles overlooks what makes that ethnic or racial group unique. Clearly there is no easy answer to this issue, and theater practitioners of all races remain divided on what the most appropriate solution should be.

My own position on the matter may strike some as both conservative and narrow-minded. I admit it is an argument that leaves me uncomfortable too, because I would hardly want to be denying work to talented individuals, especially in a field where good parts are hard to find. Yet I fear that by practicing one-way racial casting, we are not really changing the system. We are offering token opportunities to actors of color while keeping the normalizing system of whiteness firmly in place. Is there a solution? Richard Schechner, a founder of the field of performance studies, suggested provocatively in 1989 that casting in a color-blind fashion doesn't go far enough; rather, Schechner questions if it is possible to look past physical qualities altogether. He writes that there are "times when perceiving the race, gender, etc., of performers matters; times when spectators perceive the categories but it doesn't matter; and times when it should not even be perceived—not because of disguise . . . but because spectators have been trained to be race, gender, age, and body-type 'blind.'"[68] And yet how do we determine what defines each of those scenarios? When does race matter and when does it not? I would suggest that in the United States, race is all-pervasive, especially whiteness, and can determine social situations even when it seems part of the background.

The history of the Broadway musical is what it is, racism, stereotypes, warts, and all. Going forward, composers, lyricists, and librettists, including hopefully more writers of color, will create shows that will provide jobs for nonwhite actors, not for economic reasons or simply for the sake of doing so, but because the stories they tell will *require* multicultural casting that reflects the inherently integrated and diverse world in which we live. Rewriting the past or, in this case, recasting it with actors of color is not a way to make a space for minority experience. These black productions were a marker of their time and have, for the most part, happily died off.[69] While certain shows that are less grounded in a particular historical reality can be cast cross-racially with little problem, the solution to casting requires a sensitivity to history that recognizes that race is almost always a defining characteristic. Not treating whiteness as a race that has its own social history does a disservice to how we understand race in America, instead seeing race as an issue that only affects people of color. Anomalies that these virtually forgotten black productions might appear to be, they actually teach us a lot about the complex ways that race and representation interface in American society.

5

A Chorus Line

The Benetton of Broadway Musicals

You do step-kicks in America and the audience applauds.
It's depressing
—Michael Bennett

When *A Chorus Line* closed on April 28, 1990, it had racked up an astounding 6,137 performances, making it, at the time, the longest-running musical in Broadway history. Grossing almost $150 million on Broadway alone, the show was a financial juggernaut and went on to earn over $280 million on tour and internationally and was seen by over 6.6 million people in its fifteen-year run.[1] The show won the hearts of its audiences from the moment it premiered downtown at the New York Shakespeare Festival in 1975 before transferring to the Shubert Theatre on Broadway, where it walked away with nine Tony Awards in 1976 including Best Musical. It even garnered the Pulitzer Prize for Drama, not a poor take for a show about a group of dancers auditioning for a Broadway musical. Of course, a great deal of *A Chorus Line*'s magic and staying power was due to its conceiver, choreographer, and director, Michael Bennett, whose staging was so integral to the show's concept and structure that even today most productions of the musical still re-create his work. The musical also featured a tuneful score by Marvin Hamlisch (his first original score for Broadway) with lyrics by Edward Kleban, plus a funny and moving book by James Kirkwood and Nicholas Dante. It was all of these elements working together that made *A Chorus Line* the hit it was.

But is there more that accounts for the musical's success? On its surface, *A Chorus Line* is about what it means to be a performer on Broadway, but what drives the show forward is the racial politics of the seventies, which were infused with ethnic multiculturalism, new sparks from a then-burgeoning gay rights movement, and the previous decade's civil rights activism. This ethos, subtly woven into the fabric of the show, imagines a world in which everyone has an equal chance to succeed in life and where one's racial or ethnic background is not a hindrance to that success but an identity to embrace and a reason to celebrate. Though some of these factors are never explicitly referenced, they color and shape the form, characters, and content of this groundbreaking work and reveal just how central race is to the American musical. In imagining a world in which race has no impact whatsoever on the hiring process or the social forces that order our world, A Chorus Line offers lasting appeal to audiences of all backgrounds because it serves up the American Dream in all its unattainable glory.

A Chorus Line epitomizes a new genre that blossomed in the seventies known as the "concept musical," whose action is not structured by a significant forward-moving plot but rather by an overarching concept or idea (in this case, dancers auditioning for a musical).[2] Nothing particularly noteworthy happens in A Chorus Line. A minor romance transpires between a dancer (Cassie) and the director (Zach). Paul, a gay Puerto Rican dancer, is injured. Performers are selected and rejected. The musical is confessional in nature and structure, with each dancer singing and talking about his or her life.

A Chorus Line opens with a mass audition already in progress in which the dancers express their desire to be picked for the job ("I Hope I Get It"). This initial sequence results in the selection of seventeen individuals, eight men and nine women, who tell us about where they grew up, how they came to dance, their moments of sexual exploration, and the difficulties of being a dancer. From this information and based on how well they move, Zach, the show's director and choreographer, will select a final eight who will comprise the chorus line of the unnamed new musical he is casting. "I need people that look terrific together—and that can work together as a group," Zach explains. A straightforward enough request, which he then immediately complicates: "I think it would be better if I knew something about you—about your personalities."[3] This desire for personal, intimate details about the dancers' lives is a more unusual request, a strange audition tactic if there ever was one. But more than that, placed side by side, these requests are completely contradictory. The first privileges the group; the second, the individual. Which matters more, and how are they to be reconciled? This tension between being part of an ensemble versus being the star is what *A Chorus Line* is all about, and it directly feeds into the show's racial politics, which are constructed in terms of the individual and the group.

A Chorus Line, using the metaphor of the audition, is a comment on what it means to be human: the desire to be picked, the desire to be loved, the desire to "make it" in the world. But the show reveals a further struggle, one that is a bit more specific to the world of dance and theater yet still pervasive in society in general: the conflict between establishing one's own individuality (being a "singular sensation," as one of Kleban's famous lyrics puts it) and belonging to a larger unit (in this case, a chorus line). Being part of a chorus line means conforming to the group, blending in, not drawing attention to oneself. It's the opposite of what it means to be the star of the show, to be an individual. The show's creators play with this concept all evening, having the characters tell us detailed, moving stories about their lives to the point where we feel as if we know each of these individuals intimately. And yet, given that they are relegated to a chorus line, their personalities are essentially vaporized, made meaningless by the anonymity that the line imposes on them.

The impact of race on this entire conflict is huge but has been an overlooked aspect of the musical. While the racial and ethnic backgrounds of many of the characters are brought into sharp focus, it's never made clear how these backgrounds are meant to fit into the final chorus line. In other words, how are individuals who are part of a minority, whether that group be ethnic, religious, racial, or sexual, supposed to assimilate into the larger whole—in this case, a chorus line, an artistic construct historically predicated not just on the uniformity of choreographic movement but also on the racial homogeneity of the line's members? How does one situate this legacy of racial separatism in light of *A Chorus Line*'s 1970s multicultural politics of diversity?

To get at the complex ways in which race is treated in the show, a look at the musical's origins is helpful. Termed "theater vérité" by some critics, *A Chorus Line* is based on the lives of actual dancers who first met in

January 1974 in a midnight rap session with Michael Bennett. Long into the night, the group of approximately twenty dancers shared stories about their lives, their disappointments, their hopes, and their fears.[4] Bennett taped it all, ultimately using some of the actual stories from that session for the libretto, which Nicholas Dante and James Kirkwood wove together and spruced up with some uncredited jokes from Neil Simon. Some of the original participants in the all-night session, which would be repeated in February 1974, included Carole Bishop, Wayne Cilento, Priscilla Lopez, Donna McKechnie, Thommie Walsh, and Sammy Williams, all of whom ended up in the original cast of *A Chorus Line* playing characters that were based on their own lives.[5] After these sessions, Joe Papp, the head of the New York Shakespeare Festival, gave Bennett and his team months of workshop time, an unprecedented creative opportunity, so that they could develop the work in an unrushed fashion. The result was one of the biggest hits in the history of the Shakespeare Festival and Broadway.

Like the actors who attended the late-night sessions, the characters who make up *A Chorus Line*'s quilt are a diverse cross-section of America, each marked individually by name, age, and place of birth. What the libretto also takes time to note, though, is the race and ethnicity of the characters, particularly those who aren't white. In fact, virtually *half* of the chorus line members are marked as being non-WASP. "Mike Costa—it used to be Costafalone" discreetly reveals his Italian heritage by telling us about his less-Italian-sounding name change, Connie Wong "was born in Chinatown—Lower East Side," and Greg informs us that his "real name is Sidney Kenneth Beckenstein. [His] Jewish name is Rochmel Lev Ben Yokov Meyer Beckenstein, and [his] professional name is Gregory Gardner." Despite the fact that Greg could pass as WASP if he wanted to—he's even chosen a stage name for that very purpose—in the show's logic of purposely foregrounding difference, he is marked as Jewish. Perhaps one of the most unusual admissions in the initial go-around is Richie's. He tells us: "My name is Richie Walters. I'm from Herculaneum, Missouri. I was born on a full moon on June 13, 1948. And I'm black."[6] Why does Richie provide us with this last bit of info? As originally played by Ronald Dennis, a dark-skinned African American, he would certainly read as black. Is Richie's reminder actually a nod that he understands that the world of casting is often *not* color-blind and wants to remind Zach of this? In the show, whiteness, as in real life, remains unmarked, and the racial background of the white dancers goes unspoken. The 2006 Broadway revival of *A Chorus Line* played with this racial silence and cast African American performer Deidre Goodwin as Sheila, a role usually played by a white actress. There was nothing in the script to suggest that Sheila couldn't be black, but this casting decision reveals how race only seems significant when it's actually marked (casting Connie Wong with a black or white actress wouldn't make much sense, for example).

Paul and Diana, the two Puerto Rican characters in the show, meanwhile, have divergent takes on their identities. Paul tells us that his stage name is "Paul San Marco," but that his real name is "Ephrain Ramirez" and that he was "born in Spanish Harlem." Diana, on the other hand, says, "My name is Diana Morales. And I didn't change it 'cause I figured ethnic was in."[7] These two admissions, coming back to back, reveal opposite strategies. Diana decides to take advantage of 1970s multiculturalism and embraces her identity. Paul also goes multicultural, but does so by becoming Italian, a white ethnic, rather than a person of color:

> ZACH. For one thing, if you're going to change your name—why go from a Puerto Rican name to an Italian one?
> PAUL. 'Cause I don't look it. . . . People say, "You don't look Puerto Rican, you don't look Puerto Rican." But I am.
> ZACH. So you figured you looked Italian?
> PAUL. I, ah—just wanted to be somebody new. So I became Paul San Marco.[8]

Does Paul perhaps recognize that white dancers—a category that now includes Jews and Italians—might have a better chance of landing a job than dancers of color? Paul's desire to pass as white seems to parallel the fact that at the beginning of the show, he also wants to pass as straight, feeling uncomfortable discussing his homosexuality.[9] In the end, the lineup of dancers includes four people of color, two of whom could potentially pass as white if they chose to do so, and another four (three Italians and one Jew) who are marked as white ethnics, providing us with a contrast to the typical lily-white chorus line.

Was there ever before a chorus line in any real Broadway musical that actually looked like this? Probably not. It's as if the creators were purposely trying to make a statement about ethnic and racial inclusivity at this particular moment. If anything, that's the show's irony. *A Chorus Line* deconstructs the old-fashioned white version of what a chorus line is but in its place substitutes a "United Colors of Benetton" coalition of dancers, a vision that is both utopic in imaging a theatrical landscape that did not yet exist and naïve in its ability to consider the ways in which the real world's engagement with race shaped hiring practices, including on Broadway.

This emphasis on the cast's diversity, racial and otherwise, turns *A Chorus Line* into a theatrical social document writ large. With resonances of Studs Terkel's documentary text *Working*, published just three years earlier in 1972, in which Terkel captured the day-to-day lives of average American workers, *A Chorus Line* clings ferociously to the American Dream of hard work and determination. And yet, while that might be the overt thematic of the show, it's an ideology that clearly does not play out in real life, or for that matter in the Broadway musical, because as much as we'd like to believe that the best, most skilled, or most talented person will get the job, we sadly live in a country where race, physical beauty, gender, and sexual identity, to name just a few categories, still factor as determining elements in the hiring process. The Broadway musical is not exempt from this hard fact, particularly the chorus line. In fact, the entire concept of the chorus line was rooted in the idea that the chorus members should demonstrate not only unity of skill, talent, and choreographic execution but also *uniformity of race*. In an early moment of its existence, the chorus line was a theatrical element that at its core was defined by white racial homogeneity.

To understand the challenge that *A Chorus Line* poses to the history of chorus lines, we need to look back at what was probably the most famous early manifestation of the chorus line: Florenz Ziegfeld and his Follies, which appeared on the Great White Way from 1907 until 1931.[10] The Follies were theatrical extravaganzas that featured lavish production numbers, comedians, singers, and entertainers—Will Rogers, Fanny Brice, and Bert Williams were all notable mainstays. What defined the shows, though, was the Ziegfeld Girls, whom Ziegfeld turned into the Follies' signature element. He went so far as to create the "Glorified American Girl" in 1922, an all-white feminine fantasy that epitomized the perfect chorus girl. In the Ziegfeld Follies, the girls not only were all costumed alike, they were also united by a shared Anglo-Saxon racial heritage. For Ziegfeld and for many other Americans during this period that saw an influx of "dark" immigrants from eastern and southern European countries, the "model of blondness and fairness associated with northern Europe was eventually claimed by eugenicists as typical of the 'American race,' a rhetoric borrowed by the Ziegfeld enterprise for its Glorified American Girl."[11] The chorus line became a metaphor for a racially homogeneous America, which kept "inferior" immigrants at arm's length.[12]

It might appear that *A Chorus Line* doesn't stray very far from its Ziegfeldian predecessors. The curtain rises on a group of dancers while Zach, the show's choreographer, barks out:

> Again,
> Step, kick, kick, leap, kick, touch . . . Again!
> Step, kick, kick, leap, kick, touch . . . Again!
> Step, kick, kick, leap, kick, touch . . . Again!
> Step, kick, kick, leap, kick, touch . . . Right!
> That connects with . . .
> Turn, turn, out, in, jump, step,
> Step, kick, kick, leap, kick, touch.[13]

Taken out of context, it might not be clear at first glance what these lines are. Military marching orders? Instructions for a new gym regimen? They are, of course, a dance combination, but their insistence on forcing the dancers to perfectly execute each move is what will divide the rejects from the selected few. The lines demand order, repetition, precision, and, most important, uniformity.

Despite the fact that the dancers must conform to prescribed choreography, the musical provides us with an ensemble that, unlike the Ziegfeld Girl, is the exact opposite of cookie-cutter racial homogeneity. The emphasis on diversity within conformity was made iconic in the logo for *A Chorus Line*: a photo featuring all seventeen aspirants, not in lockstep harmony, but each one holding his or her body in a different posture. Connie has her hand on her chin, Sheila holds one hand on her hip, head cocked, and Al and Kristine, the married couple, hold hands. The focus on difference was further played up by Theoni Aldredge's costume designs.

The original cast of *A Chorus Line*, shown here in their idiosyncratic poses on the line. From left to right: Don (Ron Kuhlman), Maggie (Kay Cole), Mike (Wayne Cilento), Connie (Baayork Lee), Greg (Michel Stuart), Cassie (Donna McKechnie), Sheila (Carole Bishop), Bobby (Thomas J. Walsh), Bebe (Nancy Lane), Judy (Patricia Garland), Richie (Ronald Dennis), Al (Don Percassi), Kristine (Renee Baughman), Val (Pamela Blair), Mark (Cameron Mason), Paul (Sammy Williams), and Diana (Priscilla Lopez). *Credit:* Photofest

The outfits that the dancers wear, with the exception of those in the finale, purposely look like something that the real actors might have pulled from their closets for an audition, and the variety of the clothes' styles and colors, from Al's TKTS T-shirt to Cassie's famous red leotard and skirt, is meant to further point up each character's uniqueness.

Despite this highlighting of individuality, *A Chorus Line* both references and criticizes earlier, more homogeneous chorus lines. Critics recognized a parallel between the 1975 tuner and the movie of *42nd Street* and other backstage Busby Berkeley films.[14] As the music critic Tom Sutcliffe writes:

"A Chorus Line" is the stripped-down no-shit musical for the new depression. Thrilling, dazzling, enduring and relentless as "42nd

Street," it turns the "ultimate escapism" image of the musical on its head and lays waste the whole Busby Berkeley-onwards syndrome for the heartless as well as vainglorious fake it always was. In particular, it makes those film musicals of the '30s look brightly pernicious. "Golddiggers of 1933" began with "We're In the Money," a brazen celebration of the all-embracing triumph of being in work. "A Chorus Line," born of a less wide-eyed age, begins with a song called "I Hope I Get It," with the line "Please God, I need this job." And they *don't* all get it.[15]

While both *A Chorus Line* and *42nd Street* begin with audition sequences in which eager hopefuls compete for their spot "on the line," clinging to the belief that what will get them to the finish is pure talent, not a preference for type, race, or ethnicity, the 1975 work is more self-aware about the stress and difficulty in securing a job. *42nd Street*, on the other hand, indulges in heady optimism that the critic Michael Feingold notices:

> "You're going out there a dancer—but you're going to come back a star!" That line was just as silly when Warner Baxter first grabbed Ruby Keeler's elbow [in *42nd Street*] as it is now to people who call it camp or kitsch or whatever. But the myth was convenient to the movies. . . .
> Michael Bennett's "A CHORUS LINE" is a show about the kids and myth. It never questions the assumptions of the myth, which is a major drawback, but its creators have taken pains to be accurate to the lives of the people who worship at the shrine of Broadway.[16]

A Chorus Line becomes *42nd Street*'s contemporary sibling, but in some ways, it reads as more naïve than the latter work because the show's logic holds that all people, regardless of race, have equal opportunity in society, when in fact they don't. America might have come a long way since the segregationist politics of the 1930s, but race, unconsciously perhaps, still affected job and hiring decisions. *42nd Street*, on the other hand, just removes racial difference from the picture by casting its chorus line with only white dancers; African Americans and other people of color aren't even considered in the running. In *A Chorus Line*, the makeup of the line has changed but the myth of the American Dream still persists, with results that are now unrealistically color-blind.

In short, *A Chorus Line* alternates between alerting us to the racial and/ or ethnic makeup of the various dancers on the line and reinforcing the idea that one's racial background doesn't matter at all. In the show's opening number, "I Hope I Get It," the wannabe chorus members sing of their desire to be chosen:

> ALL. God, I hope I get it.
> I hope I get it.
> How many people does he need?
> . . .
> Look at all the people!
> At all the people.
> How many people does he need?
> How many boys, how many girls?[17]

The dancers sing without expressing any fear of racial bias. The director just needs "people," some men and the rest women. Throughout the number, Zach offers instructions and feedback to the dancers, and in identifying them, he is careful never to mark them racially but simply by gender and what they wear: "Boy in the headband" and "Girl in brown."

The number culminates in one of the most visually iconic moments of the show. As Zach chooses his semifinalists, they line up, and on the final chords of "I Hope I Get It," "*the lights bump up revealing the line with their photos in front of their faces.*" This stage image is striking: the three-dimensional body replaced by the flat glossy. This moment segues directly into Paul singing:

> Who am I anyway?
> Am I my resumé?
> That is a picture of a person I don't know.
> What does he want from me?
> What should I try to be?
> So many faces all around, and here we go.
> I need this job, oh God, I need this show.

This existential moment for Paul, a feeling that arguably all the characters on the line share, has particularly racial overtones. The separation of the face from the individual behind the photo asks the audience to look past race and the body, to not see skin color as any sort of true indication of who a person is, but rather to find the person *behind* the picture.[18] As the theater scholar Josephine Lee writes regarding the connection between race and color-blind casting, "Race thus became the actor's false mask over a more 'universal' humanness; nonetheless it was a mask that maintained its stubborn presence no matter how hard one worked to eradicate it."[19] This signature *Chorus Line* moment challenges us to rethink where a person's true identity lies, not located in his racial background, which is often, though not always, written on the skin and revealed by a photograph, but in the personal and unique details that make up his life.

While the final version of *A Chorus Line* addresses race unevenly, a look into the archives of its lyricist, Edward Kleban, turns up some cut musical numbers that offer a more direct acknowledgment of racial difference. Connie and Richie were given the song "Confidence," which speaks to their own perceived sense of internal strength in the world of showbiz despite being pigeonholed as actors of color:

> RICHIE. Most a them
> Out-sing me and out-kick me
> Still I feel
> This guy is gonna pick me
> I have got
> One thing the others lack . . .
> Confidence . . .
> Confidence . . .
> That separates me from the pack
> Most a them
> Know jus' what they are doin'
> But I look
> Around and I'm a shoo-in
> I have got
> One special quali*teeee*

Confidence . . .
Confidence . . .
It's written plain all over
And will remain all over me

. . .

CONNIE. I am sure
That Richie thinks he's got it
But he's wrong
If only he could spot it
He forgets
That I go either way
Confidence . . . Ma'am . . .
Diffidence . . . Madam . . .
That is the wonder of Cathay
I've passed for Ethel Merman's little girlie
I've also done a year or two in *Purlie*, Dig it!
That is
Confidence . . .
Confidence . . .
By the by
This guy needs a confident person
I can be a confident person
. . . But I can also be shy[20]

In his book about Bennett's work, Ken Mandelbaum explains the genesis of the song: "The new character, Richie, played by Ron Dennis, was given a duet with Connie . . . in which the two 'token minority' figures on the line—the black boy and the Oriental girl—sang of the confidence instilled in them by the knowledge that the director of the show could not really do without them, no matter what he thought of their talents." "The song was about how we were always the only minorities in all-white casts," says Ron Dennis, the original Richie. "It was cleverly and subtly written. . . . When it was cut, Baayork [Lee, who played Connie] and I sat around for weeks not knowing how they were going to use us. They came up with the '4 foot 10' section of the montage for her, but I didn't get my song until just before we started previews, because they really didn't know what to do with me."[21]

"Confidence" didn't make it to the stage, but neither did another number of similar ilk, called "Token":

> There's a new dance that's sweepin' the country
> From Chinatown to Watts
> If you love to dance you really hafta learn it
> For it's ev'rywhere if only you discern it
> It's called the Token
> It's the Token
> And it's colorful and very thought provokin'
> Though not a single word is ever really spoken
> It's called the Token
> Just between you and me
>
> . . .
>
> Can't be two, now
> Uh-Uh-Uh
> Wouldn't do, now
> Uh-Uh-Uh
> Never three or four or more
> I'm tellin' you, now
> Uh-Uh-Uh
> Just a smidgen
> Lonely pigeon
> Short shrift
> If you catch my drift
> It's called the Token
> It's the Token
> Came from Africa and Asia and Hoboken
> And it's danced wherever promises are broken
> It's called the Token
> Just between you and me[22]

The song reveals the prevalence of racial tokenism in 1970s society while cleverly never mentioning race at all. Ironically and perhaps inadvertently, though, *A Chorus Line* reinforces its own tokenism by casting the show the way it does, identifying what race or ethnicity most of the characters should be and thereby limiting who can play those parts. Both of these cut numbers go against the grain of the libretto, which ultimately pushes for giving the job to the most talented individual, regardless of background. Race is treated as a minor detail, no more important than where someone grew up. After all, Richie gets a job on the line, but Connie does not, proving that race neither guarantees nor denies people work.

That said, *A Chorus Line* well reflects the racial and cultural zeitgeist of the 1970s, a decade of multiculturalism, ethnic and racial pride, and gay rights in which cultural and racial minorities were finding new ways to perform and exhibit their identities. Black was beautiful, and ethnic whites such as Jews, Italians, and Irish were eschewing assimilation to identify with their cultural roots, while reaping the rewards of mainstream white racial identity. The sociologist Herbert Gans termed this latter phenomenon "symbolic ethnicity" in 1979, claiming that it is "unnecessary for [white] ethnics to surrender their ethnicity to gain upward mobility, and today ethnics are admitted virtually everywhere, provided they meet economic and status requirements."[23] White ethnics in the 1970s could now indulge in the cultural side of their ethnicity without having to endure any of the bigotry they might have faced earlier in the twentieth century. They could be ethnic *and* white at the same time.

For many social scientists, though, the relationship between race and ethnicity remained unclear. Are they interchangeable terms? Is one a subset of another? Is one biological but the other cultural? One thing was certain, the seventies were perceived as the decade of ethnicity. Werner Sollors, a literary and racial theory scholar, writes that the publication of Nathan Glazer and Daniel Patrick Moynihan's *Beyond the Melting Pot* in 1963 not only "marked the end of an era. It paved the way for the revival of American ethnic identification in the 1960s and 1970s when attacks on the melting pot became the battle cry of 'unmeltable ethnics' who admonished their audiences to pay attention to ethnicity and to give up the assimilationist hope that ethnicity was going to disappear."[24] Gone was the message of *West Side Story*, with the Jets who wanted nothing more than to ditch their roots and be seen as full-blooded white Americans. Rather, this narrative allowed newly white individuals to be both proud Americans *and* culturally specific ethnic patriots.

The ethnic pride movement was a result of, if not a direct response to, the civil rights movement of the 1960s, except now it was whites, not blacks, who were standing up and claiming their heritages as Italians, Jews, Irish, and Poles instead of "bland" white Americans. Posed with the question "What is an ethnic group?" Michael Novak, the author of *The Rise of the Unmeltable Ethnics* (1972), answers: "It is a group with historical memory, real or imaginary. One belongs to an ethnic group in part involuntarily, in part by choice. Given a grandparent or two, one chooses to shape one's consciousness by one history rather than another. Ethnic memory is not a set of events remembered, but rather a set of instincts, feelings, intimacies, expectations, patterns of emotion and behavior; a sense of reality; a set of stories for individuals—and for the people as a whole—to live out."[25] From a celebration of ethnic foods to religious rituals, these white ethnics were happy to wave the banner of cultural heritage, *choosing* how they wanted to identify with a culture, if at all.

Where, though, did African Americans, Asian Americans, and Latinos fit into this group? They too had rich cultures and yet also faced marginalization in society due to racial prejudice. Ethnicity might be about choice, but racial phenotypes still limited the options for nonwhites. White ethnics, on the other hand, could indicate how they wanted to be read: white all-American majority member one moment, nationalistic ethnic minority the next.

Under this model, race and ethnicity become equal and flattened out in *A Chorus Line;* racial difference is treated no differently from any other kind of difference. Suddenly being African American and Italian American occupy the same rung. For all of the show's emphasis on diversity, just what is it that makes someone different? His race? Her place of birth? The color of a T-shirt? All these things are given equal weight, thereby calling the show's ostensible utopic politics into question. Sure, it would be great if Richie's being black were no more special than Al's wearing a TKTS shirt, but that's certainly not the way the world works now, let alone in 1975.

The significance of race and its relationship to difference connects to the musical's tension between individual and group identity. "Analysts of American culture," argues the sociologist Mary C. Waters, "have long noticed the fundamental tension between the high values Americans place on both individuality and conformity." Does one conform to the group (the chorus line) or shine as an individual (the star)? For Waters, the appeal of Gans's "symbolic ethnicity" is that it allows a white ethnic to "feel unique and special" and not be like everyone else, while still getting to take advantage of all the benefits of being white. This type of ethnicity becomes something the person can turn on and off, like a light switch, invoking it when useful or desired, but able to pass as part of the white racial majority on a day-to-day basis. We see this again and again in *A Chorus Line*, where the Jewish, Italian, and even light-skinned Latino characters often assert their ethnic backgrounds but hide them when necessary behind WASP-sounding stage names. Of course, a dark-skinned African American cannot "turn off" ethnicity so easily because of the racial component, revealing the shortfall in grouping all ethnic experiences together. As Waters explains, "The social and political consequences of being Asian or Hispanic or black are not symbolic for the most part, or voluntary. They are real and often hurtful."[26] "Symbolic ethnicity" mirrors *A Chorus Line*'s racial politics, as the concept itself is inherently theatrical. White ethnicity is marked by changes in one's name (like stage names), changes in culturally specific clothing (like costumes), and the performance of certain customs or rituals (like acting).

For Michael Bennett, race and ethnicity were just two more items on a long list of differences that distinguished one person from another. As he noted in an early interview about the musical, "I mean, think about going to school. Trying for any job. Being accepted. Being rejected. Being too short or too tall or too fat or too thin—I mean, we all have the equivalent. I wasn't too tall, I was too short, but . . . you know?"[27] Applying this worldview to the show, being black and being short suddenly become farcically equivalent, as if short people had faced hundreds of years of prejudice, widespread societal discrimination, or slavery. In the show, Val sings ("Dance: Ten, Looks: Three") about how she wasn't considered pretty enough to be a Rockette so got plastic surgery to enhance her appearance. Kristine's "challenge" is that she can't carry a tune ("Sing!"), and Diana's problem is not that she is Puerto Rican but that she can't please Mr. Karp, her acting teacher ("Nothing"), hardly the stuff of social strife. Connie doesn't seem to have a problem with being Asian American; rather, like Michael Bennett, she has a height issue. "Four foot ten. Four foot ten. . . . I used to hang from a parallel bar by the hour, hoping I'd stretch just an inch more," she sings.[28] Similarly, Richie's "Gimme the Ball" solo is about his realization that he didn't want to be a kindergarten teacher. This isn't to imply that the only issues that do or should affect people of color are of a racial nature, but it's interesting that despite the attention paid to diversity, no one seems to suffer from any sort of overt racial prejudice in the show.

The only area where a real sense of otherness does emerge is in terms of sexual identity. Both Greg and Paul are explicitly marked as gay, and Paul's long and moving monologue at the end of the show focuses on his coming to terms with his sexual and gender identity. In many ways, this isn't surprising. *A Chorus Line* came along only six years after the 1969 Stonewall riots in New York that helped kick the contemporary gay rights movement into full gear. While race was still a major topic of discussion in the United States, society was now also discussing homosexuality with new candidness. Sadly, despite being a character with whom we are meant to empathize, Paul doesn't make the final cut. Shortly after telling Zach about his being gay and working as a drag performer, he joins the other actors to perform a dance routine only to collapse to the floor from a knee injury.

The conflict between the individual and the group suffuses all parts of the show and is one of the signature visual and choreographic motifs of the original staging, as Bennett had the line of dancers continually dissolving and re-forming itself onstage. The individual telling his or her story leaves the line, and the other dancers disappear into the stage darkness, only to return at the end of the number and re-form the line. "While *A Chorus Line* had remarkably little dancing, especially for a show about dancers," writes Frank Rich, "it could be said that the entire show was danced: its performers kept moving back and forth in different patterns through the depth of the stage, forever splintering and then reconstituting their chorus line. It was as if the company were one giant, undulating organism forever torn between the shadows of the wings and the footlights down front."[29]

This tension also works its way into a subplot involving Cassie and Zach. The two were once romantically involved, and now Cassie has returned to New York looking for work after her career in California stalled. Despite the fact that she had featured roles in some of Zach's earlier shows, the problem is that Cassie is too good for the chorus but isn't good enough to become a "singular sensation," a star. She's in theatrical limbo, where no one will hire her, and has come to Zach to beg him for a job. "Well, you shouldn't have come. You don't fit in. You don't dance like anybody else—you don't know how," Zach says.[30] Even though he knows she's too good, Zach lets Cassie stay at the audition because he is still in love with her.

Cassie's distinctiveness soon becomes a problem as the cast begins to rehearse a number called "One" from the show's unnamed musical. Zach first instructs everyone: "Now—this is important! I want to see *Unison Dancing*. Every head, arm, body angle, *exactly the same*. You must blend. This is one of those numbers where you back the star—you're her frame. I don't want anybody to pull my eye."[31] This raises the question: is Zach's desire to not have anyone pull his eye possible in a chorus line made of multiple races? Would a single black person in an all-white chorus, or a single white person in an all-black chorus line, pull the audience's eye? This isn't a theoretical question. This precise issue had permeated the casting practices of another famous dancing institution, the Rockettes, who until 1987 had remained an all-white troupe. Only a few years earlier their director, Violet Holmes, had claimed, "One or two black girls in the line would definitely distract. You would lose the whole look of precision, which is the hallmark of the Rockettes."[32]

The rehearsal of "One" begins, and in spite of its jaunty melody and affable lyrics, this number turns sinister, the music becoming discordant at moments. As we watch the dancers go through their paces, we see how Bennett's choreography forces them to become conforming automatons, devoid of personality and individuality. In fact, "One" deconstructs itself in this very moment to reveal this imposition of sameness. While some of the chorus line sing the song's actual lyrics—"One/ Moment in her presence/ And you can forget the/ Rest"—the others rhythmically speak the "counts" of the song, "One, two, three, four, five, six, seven, eight," revealing the driving forward beats that require that the dancers perform with complete synchronicity. As the dissonance grows, the lyrics become a mass of robotic instructions: "*One, hat, shoulder up,* walk, (*beat*) walk, (*beat*) stay pulled up, eyes front, *hat to chest, angle right hat to the head,* lead with the hip, follow thru; palm up, fill the phrase, elbow right, hat down, hat to chest, elbow up, *change the body, leave the head, shoulder left*, head, lead to the right, hat up, knee in, elbow." They all work to mold their bodies to the choreography, except for Cassie. Zach shouts corrections at her as the number progresses: "You're late," "Don't pop the head,

Cassie," "Too high with the leg, Cassie," "Too much plié, Cassie," "You're late on the turn, Cassie." Displeased by her performance, Zach forces her to do the routine again with the boys, until he can't bear to watch any more: "You're distorting the combination, Cassie. Pull in. Cool it. Dance like everybody else." This outburst results in a showdown between the two where they finally come to terms with the end of their relationship while the other dancers continue going through their paces behind them, the music grown nightmarish to underscore the "horror" of being part of a nameless, unindividuated crowd. For Zach, Cassie is too good for the chorus line, and it breaks his heart that someone whom he loves so much would be reduced to such a role. "You're special," he tells her, to which she replies, "No, we're all special. He's special—she's special. And Sheila—and Richie, and Connie. They're all special. I'd be happy to be dancing in that line."[33] That Richie and Connie get special shout-outs is interesting—are they more "special" because of their skin color?—but Cassie's claim that everyone is unique only works to reinforce the show's dogged insistence on equality of identity and background.

The show concludes with Zach's final selection of dancers, but in a musical fantasy-cum-finale, the entire company (selected and rejected dancers alike) returns to perform the song "One," this time costumed in sparkling gold outfits. The finale gives them what they wanted, the dream of being in a dazzling Broadway show, *but* at the expense of their own individuality; now costumed alike, they all blend together, virtually indistinguishable. As Michael Bennett imagined this final sequence, the audience, having spent two intermissionless hours getting to know the life story of each dancer, was supposed to view the number as a sort of hell, because each person's history is essentially obliterated as they are made to high-kick in chorus line uniformity. As Bennett told Ken Mandelbaum, "That finale is so sad. The craft is wonderful, but you ask, did they go through all that just to be anonymous?"[34] In his initial concept for the ending, Bennett says:

> You're going to get to know all these dancers as individuals and care about each one. Then, at the very end of the play, they're all going to come out in tuxedos and top hats, and you're not going to be able to tell one from another. They're going to blend. They're going to do everything you've ever seen anyone in a chorus line do. It's

going to be the most horrifying moment you will ever experience in a theatre. I have a vision of them forming a V and marching with frozen smiles, like in *Metropolis.* If I do this right, you will never see another chorus line in a theatre. Everybody will reevaluate what it is they're watching.[35]

Bennett's original concept involved not giving a final bow to the show's actual dancers, because he wanted to emphasize that the chorus members are eternally relegated to invisibility, never given their full due or acknowledgment. Instead, the chorus just keeps high-kicking as the curtain falls.

It's not just the staging of the finale that highlights this situation; the song "One" is itself a sad commentary on the lives of the dancers. "Fine irony lies in the music they sing and dance, 'One,'" observes Scott McMillin in *The Musical as Drama*, "for the number is *about* the individualist, the 'one,' the star whom they are supposed to be backing up . . . [who] never appears."[36] The lyrics are all about a woman who is sublimely special, a star. The boys sing:

> One
> Singular sensation
> Ev'ry little step she
> Takes.
> One
> Thrilling combination
> Ev'ry move that she
> Makes.

Then, later, the girls enter with a chorus of their own:

> She walks into a room
> And you know she's un
> Commonly rare, very unique,
> Peripatetic, poetic, and chic.
> She walks into a room
> And you know from her
> Maddening poise, effortless

The 2006 Broadway revival cast of *A Chorus Line*, costumed in matching gold outfits, performing the finale, "One," as seen in the documentary *Every Little Step*. *Credit:* Sony Pictures Classics/Photofest © Sony Pictures Classics

> Whirl,
> She's the special girl.

If this were a Jerry Herman musical, the "She" in question would be Mame or Dolly, but in *A Chorus Line* the woman is a nonentity who never appears. Instead, our attention is kept on the chorus in what is a strange moment of doubleness. We see them and in some ways, *they* are the stars, now dressed to the nines in their shimmering finale costumes, but at the same time, the dancers have been reduced to the background, made invisible, singing about a star who is much more famous than they are, made even more ironic and devastating by the fact that she is missing in action. Writes the drama critic Jack Kroll:

> It's a thrilling finish, but the thrill is laced with a kind of horror. All the sweat and desperation have exploded into this apotheosis of anonymity, in which the dancers' skills and personalities are welded into a banal kicking machine whose very mindless precision sends

thrills down the most sophisticated of spines. It's a sensational double image of the popular culture of our mass society. Those practical monosyllables we heard at the beginning—"Step, kick, step, kick,
kick . . ."—have finally conditioned the desired response in both the
dancers and ourselves. "A Chorus Line" ends on a fanfare that is also
a lament, the most moving tribute this show could make to its heroes
and heroines, the shock troops of an overentertained society.[37]

This finale is the American Dream theatricalized for the Broadway stage. It
enacts the same philosophy that Sean O'Brien, a white ethnic interviewed
by Mary Waters, articulates: "I think everybody has the same opportunity.
It doesn't matter what their background is. The education is there and if
they have the gumption to go after it, they can do anything they damn well
please. It doesn't make any difference if they are Irish, German, Jewish,
Italian, or black. There are all different groups who are multi-millionaires.
They have the same opportunities. I think a black kid has the same opportunity as one of my own."[38] This is the philosophy of A Chorus Line and
explains the current appeal of reality competition shows like American
Idol and So You Think You Can Dance.

Yet a problem with A Chorus Line remains. The show wants us to read
society as color-blind in a way that is not tenable. It acknowledges race
and then disregards it. This is not to say that the goal of color-blind casting
is not admirable or that theater should not continue to strive to be a utopic
place. Harry Newman, cofounder of the Non-Traditional Casting Project,
urges that "non-traditional casting does not of necessity imply tokenism
or loss of identity. It's about having all artists considered as individuals
with individual qualities, apart from belonging to groups based on often
arbitrary distinctions such as skin color or ethnic origin. To be judged on
individual ability is not 'playing white' either. It is allowing each artist to
bring whatever she is to her work."[39] Indeed, such a statement should be
an aim not only for theater but for society as a whole. Rather than trying to address race by pretending it does not exist in some sort of color-
blind fashion, what if theater could be used as a mirror to reveal the deep
complexities of race as a way to truly grapple with and repair the racial
inequalities that exist in society? This latter option, arguably being more
painful to engage and illuminating things that might be uncomfortable to

talk about, might also be more productive in the long run. After all, we still operate in a society that is *not* color-blind and in which race plays a profound role. Thus, to function as if race is not a factor may be more of a disservice than a boon.[40]

A Chorus Line, then, is both utopic and dystopic in its view of American society. It's a place where everyone has an equal opportunity, but in the end it doesn't matter, because the individual is ultimately discarded. This ideology was not unique to *A Chorus Line*. In 1981, Bennett staged what would be his last great show, *Dreamgirls*, a musical about an African American girl group in the 1960s that achieves fame despite a plethora of personal and societal battles. The show was loosely based on the Supremes, but the music by Henry Krieger and the book and lyrics by Tom Eyen were wholly original. Yet even though much of the show is about the particular struggles of *black* artists, Bennett claimed that "the problems that the black characters in *Dreamgirls* have are just problems about life as an American, the problems you have when you're in your 20's and you find out that happily ever after doesn't mean the things you thought . . . and that you can get everything you want and it's not what you thought it was going to be, and if you're going to survive, you have to keep wanting other things." Such a statement doesn't hold, as the plot of *Dreamgirls* itself proves: a song by the Dreams is co-opted by a white musical group, Dave and the Sweethearts, and becomes a big hit, revealing the racial inequality that impacts the world of entertainment. Bennett expands further on his thoughts about *Dreamgirls*: "The important thing about *Dreamgirls* for me was that I approached the material as if cultural assimilation is something that has happened in America. . . . *Dreamgirls* is not about being black, it's about being human. It's a black musical, but it's about people. It's not a black version of a white show. It's very nice for young blacks to go to the theatre and see role models who are successful and still human."

Bernard Jacobs, president of the Shubert Organization, comments on Bennett's perspective:

Michael was really a great advocate of civil rights, and he had a very strong feeling that he wanted to do a show which dealt with black people in the same way that most shows about white people deal with white people. He didn't want it to be a show that catered to race. He wanted it to be a show about blacks as people living in our society and having the same problems other people in our society have. . . . One of the problems with the show was that the critics, to an extent, were unable to deal with a show about blacks the same way they would treat a show about whites.[41]

But ultimately, weren't the critics of *Dreamgirls* right? As much as one might like to just treat people as people, not to acknowledge the particular ways in which race has shaped the lives of *all* people in this country, whether as minorities who have been targets of prejudice or as a site of privilege for a white majority, is a significant oversight.

And that is the exact omission that *A Chorus Line* makes as well. For despite the show's good intentions in attempting to recover the individual within the context of the chorus and its celebration of diversity, the musical fails to truly acknowledge the ways in which race remains a delineating factor in America. In fact, I would argue that the show's willful blindness to race has contributed to its success and popularity. People *want* to believe in the American Dream, in the notion that they do have a chance and that differences—racial, social, sexual, or otherwise—don't really matter. The true significance of this 1975 show, then, is that in America no matter how often society says people of color have a fair chance to succeed, such individuals must continue to fight for true equality in a world that promises freedom of opportunity but doesn't always deliver on that contract.

6

Everything Old Is New Again

Nostalgia and the Broadway Musical at the End of the Twentieth Century

To create something new, we must first love what is old.
—Mei-Li, *Flower Drum Song*, David Henry Hwang, 2001

Maybe it was the 1970s energy crisis. Maybe it was Reaganomics. Or maybe, just maybe, it was *Cats*, Andrew Lloyd Webber's 1981 megaspectacular musical, that can best explain the downfall of the Broadway musical in the 1980s.[1] Yes, the reviews are in, and the 1980s, with their singing and dancing felines, have been officially deemed a new low in musical theater history. While the 1970s had brought to prominence the musical theater genius Stephen Sondheim, who was then in his writing prime with *Company*, *Follies*, *A Little Night Music*, and *Sweeney Todd*, the Golden Age of Broadway was definitely over. It seemed that the well of talent, creativity, and inspiration had dried up. In the 1980–1981 Broadway season there were thirty-six new productions on Broadway, and eight years later, just twenty-one. The number of new Broadway musicals in particular had decreased: fourteen in 1980–1981 to just six at the end of the Reagan administration. At the 1989 Tony Awards, the lineup for Best Musical was embarrassingly bleak. Of the six new musicals that had even opened that season, three were nominated: *Starmites*, an original but strange science fiction musical that was a ninety-five-performance flop; *Black and Blue*, a revue of American jazz and blues music; and *Jerome Robbins' Broadway*, an evening celebrating the work of the legendary choreographer and director, that took the top prize. Two revues celebrating Broadway's past and one new flop. Talk about dire.

A major reason for the decline in new musicals was the rising expense of productions. Technology and labor costs were quickly escalating. Shows that once cost several hundred thousand dollars now cost millions, and producers felt that what they were offering had to at least have a chance of making back their investment, let alone turn a profit. With millions of dollars and sometimes years' worth of work on the line, Broadway was becoming more artistically conservative. Furthermore, as a related symptom of rising production costs, by 1989 most Broadway musicals had raised their top ticket prices to $55 and $60 from about $20, a $40 difference in just ten years.[2] Shows had to run longer to recoup their initial investments, making producers more risk averse and looking for safer, family-friendly hits that could run for multiple years both on Broadway and on tour around the country. In this new mutually reinforcing paradigm, as ticket costs increased, audiences wanted to be wowed by what they were paying for.

Enter the British megamusical. *Cats*, based on the poetry of T. S. Eliot and set to music by Andrew Lloyd Webber, was more revue than traditional musical, but people really weren't there for the songs. Well, they were there for *one* song, the blockbuster "Memory," which would become a pop hit. No, *Cats* was a revue on steroids, a series of songs, each describing the personality of a different cat. Think multiculturalism for felines. The show culminated with a major coup de theatre: a huge tire that rose off the stage like something out of *Close Encounters of the Third Kind* to take Grizabella (she's the cat who sings "Memory," of course) to feline heaven. *Oklahoma!* this was not. Despite becoming the butt of many jokes in the years that followed, *Cats* would laugh all the way to the bank, going on to become the longest-running Broadway musical in 1997, surpassing the record set by *A Chorus Line*.

But *Cats* was just the beginning. *Les Misérables*, the pop opera based on Victor Hugo's sprawling French novel, became a sensation in 1987 and was quickly followed by another Lloyd Webber hit in 1988: *The Phantom of the Opera*. The extravagant staging of both shows—a massive turntable set in the former and a falling chandelier and subterranean lagoon in the latter—was what drew audiences in. Were these great shows? Maybe, maybe not. But it didn't matter. The buzz on these spectacles was through the roof, tickets were in high demand, and both shows (like *Cats*) won the Best

Musical Tony. That demand had an effect not just on box office but also on the availability of the theaters themselves. Long runs of megamusicals became the norm in the 1980s, and with shows running anywhere from ten years to, in the case of *The Phantom of the Opera*, twenty-five years and counting, the number of available theaters that could book new productions was quickly diminishing. Plus, because the shows cost so much to produce in the first place, they *had* to run several years in order to earn back their initial investments.[3] The economics of theater were snowballing out of control.

Spectacle-driven British imports defined musical theater in the eighties, but there were of course home-grown musicals as well. The 1980s saw works like *The Mystery of Edwin Drood* (1985) and *Big River* (1985), which would both win the Best Musical Tony, but neither one would have a lasting legacy. No, what defined American musical theater in the eighties was revivals of Golden Age shows. There were retreads of *West Side Story* (1980), *Camelot* (1980), *Brigadoon* (1980), *My Fair Lady* (1981), *On Your Toes* (1983), *Mame* (1983), *Zorba* (1983), *Sweet Charity* (1986), *Anything Goes* (1987), *Gypsy* (1989), and even *Sweeney Todd* (1989), which had premiered only ten years earlier. *Jerome Robbins' Broadway*, the 1989 Best "New" Musical, was essentially a mishmash of multiple revivals all rolled together.

As the sociologist Jeffrey Goldfarb writes, "[The revival musical] presents to its audience a pre-existing successful package. Book, music, lyrics, and choreography are identical to the past hit. Technically, this is what makes it a revival and not a new production of an older work. A 30- or 60-second television commercial evokes the success of the past hit and its nostalgic connotations. The audience comes not so much for new cultural experience, but for a reliving of a pseudo-experience." Goldfarb's astute observations on revivals have major implications for our understanding of race. What is being relived and nostalgized is not only the show itself but what the show represents and the racial context of its time period. Goldfarb expounds further:

Today, [Richard] Burton in "Camelot" recalls our hope of the '60s, and gives us the melodramatic pleasure to witness his excellence before it was corrupted. "West Side Story" awakens our sense of past innocence. "Bye Bye Birdie" rekindles a sweetened view of our personal and national adolescence. We approach each of these and other such revivals with nostalgic longings, not for things past, but for easily digested renditions of things past.

When we wish to recall the political, cultural and personal innocence of the '50s and '60s, we do not recall the anxiety of nuclear consciousness, the cold war, political purges ("McCarthyism"), and the civil rights struggles, nor our inability to confront any of these major problems which characterize the age of The American Camelot. *Rather, we long for ignorance of these problems.* The revival musicals give us such ignorance, as do, more powerfully, such television programs as "Happy Days" and "Laverne and Shirley," the contemporary versions of the situation comedies of the '50s and '60s.[4]

Unspoken, but I would argue implicit, in Goldfarb's critique is a desire shared by much of the theatergoing public, a predominantly white, older, middle-class audience, to return to white America, for it is that "innocence," a knowledge that is devoid of racial conflict, indeed of racial Others, that seems to be the domain of the revival. As distance from the original production increases, musicals begin to operate on two levels: as the shows themselves, but also as nostalgic touchstones of the time periods in which they were first produced.[5]

Not all of the musical theater revivals of the 1980s were successful—*Camelot* ran for only fifty-six performances—but they do reveal a producerly desire to stage work that was artistically safe, pretested, and therefore economically viable. This craze for revivals would go unabated into the 1990s, so much so that in 1994, the Tony Awards committee decided to split the Tony Award for Best Revival into two categories, Best Musical Revival and Best Play Revival, to address the sheer number of revived musicals that were popping up.

While I don't want to downplay the economic factors that contributed to the revival craze, to look only at the economics is a bit limiting. Instead, I would argue that the political landscape of the eighties and its concomitant racial politics were also determining factors. The decade witnessed a new political turn to what had been termed *neoconservatism* under the presidency of Ronald Reagan. His eight-year tenure was marked by economic policies that reduced taxes and decreased spending on social programs while increasing overall spending that swelled the national debt. The Reagan administration played its conservative card on the issue of race by opposing affirmative action and cutting back on social welfare programs that would aid lower-income individuals, who were often people of color. High price tag plus conservative politics? Sounds like the Broadway musical at the end of the twentieth century.

Three types of musicals emerged out of this social landscape: 1) "new" musicals such as *42nd Street* and *The Will Rogers Follies* that were based on classic 1920s and 1930s Broadway shows or movies;[6] 2) "revisals," which were rewritten revivals of classic shows such as *Annie Get Your Gun* and *Flower Drum Song*; and 3) jukebox musicals of the 2000s such as *All Shook Up*, *Mamma Mia*, and *Jersey Boys*, constructed from the song catalogs of famous composers and recording artists like Elvis Presley, ABBA, and Frankie Valli and the Four Seasons. Despite the seeming diversity of these styles, these works share a love of nostalgia; they're postmodern pastiche, recycled and repurposed with shiny new veneers, but reflecting Broadway content and musical styles that had been around for almost the entire twentieth century. Lamenting the state of the Broadway musical in 1982, the *New York Times* critic Frank Rich wrote that "escapist musicals still exist on Broadway, but . . . they're mostly repackagings of old material rather than new works with fresh books and scores. If they're not stage adaptations of movie musicals (from '42nd Street' down to 'Seven Brides for Seven Brothers'), then they're revivals of past Broadway hits or vintage songbook anthologies. The assumption seems to be that because we already know the jokes and tunes going into the theater, we'll respond by Pavlovian habit."[7] Indeed, the "quaint" Broadway musical had become the epitome of postmodernism, which fetishized the past and turned older works into new commodities in a consumer-driven age.

To place *42nd Street* and *The Will Rogers Follies* in the camp of postmodernism may sound strange to some. After all, on the surface, they are just lighthearted musicals with attractive chorus girls, catchy songs, and lots of tap dancing. But they are also perfect examples of pastiche, which in its broadest sense is an artistic mode that attempts to imitate or recall an earlier style. While pastiche can have a parodic effect—spoofing or laughing at an earlier time period—postmodern pastiche is what the cultural theorist Fredric Jameson terms "blank parody": "Pastiche is, like parody, the imitation of a peculiar or unique style, the wearing of a stylistic mask, speech in a dead language: but it is a neutral practice of such mimicry, without parody's ulterior motive, without the satirical impulse, without laughter, without that still latent feeling that there exists something *normal* compared to which what is being imitated is rather comic."[8] It is imitation without commentary. Rather than recalling a previous era with historical accuracy, pastiche invokes the *feel* of the era. (The TV show *Mad Men* with its evocation of the sixties illustrates this well.) Could the musical genre, which often revels in style over substance, be any better suited for this task?

The theater scholar Rebecca Ann Rugg says that nostalgia in relation to the musical is "a longing for something in the past that never actually existed, at least not as remembered. All memory is selective, but nostalgic memory selects only the carefree, blissful past."[9] Nostalgia and pastiche happily cohabitate, but the shows here are more than just pastiche. Many might be more properly termed *simulacra*, a postmodern term for a copy with no original. In the case of *42nd Street*, for example, the show looks back to a 1933 film, but it is not a slavish re-creation of that work; rather, it is a contemporary take that attempts to evoke the lost era of 1930s film and stage musicals. From a racial perspective, these nostalgic postmodern musicals offer audiences a return to an uncritical, deracialized past where people of color are often absent, historical racial conflict has gone missing, and racial history is rewritten to be both palatable and easy to digest.[10]

Fredric Jameson defines postmodern pastiche as a style that emerges out of a consumerist, capitalist society where the corporate is valued over the idiosyncrasies of the individual. While Jameson's articulation of the factors that contributed to postmodernism are purposely quite broad and far-reaching in scope, his focus on the shift from the individual to the corporation also serves as a spot-on assessment of the transformation of theatrical producing in the 1990s and beyond. Gone were the handful of forceful visionary producers like Hal Prince and David Merrick, and in their place came corporations. Musicals are now produced by Disney, Warner Bros., and a slew of other Hollywood studios that are keen to turn their catalogs of popular films into money-making stage adaptations. Just pick up almost any Broadway playbill nowadays and count the number of producers that precede the title of any show. It's not uncommon to see ten or more names, both individuals and organizations, listed. The days of the individual producer and the auteur are over; welcome to theater by committee.

This chapter examines a handful of musicals, both new shows and revivals, that exemplify this postmodern turn to nostalgia in the eighties, nineties, and beyond, and particularly looks at the ways in which such shows articulate, or more importantly *don't* articulate, an overt policy of race. This might seem an unusual argument. After all, the logic might hold, the lack of attention paid to race by the musical could mean that racial issues were no longer a matter of concern in our society. Maybe W.E.B. Du Bois was wrong. Maybe race wasn't such a big deal anymore. But that, as we know, was hardly the case. From new policies that upheld affirmative action to the violent beating of Rodney King in Los Angeles in 1991 that set off a series of race riots the following year to the election of Barack Obama, the country's first black president, the topic of race continues to permeate U.S. society.

And where was the American musical on all of this? If the 1970s had been a moment of multiculturalism and ethnic pride, the 1980s would witness a firm turn back to whiteness and the mythologies of the American Dream. By invoking the past, the Broadway musical came to represent something larger than itself. Not only did the content of many popular shows imagine a world that was mainly if not entirely white, but the Broadway musical became a touchstone for a lost America, a more "innocent" and whiter America of the thirties, forties, and fifties where life was "simpler" and "better." As throwbacks to earlier time periods, these shows recovered not just the songs and style of previous generations but also the racial politics of those eras, much of which privileged whiteness. Musicals would begin to lose their widespread cultural currency in this moment and be deemed old-fashioned by a younger generation, but it was precisely this "antiquated" aspect that made the musical so perfect for evoking a lost all-white society that never actually existed.

The shows I examine in this chapter might at first appear to have nothing to say about race at all, either because people of color don't appear in them or because thematically they don't talk about race, but the challenge of seeing race doesn't mean that it isn't there. If anything, the fact that these shows don't articulate their racial politics when race is clearly at work gives them, one might argue, a more subversive impact. These shows, which uphold a reactionary white view of the world, succeed precisely because they don't broadcast their politics; rather they assume that whiteness is the normative way of looking at the world. In turn, whiteness maintains its place of authority, power, and influence by going unchallenged and unmarked. Rather than something that authors add to a show or decide to highlight, race is "always already" there, whether we think it is or not.

42nd Street: Hear the Beat of Postmodern Feet

For me, no other musical personifies Broadway as does *42nd Street*. From its battalions of tapping chorus kids and hummable melodies to its backstage milieu, the show is pure old-fashioned theater magic. Yet despite the fact that it exudes "classic" vibes, the musical is actually a new creation, dating to 1980. It is based on the famous 1933 film of the same name, which was directed by Lloyd Bacon and choreographed by Busby Berkeley (then a rising talent), and starred Ruby Keeler, Warner Baxter, Bebe Daniels, and a young Ginger Rogers. The stage version used the film's original score by Harry Warren and Al Dubin, while interpolating songs from the team's other Warner Bros. films. Directed and choreographed by Gower Champion, it featured not a book but "Lead Ins and Crossovers" by Mark Bramble and Michael Stewart, which reinforced the show's pastiche qualities. As the film critic J. Hoberman writes of the stage incarnation, *42nd Street* "is a prime example of a vulgar postmodernism—a remake without an original, the revival of a non-existent show."[11] The musical is a racial fantasia whose casting evokes the all-white 1930s world in which the show is set.[12]

42nd Street follows Peggy Sawyer, a chorus wannabe from Allentown, Pennsylvania, who shows up late to her first Broadway audition and through sheer luck and talent taps her way into *Pretty Lady*, the latest musical by the director Julian Marsh. All is going smoothly until Peggy crashes into the leading lady, Dorothy Brock, during a dance sequence and injures her, thereby throwing into question the future of the entire show, which rests on Brock's star power. Peggy is fired and decides to return to Allentown, but in a strange turn of events that could only happen in a

Broadway musical, the same Peggy is called on to replace Dorothy and thereby saves the day. Big production numbers, lots of melodrama, and a hint of romance make for the perfect backstage musical.

42nd Street was a huge hit and ran for almost ten years, closing in 1989. Much of its success was due to its producer, the legendary David Merrick, who had built a career by pulling every known stunt in the book (and creating a few himself) to draw in audiences. He was known as egomaniacal, controlling, and duplicitous, but it didn't matter. Merrick had produced some of the greatest musicals of Broadway, including *Gypsy, Hello, Dolly!, I Do! I Do!,* and *Oliver!*—he seemed to have an affinity for musicals with exclamation marks in their titles—and had earned his tantrums and fits. *42nd Street* would not be Merrick's last show, but it would be his final hit. Merrick was up to his usual tricks during the tryout of the initially troubled show, going so far as to ban reviewers from previews and even having the cast play to empty houses so they could work out the show's problems in private.[13] Always the showman, when the musical played across the street from the megahit *The Phantom of the Opera* in the mid-1980s, Merrick moved *42nd Street*'s curtain time to 8:15 P.M. so that theatergoers who were turned away from *Phantom* could cross the street and see his tap-dancing extravaganza.

The show's success, though, was really generated by the director/choreographer, Gower Champion, who was working at the top of his game creating dazzling and innovative tap sequences (with the help of Randy Skinner and Karin Baker). Tragically, Champion, a beloved figure in the theatrical community, died of blood cancer on the afternoon of the show's opening night, August 25, 1980. Merrick kept Champion's death a secret through the opening performance to shield the cast from the news and only announced at the curtain call that Champion had passed, creating a scene of tears and grief that was quite devastating to actors and audience alike. Critics, who had leapt out of their seats and headed for the door so they could file their opening night reviews, ended up rushing back to the theater to report on what was the real story of the evening.

42nd Street was a good musical, but Champion's death and the attendant media coverage helped give it the kind of buzz that a producer like Merrick hungered for. It turned into a hot ticket that went on to win the Tony for Best Musical in 1981. But a beloved artist's death and good tap numbers do not ensure the staying power of any show. *42nd Street* was popular because it told the great American rags-to-riches success story, a combo of luck, hard work, and talent that has the hero come out on top.

By the time *42nd Street* closed in 1989 after 3,486 performances, it was the second-longest-running musical in Broadway history, only bested by that other show about chorus kids trying to catch a break in a big Broadway musical, *A Chorus Line*. That show was blunt about the difficulties of finding a job "on the line," though optimistic in its racial politics, suggesting that people of any background have equal opportunity; *42nd Street*, by contrast, is pure white fantasy. To my knowledge, no nonwhite actress has ever played the leading role of Peggy Sawyer in any major professional production. While the show is predicated on the idea that hard work will pay off and that anyone can get the job as long as he or she has talent, what is unspoken is that this mythology only holds for whites. *42nd Street* takes place in 1933, thereby placing the contemporary audience within the racial politics of that specific historical moment. How do we reconcile the 1930s milieu of *42nd Street* with the world of the stage production in 1980, which was quite different, racially speaking?

42nd Street seems not to be about race simply because the musical refrains from explicitly invoking racial ideologies, but it is a work that is very much about white privilege in American society. It's sometimes hard to grasp such an ideology in the show, especially for the casual viewer, who often sees only the tap dancing and musical spectacle and not the undergirding policies that drive the plot forward. Then again, *42nd Street* is not a show that moves forward at all. The dancers keep tapping in place, their eyes firmly looking backward to a lost and mythologized past in which a belief in talent and hard work will win the day.

Despite the fact that forty-seven years separated the original *42nd Street* film and its stage adaptation, there was much that united their two worlds. The critic John Beaufort writes, "'42nd Street' celebrates a time as well as a genre. 1980 looks at 1933 with affection and humor but no patronizing. It reminds us how close here and now can be to there and then. The time gap dissolves."[14] The original movie, of course, was a product of the Great Depression, when millions of Americans were out of work. Theater too had been hurt by the economic catastrophe, and *42nd Street* was Hollywood's optimistic response to society's financial woes. Despite being hard

Billy Lawlor (Lee Roy Reams), surrounded by chorus girls all outfitted in matching costumes and blond wigs, jumps high in *42nd Street*'s "We're in the Money." *Credit:* Photofest

hit by the financial collapse and cutting back on their output of musical films, Warner Bros. optioned the 1932 novel *42nd Street* by Bradford Ropes and turned the backstage potboiler into one of the most successful movie musicals of the thirties. *42nd Street* was the number-one film attraction for the first half of 1933, no small feat considering that 1933 was also the worst year of the Depression.[15] In fact, J. Hoberman writes, "*42nd Street* is inextricably bound up in the experience of the Depression and the coming of the New Deal. Its production spans the 1932 Presidential election campaign and its release—together with that of *Gold Diggers of 1933*, which opened in Los Angeles and New York the very week that Congress passed the National Recovery Act—coincided almost exactly with the celebrated 'first hundred days' of the Roosevelt administration."[16] The movie reinvigorated the Hollywood musical and would become the model on which other backstage films would be based; a by-product of the film was that more than twice the number of movie musicals were released in 1933 than

in 1931 and 1932 combined.[17] The film's story offered the promise of jobs
and the belief that hard work and talent would ultimately be rewarded.
The entire world of *42nd Street* and the Ziegfeld Follies, which are fairly
contemporaneous, is predicated on this notion. "The ideal chorus girl," J.
Hoberman observes, "was a Horatio Alger heroine, an American Cinderella, free to sing and dance her way up the staircase of success."[18] As the
chorus girl Anytime Annie sings in the stage version of *42nd Street*, "A raw
beginner can be a winner," to which Peggy Sawyer responds, "Just give me
a chance!" indicating that the promise and opportunity of work are available to everyone.[19]

The America of 1980 was not the America of the Great Depression, but
coming out of the Carter presidency, the country was facing its own economic challenges, including raging inflation and high oil prices. America
was looking for a new direction and would find it in Ronald Reagan, who
would be inaugurated as the country's fortieth president just five months
after *42nd Street* opened. As the critic Stanley Kauffman wrote of the
musical, "For a couple of hours that brisk tapping protects us from the
uncertainties of today. (It didn't do much for the people actually *in* the
1930s, but nostalgia is a drug, not history.)"[20]

Yet despite the rough times of the Depression, the stage incarnation
wants us to look at the 1930s with a sense of quaint nostalgia. In one of the
musical's opening lines, Maggie Jones, the co-writer of *Pretty Lady*, the
fictitious show in *42nd Street*, says, "They're paying four-forty a seat out
there!" and points to the audience.[21] If only prices were so cheap; top ticket prices for *42nd Street* when it opened were $25 and $30, hardly bank-
breaking, but not the rock-bottom prices of the Depression. Sure, things
were bad then, the show seems to say, but everything was so inexpensive!
Adding to this generalized nostalgia, the musical's score is a hodgepodge
of songs from a variety of sources, all written by the composer/lyricist
team of Harry Warren and Al Dubin. "Shuffle Off to Buffalo," "You're Getting to Be a Habit with Me," and the title number are all present from *42nd
Street*, but in a trend that would define the musical in the eighties and
nineties, other classic and famous numbers were inserted as well: "Lullaby
of Broadway" from *Gold Diggers of 1935*, "Dames" from the film of the
same name (1934), and "We're in the Money" from *Gold Diggers of 1933*.[22]
The pastiche creates what the theater historian Alan Woods has called

"ersatz nostalgia," a term he reserves for "productions which intended to evoke a simpler (and safer) past for their audiences, but did so without reviving work which might be uncooperatingly complex. . . . These 'ersatz nostalgia' productions essentially remade the past, revising it to meet the interests and concerns of contemporary audiences while suggesting that they were actual recreations of the past."[23] The appeal seems clear. In a moment of economic distress, looking back to the Depression for inspiration and motivation was a terrific morale booster. If America could get through hard times before, it could overcome them again. That such a philosophy glossed over the racial issues at stake was a secondary detail.

For some critics, though, the show's pastiche qualities proved confusing. In his generally laudatory review in the *New York Times*, Frank Rich wrote: "Mr. Stewart and Mr. Bramble [the book writers] have not really spoofed the old Warners musicals in the winning manner of such latter-day parodies as the Off-Broadway hit 'Dames at Sea' or the recent film 'Movie Movie.' And yet they haven't exactly played the old clichés straight, either. When we watch their characters overcome quintessential showbiz adversities to bring their musical to Broadway, it's hard to know whether we are to laugh or to cheer or merely to float off on a cloud of nostalgia."[24] Similarly, John Simon saw the show as walking the line between nostalgia (the songs) and camp (the plot), bridged only by Gower Champion's remarkable choreography.[25]

The choreography definitely was the star of the show, but it owed its debt to the choreographer of the 1933 film: Busby Berkeley. Berkeley, born William Berkeley Enos, spent time as a young man in the military, where part of his responsibilities as an entertainment officer involved choreographing military marches and other drills.[26] His attention to precision and detail became the hallmark of his career, in which he would turn the chorus into an elaborate and intricate choreographed machine.[27] Setting his camera at a variety of angles, including his famous overhead shot to capture the clever geometric patterns he created using the bodies of the chorus members, Berkeley's choreography defined a generation of Warner Bros. films. But more to the point, the chorus lines of the twenties and thirties, as choreographed on film by Berkeley and produced onstage by Ziegfeld, were marked not only by their exactness but also by their racial uniformity. *42nd Street* both in 1933 and in 1980 capitalizes on this homogeneity. The world of Broadway in the 1930s was a white world, and the film and stage musical are paeans to the rhythmic sound of uniform tap dancing, where sameness is the ideal. Of course, what is particularly ironic about all of this homogeneous white tapping is that its origins are in black culture and Irish dance, but here, as happened with ragtime and rock and roll, tap has been denuded of its black past. As white performers from Shirley Temple to Fred Astaire came into prominence, tap's black roots were given a white makeover that made this style of dancing both "palatable" and accessible for a white mainstream audience.

Much of *42nd Street*'s premise is based on the chorus kids' optimism that they will get jobs, and the theater becomes a place where, clichéd as this may be, dreams can come true. In one of the musical's most famous lines, Julian Marsh tells Peggy Sawyer without a trace of irony to "think of musical comedy, the most glorious words in the English language!"[28] We perhaps laugh at this line today, but there is a naïve charm about the musical that explains its staying power. We *want* to believe in its optimistic message, even as we know, deep down, it's not true. Why else would people continue to return to the theater year after year to see musicals and pay, now, upwards of $140 a ticket for something so "frivolous"?

Halfway through the first act of *42nd Street*, Marsh ridicules Sawyer for her musical theater "greenness": "Broadway dreams, Sawyer! We've all had 'em!" "Well, I mean to hold on to mine, Mr. Marsh!" she replies.[29] The Broadway musical becomes synonymous with the American Dream itself, a goal that early in the show has become a source of disillusionment for Marsh, given the economic downturn. But *Pretty Lady* becomes a hit (as we knew it would), and Marsh—a softy at heart—is given *42nd Street*'s final moments onstage, singing a short but searing reprise of the title number, an anthem of Broadway that serves as a testament to his own undying love for what Broadway represents. *42nd Street*, after all, is a symbol for a lost era. 42nd Street, the place, and Times Square were not the overly commercial, Disney-driven, tourist-friendly locales they are today. In the early eighties, this was a rundown area, inhabited by drug dealers, prostitutes, and porn shops amidst the theaters.[30] It was hardly a pleasant place to visit, and *42nd Street* opened at the Winter Garden Theatre at 50th and Broadway, located at the northern reaches of Times Square, as if trying to escape the area's seediness. When Julian Marsh and the chorus sing

"42nd Street," the song's lyrics conjure up not the then-faded Broadway of 1980 but a lost New York in its glittery heyday.

Like the title song, "Lullaby of Broadway" celebrates the theater and the excitement of New York. In the context of the musical, the cast, led by Marsh, sings the song to Peggy, who wants to run back to Allentown and give up theater rather than save *Pretty Lady*. When she acquiesces to their request and does her duty by helping out her fellow cast members, Peggy simultaneously reaffirms both the promise of Broadway and the American Dream, which are directly linked. As Annie tells Peggy moments before she is going to go on as the star of *Pretty Lady*, having just learned and rehearsed the entire show in an unbelievable twenty-four hours, "[You've] gotta come through! Not for Jones or Barry or any of those stuffed-shirts out there, but for us! The kids in the line. You're not just Peggy Sawyer tonight, you're every girl who ever kicked up a heel in the chorus. Get out there in front, kid, and show 'em what *we* can do!" Like the common man who fights for good, Peggy redeems the downtrodden chorus kids. Julian Marsh says as much after Peggy has made it through the fire of opening night: "You're quite a girl, Miss Peggy Sawyer. Quite a girl. And you're on your way to becoming quite a star. You've broken through, Peggy. You're the million-to-one shot that comes home a winner. For years to come, thousands of little chorus girls will go to auditions and say to themselves, 'Who knows? I might come out of this another Peggy Sawyer!' I ask you only to be the sort of star those little girls would want you to be. Shine your light over this glorious gulch they call Forty-second Street!"[31] Invoking a Statue of Liberty–like image here, Peggy becomes the symbol of Broadway, lifting a torch to lead the way for all who come after her. *42nd Street* is the epitome of Broadway musicals, not just because it is a metatheatrical show that celebrates theater but because the show connects American nostalgia to the musical itself. It wants us to believe that we all have a chance and that real rewards still exist.

Meanwhile, in the "real world," a different message was being constituted about work, rewards, and race. In 1978, two years before *42nd Street*'s debut, the landmark Supreme Court case *Regents of the University of California v. Bakke* changed the social landscape by making a legal case for affirmative action. Allan Bakke, a white male medical school applicant, sued the University of California–Davis Medical School when he was not admitted to its program. Despite other extenuating factors that could explain Bakke's failure to be admitted, Bakke believed he was the victim of reverse discrimination, as students of color with poorer academic records were accepted to the medical school. The Supreme Court found in Bakke's favor, but the justices simultaneously upheld the school's right to use race as a determining factor in selection, thereby giving official support to the policy of affirmative action while ruling against racial quotas. The case would make affirmative action a contentious but prime policy in the worlds of education and hiring in the 1980s and beyond.

42nd Street, on the other hand, is an anti-affirmative-action fantasy. Forget about giving jobs to people of color; in a 1930s musical, people of color weren't even present except as maids or servants. Instead, 42nd Street makes a case that the job will and should always go to the person with the most talent and that the world is a level playing field. This is clearly different from the racial politics of Dreamgirls, another musical that ran in 1981, about the Dreams, an African American girl group from the sixties (loosely modeled on the Supremes), who encounter their own struggles in trying to break into a white-dominated music industry. Where Peggy Sawyer becomes an overnight success, the Dreams face decades' worth of institutionalized racism that imposes a glass ceiling on just how high they can rise in the world of pop music.

This emphasis on talent is marked at the beginning of act 2 when the fate of Pretty Lady is in doubt. Dorothy Brock, the show's not so talented star, has been injured, and it seems that without a decent replacement, the show will have no option but to close. Anytime Annie, though, has figured out a solution to their predicament:

> ANNIE. Mr. Marsh, wait a minute! You don't have to close the show!
> JULIAN. What?
> ANNIE. We've got someone right in the company who can replace Brock!
> JULIAN. My dear Miss Reilly, if there were someone in the company with that much talent, don't you think I would have noticed her?
> BERT. Maybe not in this case.
> JULIAN. We're wasting our time.

MAGGIE. All you have to do is give her a chance! Isn't anything better than closing the show?

JULIAN. Who is she?

ANNIE. Peggy Sawyer!

MAN. That kid?

ANNIE. Yes, Peggy! She's got a voice that'll panic 'em and she can
dance rings around Brock.

JULIAN. A raw beginner! This is her first job in the chorus!

ANDY. No wait, Boss. She *is* the best dancer in the line.[32]

This sequence indulges in the showbiz mythos of the understudy who
becomes an overnight success. We want to believe in Peggy, because if we
don't, it's as if we've given up on the promise of America itself. The critic
Richard Barrios writes that the famous line Marsh utters to boost Sawyer's confidence—"You're going out there a youngster, but you've got to
come back a star!"—"has passed beyond camp into folklore, encapsulating
a triumphing-over-the-odds myth that Depression spectators were ready
to believe."[33] Of course, this entire narrative is told against the unspoken
context of whiteness, and in the logic of the Broadway musical, there are
happy endings, but only if you're white.

It's interesting that the run of *42nd Street* coincides almost perfectly
with Reagan's two-term presidency, coming to exemplify his administration's capitalist, money-hungry politics. Could there have been a better
song to sum up the philosophy of Reagan and his followers than "We're
in the Money"? In terms of Reagan's racial politics, though, after the
multicultural 1970s, there was, not surprisingly, some pushback from
the conservative Republican Party, who wanted to stop giving "special"
attention to nonwhites. According to the political historian Allan J.
Lichtman:

Reagan's racial policies also generated a mixed response from the
conservatives. The [Reagan] administration drew upon rhetoric
fashioned in the 1960s to uphold the ideal of a colorblind society. It assailed affirmative action quota systems. It criticized welfare for creating dependence and touted economic programs that
opened opportunities for minorities to find jobs, buy homes, and

start businesses ("black capitalism") instead of idling on the dole or depending on civil rights programs.[34]

While it's true that in 1982 Reagan signed a twenty-five-year extension to the Voting Rights Act of 1965, he had long been on the books as being opposed to the act, calling it "humiliating to the South."[35] The Reagan administration wanted to bring about a color-blind society, but in doing so overlooked the actual racism that was still causing severe inequality in America. According to the legal scholar Herman Schwartz, "President Reagan and his allies present[ed] two related arguments: (1) hiring and other distributional decisions should be made solely on the basis of individual merit; (2) racial preferences are always evil and will take us back to *Plessy v. Ferguson* and worse."[36] Is not the first point the modus operandi of *42nd Street*, which is predicated on the notion that individual talent should and will be rewarded? As Michael Omi and Howard Winant claim about Reagan's racial policies: "In the neoconservative view opposition to affirmative action is consistent with the goals of the civil rights movement; it is a challenge to 'race-thinking.' According to this logic, only individual rights exist, only individual opportunity can be guaranteed by law, and only 'merit' justifies the granting of privilege."[37] Of course, the world is not a level playing field and never was. Affirmative action was meant to remedy years' worth of inequality, mainly affecting a large African American working-class population that even 150 years later was still experiencing the reverberations of once being a slave class in America. The *42nd Street* of 1933, on the other hand, didn't have to bother with the pesky issue of racial inequality. People of color "knew their place" and weren't expected to rise. Even if the American Dream has always been just that—a dream—whites have always had a leg up on people of color in trying to achieve that goal.

The Return of the Ziegfeld Follies

If Florenz Ziegfeld had been brought back to life in 1991 and dropped off at the Palace Theatre on Broadway, he might have been momentarily confused. There, in gorgeous Technicolor-inspired sets and costumes, were the Ziegfeld Follies onstage, complete with chorus girls, a dog act, and Will Rogers himself. What was going on?

Okay, so it wasn't *really* the Ziegfeld Follies, but it was a close postmodern facsimile. The show was *The Will Rogers Follies*, a Broadway musical about the life of American celebrity, raconteur, and entertainer Will Rogers, with music by Cy Coleman, lyrics by Betty Comden and Adolph Green, libretto by Peter Stone, and direction and choreography by Tommy Tune. The show's conceit was to tell Will Rogers's life story against the backdrop of the famous Ziegfeld entertainment where he was a headliner from 1916 to 1925. This wasn't a straightforward version of the Follies, though, but a postmodern, time-bending reinterpretation. Not only did Ziegfeld himself have a presence (embodied by the prerecorded voice of the legendary actor Gregory Peck), but Rogers himself (played by Keith Carradine) narrated his life from beyond the grave.

Like *42nd Street*, *The Will Rogers Follies* is pastiche, evoking the style of a long-gone era. But where *42nd Street* looked toward the past in almost oblivious disavowal of the present, *The Will Rogers Follies* is both a contemporary neoliberal multicultural fete of American diversity *and* a backward-looking celebration of early twentieth-century racial homogeneity. From a racial standpoint, everyone is represented but whiteness wins out.

Despite Tune's denial that it is a pastiche,[38] the show is confusing as to when it takes place, conflating earlier time periods with the present moment of performance. In the opening number, "Will-a-Mania," the chorus calls Rogers "a brand new sage for a brand new age," but it's not clear which "age" they're referring to. Rogers's or our own?[39] The script doesn't say, and it's as if we're in theatrical limbo. Similarly, in his opening monologue, Rogers plays on a typical routine that he would perform in the Ziegfeld Follies: reading the headlines of the day and commenting on them. In the 1991 musical, Rogers uses an actual newspaper from that day's performance for fodder and jokes but then asks for a paper from 1935 to show just how little has changed over time. This might not be news, so to speak, but from an ideological and racial perspective, *The Will Rogers Follies* is a place where time has basically stopped, collapsed in on itself.

Like another Cy Coleman show, *Barnum*, about the showbiz personality and circus creator P. T. Barnum, *The Will Rogers Follies* is a plot-light musical bio. Not much happens to Rogers; we watch him fall in love and marry Betty Blake, have kids, feud with his father, become a famous radio personality, run for president, and weather the Great Depression. While the show didn't have much to recommend it in terms of story, *The Will Rogers Follies* was all about production and was staged with a fine eye to detail by Tommy Tune. From lavish dance routines featuring scantily clad chorus girls to Tony Award–winning eye-popping costumes (designed by Willa Kim) to a light-up rainbow staircase that filled the entire stage, the show kept its audiences more than entertained and dazzled. The show wasn't high art, but it was good enough to win the Tony Award for Best Musical that season, beating out the black Caribbean-inspired *Once on This Island*, a musical version of the classic children's book *The Secret Garden*, and the British megaspectacle *Miss Saigon*, a contemporary retelling of *Madame Butterfly* that featured a facsimile of a helicopter landing onstage.

Rogers was known for his folksy, homespun ways of speech and his appeal as a "regular Joe" who could relate to the common man. The musical's overarching motif is that Will Rogers was a friend to everyone, a point encapsulated in the song that both opens and closes the show, "Never Met a Man I Didn't Like." Rogers sings:

> Never met a man I didn't like,
> Hi-falutin' gent or Bow'ry bum,
> Yes I've come a long way down the pike
> Never met a man I didn't like . . . [40]

The song reads as a manual of tolerance, encouraging us to embrace people from all walks of life. Rogers tells his wife, "People. I just can't get over 'em, Blake. No matter how different they look and talk, they're all just the same. Of course, there's gettin' to be too many of 'em—but the one thing I've learned is they all want exactly the same thing—three meals a day and a good night's sleep."[41] In his day, Rogers was a champion of the people, regardless of a person's race or social class, but are we meant to see this show as a celebration of the past or to embrace Rogers as the voice of the present and the future?

Despite this "let's all hold hands" message, an earlier number in the show, "Give a Man Enough Rope," offers a more Darwinian perspective on humanity. Rogers, backed by a male quartet, sings of how he got to where he is in life by learning how to perform rope tricks. Rogers introduces the song claiming, "Believe it or not, there's a lotta people who say this ain't respectable work, my father having been one of them. But there's nuthin' wrong with swinging a rope. Long as your neck's not in it."[42] This statement may be delivered as a glib joke, but in a country with a history of lynching black people, it's a pregnant image. Lest one think that this is a throwaway line, "Give a Man Enough Rope" presents the themes of work and success with racial overtones:

> Give a man enough rope,
> Give a man enough rope,
> And he can hang himself or not,
> That is the choice that he has got.
> He could wind up
> Hanging down from a tree,
> Or he could spin himself a life,
> That's what happened to me.[43]

What polarized options the song offers us! The rope here becomes a marker of either death or success, and in the logic of the song, life is what you make of it. The song is a return to the worldview of *42nd Street* with a Horatio Alger "pull yourself up by your bootstraps" logic. If we think about the relationship between race and economic opportunity in this country, the American Dream holds that people can make of themselves what they want, and Rogers paints himself as the poster child of this ideology. Part Native American and from a poor background, Rogers became one of the richest and most influential individuals in early twentieth-century America. The song presents us with the possibility of success via hard work or demise via suicide, but like *42nd Street*, the equality of opportunity is available fairly to all Americans.

> ROGERS. You hand two guys
> A pile of dough,
> One spends it fast,
> One saves it slow.
> You make a choice,
> Up to you what you do.
> This act ain't much,

But through it I've met
Kings and queens
And I got to meet you.[44]

Each individual just needs to grab the rope that he's been handed and make something of his life. Of course, we know that society doesn't really work this way, particularly for African Americans and other people of color. By 1991, when this show premiered, affirmative action permeated society, a fact that was not without its critics, who saw the policy as basically giving jobs to undeserving people of color and engendering reverse discrimination against whites. For many white Americans, affirmative action was a slap in the face of the traditional "work hard and you'll succeed" ideology on which the country based much of its national identity. *The Will Rogers Follies* evokes the racial ideologies of the early twenties, now wedded to the *neo*conservative policies of the eighties and nineties, which were grounded in a color-blind America. In evoking the Ziegfeld Follies of an earlier age, the creators offered audiences a nostalgic image of America where the American Dream still holds and whites are in charge, but now glossed over with a touch of late twentieth-century multicultural varnish.

The show's unspoken fascination with whiteness transcended its content; it permeated the casting as well. When the musical opened, it did not feature a single actor of color. Actors' Equity brought a grievance before the League of American Theaters and Producers, "charging that the show had failed to hire minority-group actors." Phillip Oesterman, the show's associate director, refuted the accusation, claiming that "despite our posting casting notices at Actors' Equity and contacting agents to get people of color to the auditions, by the time we opened in May only 37 African-American women had auditioned." The rumor surrounding the production, though, was that Tommy Tune, in trying to evoke the early days of the Ziegfeld Follies, had purposely only hired white actors to maintain Ziegfeld's tradition of glorifying the all-American (that is, white) girl. After the show opened and following the outcry, three African American actors were added to the cast.[45]

While the show looked "all white," the creators were clear to highlight Will Rogers's Native American background. Clem Rogers, Will's father, says: "You're not a redskin, Willie—you're an Indian. Our people didn't

Keith Carradine (as Will Rogers) poses with a bevy of white chorus girls in *The Will Rogers Follies*. *Credit:* Photofest

come over on the Mayflower—we met the boat. Just remember one thing: I'm three-eighths a Cherokee and your ma's one-quarter," to which Will responds, "I guess if I'da ever finished the fifth grade I'd know just how much of a Cherokee that made me."[46] This exchange leads into a short sequence in which, Ziegfeld-style, the cast creates a living tableau of Custer's Last Stand. The Indian characters in the show are hardly the stage Indians seen in *Annie Get Your Gun, Little Mary Sunshine,* or *Whoopee!* They have no lines and appear mainly as exotic figures in the opening sequence, which theatrically portrays Rogers's Indian heritage. The chorus sings:

> In those primeval days
> When the world first began
> Each man tried to communicate with fellow man.
> Will Rogers' Grandpapa and other Indian folk,
> Cherokee, and Tutelo from Roanoke,

Sent the news by banging drums
And blowing smoke.[47]

This sequence was cause for criticism and outrage from some Native Americans. Despite the fact that Tommy Tune himself is part Native American, *The Will Rogers Follies* was accused of depicting Indians in a poor light. According to a letter sent by representatives from the American Indian Community House in New York, "The life and work of one of the Cherokee Nation's most famous citizens is currently being butchered and distorted at the Palace Theater in 'The Will Rogers Follies.' The show is replete with racist caricatures and stereotypes; everything from a braided man in buckskin crashing a unicycle to Tommy Tune's interpretation of Indian dance, which is more suited to an episode of Scooby-Doo than Broadway." They took special offense at a piece of choreography that featured an actor costumed as a Native American dancing on a drum, and summed up their comments by stating: "These antics are applauded and laughed at by an audience who doesn't know any better and thinks that this Indian version of 'Stepin Fetchit' is totally acceptable. . . . What is most hurtful about this show is that Tune, its director as well as choreographer, is a self-identified Choctaw Indian." Marty Richards, a coproducer for the show, responded that "the show was not intended to offend people. It was intended as an entertainment."[48] But Richards illuminates an issue that has plagued many of the shows in this book, namely that certain representations or performances can be read as racist by one group of people and seen as mere "entertainment" by another.

The "entertainment" that the show is purportedly interested in is resolutely nostalgic. Playing up the Americana aspect, *The Will Rogers Follies* even features a scene that takes place at a Wild West show, complete with "genuine cowboys and Indians displaying their incredible skill and mastery of the untamed broncos and mustangs of the great American prairie!"[49] While happily no battle between cowboys and Indians actually graces the stage—the creators opted instead to give us "Texas Jack's Dog Act," complete with trick dogs—the fact that the show invokes this mythology that we've seen in *Oklahoma!* and *Annie Get Your Gun* speaks to the lasting appeal of the Wild West. The Wild West show is all over *The Will Rogers Follies*, from Tony Walton's cowboy-inspired sets and cowboy-hat proscenium, outlined in rope, to the buckskin outfits worn by the chorus girls. As the *Backstage* writer Michèle LaRue described it, "Walton and his fellow designers . . . created a 'Cowboys and Indians Follies' seen through 1990's eyes."[50] The musical evokes white Americana, and despite the image of Will Rogers as the multicultural everyman, the show paints him as the epitome of white old-school patriotism. The show literally turns red, white, and blue in the second act, complete with streamers and skimmer hats when Will Rogers recounts how he ran for president on the Anti-Bunk Party's ticket and the cast performs the show-stopping patriotic "Our Favorite Son." But the overarching color of the show seemed to be the rainbow itself, as reflected in the show's massive light-up staircase that could change to any color imaginable but was often lit to look like a rainbow. Was this perhaps a nod to Jesse Jackson's 1984 National Rainbow Coalition, a political movement meant to reflect a wide variety of races, or simply a generalized symbol of multiculturalism?

As *The Will Rogers Follies* reaches its conclusion, it takes a maudlin turn. America has entered the Depression, and Rogers becomes the voice of the masses, using his fame to give them solace and support in their difficult hour. Rogers offers up a monologue in which he reflects on his lifelong belief that people are really all the same once you get to know them and invokes his Indian heritage to explain how he sees the world:

> Y'see, an Indian always looks back after he passes something so he can get a view of it from both sides. A white man don't do that— he just figures that all sides of a thing are automatically the same. That's why you must never judge a man while you're facing him. You've got to go around behind him like an Indian and look at what *he's* looking at. Then go back and face him and you'll have a totally different idea of who he is. You'll be surprised how much easier it is to get along with everybody.[51]

A little *Afterschool Special* in its message, the musical asserts a theme of tolerance and of difference—but as in *A Chorus Line*, difference that's flattened out. *Everyone* is different and special, Rogers says, but not in ways that are worth distinguishing. The show ends with a longer version of the song "Never Met a Man I Didn't Like," and the stage directions call for the song to "be accompanied by various slides projected on the scrim—stills of Will Rogers (the real Will Rogers), of his family and friends: presidents, celebrities from the Follies, movies, politics, sports, world figures, etc., and of common people: Indians, farmers, Depression bums, etc. Masses of people")[52] Rogers sings:

> Never met a man I didn't like
> Hi-falutin' gent or Bow'ry bum
> Yes, I've come a long way down the pike,
> Never met a man I didn't like.
>
> . . .
>
> In all my wand'rin',
> I've bumped into all kinds of people;
> Fancy cinema stars,
> Fake evangelists,
> Politicians,
> Morticians,
> And I have reached the conclusion,
> While hiking the pike.
> Though I try and I try,
> Never once met a guy that I didn't like.

The song reinforces Rogers's Native American background while celebrating a wide spectrum of American identities. While the racial politics of the 1980s offered a rejection of affirmative action and a renewed focus on the individual, here we see the incipient markers of what would be a renewed turn to liberal multiculturalism in the 1990s. The Will Rogers Follies articulates a politics of race that is a mash-up of multiculturalism, individual chutzpah, and an embracing of whiteness. The show provides a liberal ending to make white audiences feel good about themselves, making them think they've become more enlightened while really reinforcing their own conservative stance. The Will Rogers Follies, like 42nd Street, is very much a show about spectacle, and while spectacle entertains, it can also blind, forcing us to see what it wants us to see and not the uncomfortable truths that have defined U.S. society.

Revisals: Haven't We Met Before?

On April 1, 2000, the following announcement was posted on the CAST-RECL listserv:

> April 1 is a busy day for reissues, with long-awaited CD transfers of SUBWAYS ARE FOR SCHIZOPHRENICS, WHAT MAKES FORBES RUN? and THE BEST LITTLE WHOREHOUSE MERGES WITH TIME-WARNER finally appearing. Also due is ANNIE GET YOUR PEPPER SPRAY, a politically correct "revisal" of the Berlin classic, in which Annie sings "I'm a Native Peoples Too," resigns from the Wild West Show in protest over Buffalo Bill's disrespectful treatment of animals, and goes off to start a radical feminist separatist vegan commune with her new lover Calamity Jane.[53]

The release was part of CASTRECL's annual April Fools' Day parody postings; however, the humor surrounding a radically revised ultra-PC vegan, lesbian, animal-rights version of Irving Berlin's 1946 musical *Annie Get Your Gun* emerged out of an ongoing anxiety concerning a trend to rewrite classic musicals for contemporary audiences, in particular the 1999 Broadway arrival of a new politically correct version of *Annie Get Your Gun* starring Bernadette Peters.

This new production was just one of a handful of musicals to go under the scalpel at the end of the twentieth century to excise "racist tumors." While new musicals in the eighties, nineties, and beyond looked to the past for inspiration, classic musicals from the Golden Age also began to reappear on Broadway, but not in the paint-by-numbers fashion that some audiences were expecting. These shows had undergone plastic surgery with varying results. Some revisals, like the 1998 Sam Mendes production of *Cabaret*, were given new life, while in other cases the result was more spackle and less sparkle. Given all the charges of stereotyping and racism that have plagued many an older musical, contemporary producers were faced with a conundrum: How does one revive a show that features problematic or, at the very least, dated racial content? Are some older shows unrevivable? Can objectionable material simply be excised? The answer that emerged was a new type of show that some people have termed a *revisal*. Bringing in new writers to update the libretto and add or subtract songs as they saw fit, producers attempted to make certain Golden Age musicals palatable for a new generation of audiences. Editing and revising shows is not new. It happens to Shakespeare all the time. But this movement stirred up a lot of anger among musical theater purists who didn't want a line of dialogue or a note of music touched. The trend was also strange because it involved rewriting shows that in some cases, unlike Shakespeare, were barely fifty years old.

A number of shows have gotten the revisal treatment. The 1995 revival of *How to Succeed in Business without Really Trying* lost the song "Cinderella, Darling," which Des McAnuff, the director, felt to be demeaning to women, while a 1999 production of *Finian's Rainbow*, a 1947 show that was already a satire of race, had some makeover work done by Peter Stone to address the show's use of blackface and make its racial politics edgier. Even chestnuts like the 1934 Ethel Merman vehicle *Anything Goes* by Cole Porter got a punchier new book for the 1987 Lincoln Center revival by Timothy Crouse (son of the show's original book writer Russell Crouse) and John Weidman.

But the changes done for those shows were pretty much nips and tucks. Two shows in the last ten years or so have experienced more thorough overhauls. The 1999 *Annie Get Your Gun* featured a new book by Peter Stone that aimed to remedy the treatment of Native Americans, while the playwright David Henry Hwang offered a *completely* revised version of the Rodgers and Hammerstein musical *Flower Drum Song* in 2001 that attempted to improve the work's portrayal of Asian Americans.

The representation of the Indian characters in *Annie Get Your Gun* has been a sticking point for quite some time, particularly the number "I'm an Indian Too." Peter Stone wanted to address the concerns of a politically correct generation, and to do so, he eliminated the songs "I'm an Indian Too," "Buffalo Bill," and "I'm a Bad, Bad Man" as well as references to Indian scalping and the use of nonsense Indian words. Stone reinstituted the pair of juvenile lovers, Tommy and Winnie, who were in the 1946 production but cut by Berlin himself in the 1966 Lincoln Center revival. Stone went further, though, making Tommy half Native American, thereby creating the conflict of an interracial romance with the white Winnie.

In an unusual conceit, Stone reframes *Annie Get Your Gun* as a show within a show. The inner show is now explicitly set in 1888 to more firmly ground the events in a specific historical moment as opposed to a generalized nostalgized past, but the time and location of the surrounding framework remain confusing. The 1999 version opens with the actor playing Frank Butler singing "There's No Business like Show Business." This song, perhaps the show's most famous and recognizable, evokes nostalgia. The song also works, though, as an anthem that emphasizes the recurring theme of performance: everything is show business. Buffalo Bill then enters: "I am Colonel Buffalo Bill Cody, the owner and founder of the most famous Wild West Show on earth! You are now going to see my own personal version of the tempestuous and romantic story of Annie Oakley and Frank Butler, featuring my celebrated troup [sic] of western actors . . . all of it exactly as I've presented it over the years, right here under my big top!"[54] Where exactly is Buffalo Bill speaking from? Is he dead? Where and when are we? The present? The recent past? 1946? Theatrical limbo? Having Buffalo Bill reveal the show as a performance is a productive move, emphasizing the theatricality of what we are watching, but his own character, taken out of historical context, emphasizes Wild West nostalgia all over again. Peter Stone, though, sees this technique otherwise: "I used something that I had tried with *Will Rogers Follies:* that is, that *we* were not telling the story of Annie Oakley and Frank Butler; Buffalo Bill was telling it, under his big top. By switching the point of view that way, the show could be as naïve and even as corny as we wanted, because those big top shows *were* naïve and corny."[55] Stone plays into the stereotype that the Broadway musical (in this case by way of the "big top") has little to say of importance. At the heart of this statement is a nostalgic impetus to run away from context and meaning and just have a good time.

The major impetus in Stone's rewrite, of course, was to address the issue of Native American representations. "The treatment of the Indians [in *Annie Get Your Gun*] wasn't malicious, it was part of a collective insensitivity that was very pervasive at the time," he said. "I'm trying to keep away from being oversensitive in correcting that, but all you have to be is fair. The Indians are amusing—but now they are not the butt of the humor, but the cause of the humor. I make them smarter."[56] Rather than recognizing how "I'm an Indian Too" might have been restaged in a subversive way such as was done with the "Ugg-a-Wugg" Native American–inspired number in the 2001 revival of *Peter Pan* starring Cathy Rigby, Stone simply cut the song.

If Stone kept the overall plot of *Annie Get Your Gun*, the same could not be said for the 2001 production of *Flower Drum Song*, one of Rodgers and Hammerstein's "lesser" musicals. The show received polite reviews on Broadway when it first premiered in 1958 and ran for six hundred performances. Despite a few memorable songs such as "I Enjoy Being a Girl" and "Love, Look Away," the show was never a huge hit. Probably the most notable thing about *Flower Drum Song* is that it was the first major Broadway show to feature a virtually all-Asian cast.[57] It even got a film version in 1961, but it was never mentioned in the same breath as *Oklahoma!*, *Carousel*, or *South Pacific*. The show, which focuses on the lives of native-born and immigrant Chinese Americans living in San Francisco in the 1950s and is based on the novel by C. Y. Lee, is about race, assimilation, immigration, and citizenship, but its racial politics had become dated over time. The creaky libretto, combined with the show's casting challenges, led to few productions following its premiere. That is, until the award-winning Asian American playwright David Henry Hwang entered the picture and completely overhauled the original libretto in an attempt to make the work speak to a new generation. The results of this artistic endeavor are rich with lasting implications about artistic integrity, theatrical history, and racial sensitivity.

The overarching plot in both versions of the show remains fairly similar. Ta, a Chinese American teenager, is in love with a culturally assimilated nightclub performer, Linda Low, but Ta's father, Wang, wants him to marry a more traditional girl. Mei-Li, a newly arrived immigrant, fits the bill, and after several reversals in the plot, she and Ta tie the knot. Despite the show's old-fashioned sensibility, many Asian American theater artists had a soft place in their hearts for the musical, as it was often the first show that they remembered seeing where Asian actors were not supporting players but the stars.

Hwang admits that for him the movie version of the show "was kind of a guilty pleasure and one of the only big Hollywood films where you could see a lot of really good Asian actors onscreen, singing and dancing and cracking jokes."[58] Hwang approached Ted Chapin, the president of the Rodgers and Hammerstein Organization, which oversees, licenses, and maintains control over all of the Rodgers and Hammerstein properties, with a proposition. Hwang wanted to completely rewrite the original libretto of *Flower Drum Song* by Oscar Hammerstein and Joseph Fields while preserving the score. Hwang's plan was to create new characters, eliminate or combine others, and fashion new plot and conflicts, drawing on C. Y. Lee's original novel for inspiration. Rodgers and Hammerstein's original score would remain intact, but Hwang would assign the songs to characters as he saw fit and repurpose them in ways that sometimes imbued them with meanings they did not originally possess. "I aspired . . . to write the book Hammerstein would have written had he been Asian American," said Hwang.[59] This was no simple task that Hwang had undertaken. The Rodgers and Hammerstein Organization is known for being notoriously strict about its properties and does not hesitate to shut down productions that alter the original materials in any way.[60] For the organization to endorse this experiment was quite significant.

While shows have been tinkered with in the past, this level of rewriting was unprecedented. Characters such as Helen Chao (given the lovely ballad "Love, Look Away" in the original production) were totally eliminated, while other figures got makeovers, like motherly Aunt Liang, who in the new version became Rita Liang, a fast-talking talent agent. The central love triangle between Ta, Mei-Li, and Linda Low remained, but new was a competing love interest for Mei-Li named Chao. Particularly noteworthy was an enriching of context and plot, from the opening sequence, which begins in China during the Cultural Revolution, to new scenes in a fortune cookie factory in America, which reflect the struggles of immigrant workers. Interestingly enough, many of Rodgers and Hammerstein's songs were not particularly well integrated into the show's original libretto but now found themselves layered with new meaning. The song "Grant Avenue," a toe-tapper about life in Chinatown, for example, was no longer a throwaway number, as it was in the original version, but was utilized as a sales pitch by Rita Liang to convince the other characters that Chinatown will make for good tourism.

The revised show was hardly a hit; it received mixed reviews and only played 194 performances on Broadway. I had the good fortune to see *Flower Drum Song* both in Los Angeles when it premiered at the Mark Taper Forum in 2001 and then again on Broadway in 2002, where it had undergone further changes. I remember being handed my program at the Los Angeles production and being both surprised and perturbed by the

Sandra Allen (as Linda Low) leads the cast in "Fan Tan Fannie" from the 2002 revisal of Rodgers and Hammerstein's *Flower Drum Song*, featuring a new libretto by David Henry Hwang. *Credit:* © Carol Rosegg Photography

cover. The title of the show was now *Rodgers and Hammerstein's Flower Drum Song*. Not a crazy title, to be sure, given that many classic works of theater are now being billed with the name of the author permanently, if awkwardly and brazenly, attached.[61] The problem with this title, though, is that it *wasn't* Rodgers and Hammerstein's *Flower Drum Song*, at least not anymore, and if anyone's name should have been part of the title, it was David Henry Hwang's. With Rodgers and Hammerstein's names firmly attached, the work was positioned to enter the canon of American musical theater and was now accorded the same status as other Rodgers and Hammerstein masterpieces.

But this perhaps not unintentionally duplicitous bit of marketing creates a more difficult theoretical problem. If completely revising the book of a musical causes little concern or, worse, is sold as if it were the original product, what does this do to the value of a work? When we talk about *Flower Drum Song* or *Annie Get Your Gun* or any other show that has undergone significant retooling, to what should we be referring? These works with their multiple versions are no longer the same work, and yet they are treated as such. There is a danger in this whitewashing of history, theatrical and otherwise, in which the new productions are either con-flated with the older versions or come to replace those versions altogether, and we need to be clear and careful about how we talk about such works so that the specific contexts are not lost.

This policy of revision raises a further question about where the value and definition of a musical reside: in the music or the libretto or both? Most scholars would argue that the music cannot be separated out from the libret-to; in fact, it is this aspect that defines the contemporary musical and what made Rodgers and Hammerstein such pioneers with *Oklahoma!* But in the case of the 2001 *Rodgers and Hammerstein's Flower Drum Song*, the oppo-site holds true. All that matters is the songs, which not only can be lifted out of a show, rearranged, and repurposed but become a sort of shorthand for the show itself. The libretto, even when written by someone of Hwang's caliber, becomes an inconsequential afterthought, a skeleton on which to hang pleasant music. If this wasn't the definition or purpose of a libretto in musical theater before the era of *Oklahoma!*, I don't know what is. The libretto—no one ever goes out humming the book, so the saying goes—is precisely what gives the modern musical its grounding, and yet revisals are based on the premise that all anyone cares about is the songs.

The importance of all this cannot be separated out from the larger con-cern of race. Saying that a libretto can be rewritten with little hesitation or thrown out altogether contributes to the ongoing misconception that musicals are frothy entertainment and have nothing particularly impor-tant to say or offer beyond their music in the first place. Furthermore, separating the songs from the libretto displaces them from their original context, which is informed not only by the show's plot but by the larger sociopolitical context that gave birth to the show. While Hwang may have actually deepened *Flower Drum Song's* context, should a goal of such work be to update a show to fit our current sensibilities? *West Side Story* may be a modernization of *Romeo and Juliet*, but it never pretends to be or replace Shakespeare's classic play.

I should say that I thoroughly enjoyed the Los Angeles production of *Flower Drum Song*. Indeed, the first act of the show was one of the most memorable and entertaining nights of theater I can recall (act 2 suffered from some awkward book problems, which were happily solved by the time the show got to Broadway). This *Flower Drum Song* was considered by many theater practitioners and the Rodgers and Hammerstein Organization to be a worthwhile experience, but it may be at the top of a slippery slope. In a panel on the topic of writing new librettos for old musicals set up by the Dramatists Guild, perhaps the most important organization that safeguards the rights of playwrights to make sure that their work is not tampered with, the librettists David Henry Hwang, David Ives, Peter Stone, and John Weidman exhibited little hesitation about rewriting the works of old masters. The panelists were all respected playwrights, and while wanting to honor the original work as best they could, they felt that this could be a way, in the words of David Henry Hwang, "to collaborate with major artists who are no longer with us."[62] Is this flattery or hubris? Is it really collaboration if one half of the team is dead? How would any of these authors feel if fifty years from now their own works were rewritten by someone else to reflect the social mores of the time period?

In fairness, Hwang brings up an important point concerning the critics who took issue with his revision of *Flower Drum Song*: "What I found interesting is that they don't mention other cases in which white people rewrote white people's musicals—*Anything Goes* being revised by John Weidman and Timothy Crouse, or *Crazy for You* being a rewrite of *Girl Crazy*. But, somehow, the idea of a person of color doing it and having some sort of political agenda all of a sudden made it a big, PC, artistic-freedom issue."[63] While some musical theater purists take umbrage at even the slightest tinkering with a show, it is true that revisions of white shows seem less angst-producing.[64] And yet, despite Hwang's good intentions to make *Flower Drum Song* into a more accurate representation of Asian American life, the scholar Dan Bacalzo rightly asks, "Is Hwang's version more 'authentically' Asian American than the book by Hammerstein and Fields? The simple fact that Hwang is an Asian American writer is not sufficient to make a definitive claim on the truthfulness of his depiction of Asian American characters."[65] No single person can speak for an entire race; he can only offer his unique perspective on a situation. To say that David Henry Hwang "solved" the problem of *Flower Drum Song* is not correct. He has only provided another remedy, one that reflects this current moment in time and his own personal take on what it means to be Asian American.

A larger question must be asked here. Why revive *Flower Drum Song* at all? It's not as if the show was packed with memorable show-stopping or beloved numbers. It wasn't a lost classic that changed musical theater history. Was it simply due to the almighty dollar? The Rodgers and Hammerstein Organization was intrigued by the possibility of reviving *Flower Drum Song* as a way to generate royalties for a show that was basically collecting dust on its shelves. Perhaps an updated version would breathe new life into the show and prove profitable. As much as I admire David Henry Hwang and his oeuvre, if Hwang, who is quite talented and has written numerous award-winning and insightful plays about the Asian American experience, wanted to create a musical that spoke to Asian American life, why did he not, perhaps with a collaborator, write a *new* musical as opposed to trying to resuscitate *Flower Drum Song?*[66]

The practice of rewriting shows is a dicey one. While perpetrating stereotypes is obviously wrong, revising shows to make them acceptable for the current age feels like whitewashing history. Maybe it does mean that certain shows are not revivable or can only be seen as museum pieces in venues such as the Encores! series at City Center, which produces starry, staged readings of classic but lost or forgotten musicals. While Mark Twain's *The Adventures of Huckleberry Finn* remains a contentious text because of its use of the N-word, most attempts to rewrite the book and eliminate the pejorative term have been looked at with great skepticism and even disdain. Either the book is read and taught and we discuss the context that produced the book *or* it's banned and not read. While it is beyond the scope of this work to go into the politics of book banning and *Huckleberry Finn*, the comparison to "problematic" American musicals (many of which are also thought of as "classics") is instructive.

If these postmodern inventions and revisals are conservative in their politics, at least they aimed to be something theatrical. The same cannot be said, at least from my at times cranky and opinionated point of view, of the final major development in the musical genre at the end of the twentieth century: the jukebox musical. If one form seems to be sounding the death knell of this genre, this is it. Most jukebox musicals bear only the thinnest of librettos—one-dimensional characters and unmoored plots—that serve as a minimal excuse for characters to belt out songs by John Lennon, Queen, and ABBA. I will never get back the two and a half hours I spent watching the Beach Boys musical *Good Vibrations*. As it is for revivals and the postmodern "old" new musicals, the currency of jukebox musicals is familiarity. In a particularly odd turn, the nostalgia that jukebox shows evoke is not even for an earlier show but for one's own personal memories of the time when one first heard a certain song. Most musical catalogs that populate jukebox shows harken back to the youth of baby boomers, so hearing a character sing "Help Me, Rhonda" or "My Boyfriend's Back" recalls fond memories of adolescence. Baby boomers are, for the most part, a generation with money, and so it's not surprising that in the multimillion-dollar world of Broadway, shows are pitched to that demographic. (Although I'm sure it's only a matter of time until there are shows based on the catalogs of Lady Gaga and Katy Perry.) But in evoking the music of the fifties, sixties, and seventies, there is also the con-comitant evocation of the time period's social milieu when things seemed "better" and "simpler" and, yes, "whiter." With the exception of the 2011 flop *Baby, It's You!*, a musical about the creation of the African American girl group the Shirelles, and *Motown: The Musical* (2013), which tells the history of the Motown sound, there have been no significant black juke-box musicals.[67] Even in the case of *Baby, It's You!*, the star of the show was the white Jewish housewife Florence Greenberg (played by Beth Leavel), who discovered the Shirelles.

If you're expecting a close reading of *Mamma Mia* or *Jersey Boys* at this point, I can happily say that I will be sparing you. Suffice it to say that these shows are nostalgic vehicles for pop music that, despite whatever accolades they might have garnered, are hardly making a lasting or indel-ible contribution to the canon of musical theater.

While we can wring our hands over the state of major new musicals in the last thirty years (an action I find myself doing all too much), to reduce these shows to mere symptoms of cultural decline overlooks the way in which race, particularly whiteness, continues to be a driving force, invis-ible at times, in the selection and production of many shows. Broadway continues to do big business, and it's significant that the form's content, with few exceptions, seems to stay resolutely fixated in the past. Whatever we make of the phenomenon, the short of it is that we can't take "classics" for granted anymore. These shows, old and "new" alike, are invested with racial significance even when they seem not to be.

Exit Music

In the summer of 2011, a new production of the famed 1935 opera *Porgy and Bess* was gearing up for an out-of-town tryout at Boston's American Repertory Theatre. But this was no paint-by-numbers revival of the show; rather, the director Diane Paulus, having garnered critical acclaim for a new Broadway production of *Hair* that won the Tony for Best Revival in 2009, was working with the Gershwin Estate to turn the classic three-hour opera into a two-and-a-half-hour commercial Broadway production. Some cutting of the score would of course be necessary, but this was hardly new to *Porgy and Bess*; other productions had played with the show's running time. But Paulus and the playwright Suzan-Lori Parks, who was also attached to the production, had more in mind than a few nips and tucks. They were planning to rewrite the show to flesh out the characters and dramatic narrative, going so far as to give the show a "happy ending." Despite the fact that other musicals had done wholesale rewrites before, one person in particular was upset about the situation. The August 10, 2011, edition of the *New York Times* featured an open letter from the master of musical theater himself, the man whom all others, artists and audiences alike, bow down to: Stephen Sondheim. In his open letter to Paulus and her creative team, Sondheim, not having seen the production, which hadn't even started previews, had a lot of bones to pick. He was infuriated that the show was now called *The Gershwins' Porgy and Bess*, thereby ignoring the work of DuBose Heyward, the librettist, who also wrote the book on which the opera was based. Sondheim also took the artistic team, including the leading lady, Audra McDonald, to task over their assessment of the character of Bess, claiming she wasn't a particularly three-dimensional character. Sondheim wrote: "She's always full-blooded when she's acted full-bloodedly, as she was by, among others, Clamma Dale and Leontyne Price. Ms. McDonald goes on to say, 'The opera has the makings of a great love story . . . that I think we're bringing to life.' Wow, who'd have thought there was a love story hiding in 'Porgy and Bess' that just needed a group of visionaries to bring it out?"[1] Sondheim felt that Paulus et al., rather than letting the work speak for itself, were wrongly excavating the text in ways that were both unnecessary and misguided.

Sondheim concluded his excoriating diatribe: "In the interest of truth in advertising, let it not be called 'The Gershwins' Porgy and Bess,' nor even 'The Gershwin-Heyward Porgy and Bess.' Advertise it honestly as 'Diane Paulus's Porgy and Bess.' And the hell with the real one." The letter, despite the discussion it sparked online on message boards, Facebook posts, and a variety of other forums, received no response from Paulus, who had her hands full readying the show for audiences. Whether or not Sondheim's words had any substantial effect on the show is not clear, but the proposed rewritten ending for the musical never manifested in Boston or on Broadway. Paulus was quoted by the *New York Times* on November 14, 2011, as saying: "We were learning about the work as we were living it, experimenting with different scenes and endings, and by the culmination of our journey with Porgy and Bess—the show and those characters—we found its strongest version. . . . It had nothing to do with Mr.-Whomever-we-are-not-talking-about, or the producers or the estates."[2]

Sondheim's critique was uncharacteristic; this rant was surprising, but perhaps telling as well. The question of how to treat musical theater, particularly in this day and age, must weigh heavily on the mind of someone who has dedicated his life to musical theater and received as many accolades as he has, especially as his own confrontation with mortality approaches. Perhaps Sondheim was worried that someone might rewrite one of *his* works after he died. Would the end of *Company* have Bobby getting married? Would none of the characters in *Sweeney Todd* die? Would Sally and Phyllis wrestle in Jell-O in *Follies*? The possibilities seem both endless and horrific. Why, Sondheim must have been thinking, would one want to tinker with one of the great shows of all time written by the Gershwins? Of course, part of the answer is in the question. The appeal of *Porgy and Bess* for a mainstream audience has always been its hummable and excerptable score with classic Gershwin show tunes like "I Got Plenty o' Nuttin,'" "It Ain't Necessarily So," and of course that chestnut "Summertime."

While Sondheim's outcry may have seemed to at least a few people like the grouchiness of an old man, his comments point to society's ongoing uneven response to the musical. The appeal of musical theater, despite the fact that what defined it in the twentieth century was its structurally integrated nature, is really the music. Time and time again, the music becomes dissociated from the libretto and by association the show's sociohistorical context. As we get further and further away from the Golden Age of Broadway and become more entrenched in our postmodern world that is marked both by a dearth of new classic musicals—new musicals *are* being written, but only a handful will enter the theatrical canon—and a glut of revivals, our understanding of musicals will diminish. Musicals will lose their importance as socially transformative and meaningful texts and instead devolve into postmodern pastiche, where all that remains is the hit songs. Just watch an episode of *Glee* to see this in action, as the young characters perform flattened-out versions of show tunes with all sense of context eviscerated. Audiences will go to musicals to recall, most likely with fondness, classic songs, but the shows themselves, their plots and contexts, will fade into the background. Older musicals will become nostalgia for graying audiences who may have been lucky enough to witness the original productions and serve as quaint artifacts of another time for younger theatergoers, if younger individuals even decide to go to the theater at all.

The upshot of all this in terms of this book's concern with race cannot be overestimated. In the case of *Porgy and Bess*, while race was never directly invoked as an issue at stake, one might argue that Paulus and her team's concerns over the nature and depiction of the show's characters had racial overtones. It was no accident that the esteemed playwright Suzan-Lori Parks, known for her body of work about African American life, was brought in, presumably to lend a stamp of authenticity to the drama. Were the producers or creative team concerned that the African American characters came off as two-dimensional and needed to be redeemed for contemporary audiences? It would not be the first time such a charge was made. *Porgy and Bess* has often been called racist, or at least stereotypical, in its folksy, backwater portrayal of the people of Catfish Row. It didn't help matters that the show was written by white folks. But does the desire to remedy past wrongs go too far? At what point do we do more harm than good by rewriting theatrical history and the Great American Songbook by revising shows to fit our contemporary mores? At what point did *Porgy and Bess* get lumped into the same category as *The Birth of a Nation*?

Perceptions and definitions of race change over time. We've seen that in the racial theories discussed in this book and in the musicals themselves. If a show is truly racist or simply offensive to our current sensibilities, maybe it is best to forget it. Indeed, many straight plays, popular in their day, have been relegated to the dustbin because they no longer speak to audiences or because the worldviews they articulated are too removed from our own society. *Abie's Irish Rose* (1922) might have once been the longest-running play in Broadway history, racking up an outstanding 2,327 performances, but today the play is hardly remembered or performed; it isn't even in print. The musical consistently bucks that trend because of the songs. Somehow the songs make it "okay" for a show to find new life, no matter how unworkable the libretto may be.[3]

Perhaps the answer to this problem is simply to invest in the future, in new writers, particularly nonwhite creators, and musicals that actually speak to our current moment. That, however, is easier said than done. The prognosis for the musical in general seems grim. Forget telling important stories about who we are as a nation; Broadway has become an offshoot of Hollywood, turning out stage versions of popular films at a seemingly exponential rate. Recent examples of this sad phenomenon include *Legally Blonde*, *The Full Monty*, *Billy Elliot*, *The Producers*, *Thoroughly Modern Millie*, *9 to 5*, *Ghost*, and *Dirty Rotten Scoundrels*. Other shows in the pipeline to Broadway from earlier runs in London include musical versions of *Dirty Dancing* and *Flashdance*. Just writing that last sentence depresses me. While the occasional show like *Billy Elliot* has been a thoroughly theatrical rethinking of the original source material, most adaptations are overly faithful reproductions of the films, cleaving closely to the original dialogue and inserting subpar songs that extend the running time of the work without adding much new value. The future of truly new shows with original books and scores seems bleaker by the moment. Occasionally, an original juggernaut like *The Book of Mormon* does appear, but even in that case, much of the show's (initial) draw stemmed from the fact that its creators, Matt Stone and Trey Parker, were also creators of the über-popular cable show *South Park*. Producers simply do not want to take the risk of producing untested work that may or may not find an audience, regardless of how good the material may be. On the other hand, *The Addams Family* (2010), which was universally panned, managed to run for a year and a half on Broadway and embark on a national tour, simply on name recognition alone.

And yet, amid the revivals that continue to be produced at a frenzied rate and the jukebox mash-ups, there have been some glimmers of hope. In 2007, a young Latino musical theater composer named Lin-Manuel Miranda hit the New York theater scene with *In the Heights*, a contemporary hip-hop, salsa-inflected musical about the Hispanic community in New York's Washington Heights neighborhood. Miranda began writing the show, in which he also starred as the protagonist, Usnavi, when he was just nineteen and saw it through multiple rewrites and workshops during his time at Wesleyan College.[4] With a book by the Latina playwright Quiara Alegría Hudes, the show premiered off-Broadway to strong reviews and transferred in 2008 to the Richard Rodgers Theatre on Broadway, where it won several Tony Awards including Best Score and Best Musical. While on the surface *In the Heights* might have seemed a risky bet for Broadway, its depiction of Washington Heights was quite tame, and the score owed as much to Cole Porter and traditional musicals as it did to Jay-Z. The show became a hit and ran for over two years in New York, before traveling around the country. If *In the Heights* didn't exactly revolutionize the Broadway musical, it at least happily brought new sounds, faces, and stories that had not been previously told to the Great White Way. *In the Heights* was what *West Side Story* might have been if told from the point of view of the Sharks.[5]

The 2008 Broadway season also saw *Passing Strange*, a show by an African American artist known simply by the moniker Stew. Part traditional musical, part rock concert, *Passing Strange* premiered at the Public Theater downtown and later moved to Broadway. The autobiographical work with book, lyrics, and music by Stew recounted his journey growing up in L.A. and his travels through Berlin and Amsterdam in a search to define himself both as a musician and as an African American.[6] The format pushed at generic boundaries; the band, led by Stew as front man, remained onstage for the duration of the evening, while a company of actors also enacted the adventures of Stew's life story. *Passing Strange* only ran for five months— it was probably a bit too avant-garde for uptown—but it received strong notices and was even filmed for television by the acclaimed director Spike Lee. It also had the distinction of being one of the few *original* book musicals to deal with contemporary African American life in the past twenty-six years.[7] Broadway musicals gravitate toward nostalgia and the past, so for a show like *Passing Strange* to offer a contemporary nonwhite look at the world was a welcome addition.

In a further promising move, musicals of the last ten or so years have seen an increase in the number of nonwhite characters appearing onstage. From *Hairspray* (2002), which is set in the civil rights era and has both black and white characters, to *Avenue Q* (2003), whose denizens are not only multiracial but also nonhuman (the show features *Sesame Street*–like puppets) to the Bollywood-inspired *Bombay Dreams* (2004) that had a mainly East Asian cast, Broadway has begun to diversify. Add to that a musical version of *The Color Purple* (2005) produced by Oprah Winfrey and *Fela!* (2009) about Nigerian singer/songwriter Fela Anikulapo-Kuti, and there are a few reasons to cheer.

But these shows make up just a small percentage of current Broadway musicals. If one thing remains constant in all of this, it's that whiteness has not diminished its hold on the Broadway stage. The incorporation of nonwhite actors and characters into works has increased, but in the end, whites are still the stars. Take *Lysistrata Jones* (2011), a modern musical retelling of Aristophanes' Greek comedy *Lysistrata*, set in a present-day high school and concerning the welfare of the school's losing basketball team. The cheerleaders hatch a plan to stop "putting out" until the team commits to winning a game. The show featured a diverse multiracial cast and yet, while the cheerleading squad was made up of Lampito (Asian), Robin (black), Cleonice (Latina), and Lysistrata Jones (white), Lysistrata was of course the star. With the blond actress Patti Murin in the title role, the show did little to upset racial hierarchies. Nonwhites may now be present onstage, but they're still relegated to secondary roles. There was no reason why Lysistrata needed to be white, no historical or geographical motivation requiring such a choice, but the status quo remained.

I want to end with one final discussion of a musical: *The Scottsboro Boys* (2010), which I personally find to be one of the most devastatingly moving and beautiful musicals of recent years.[8] Written by David Thompson, directed and choreographed by Susan Stroman, and featuring a score by the legendary songwriting team of John Kander and Fred Ebb—Ebb died before the show was finished—the musical is about the nine African American boys who were wrongly accused and unjustly found guilty of raping two white women in Alabama in 1931. Their lives were destroyed by a series of endless trials and imprisonment that stretched on for years. Not light material by any means for a musical, but Kander and Ebb had made a career of musicalizing difficult subject matter in shows such as *Cabaret, Chicago*, and *Kiss of the Spider Woman*. *The Scottsboro Boys* is no exception, and it deals with the harsh realities and uncomfortable truths of this often forgotten moment in U.S. history. What makes the production further stand out is that the creators frame the musical's action within the structure of a minstrel show. Nine African American actors play the Scottsboro boys, while two other African American actors play the minstrel roles of Mr. Tambo and Mr. Bones.[9] A single white male actor serves as the minstrel show's Interlocutor. This daring theatrical conceit is turned on its head as the show proceeds, revealing the ways in which African Americans are forced to perform minstrel-like roles in American society. In a particularly chilling finale, the actors playing the Scottsboro boys appear in blackface, hammering home the show's minstrel conceit.

The Scottsboro Boys received rave reviews but closed early due to slow ticket sales. The show earned twelve Tony nominations but walked away empty-handed in light of *The Book of Mormon*, which cleaned up. Both musicals received positive critical notices (with out-and-out raves for the latter), but *The Scottsboro Boys* was much darker and even unsettling in its thematic content in comparison to *The Book of Mormon*'s purposely vulgar, foul-mouthed, crowd-pleasing material. *The Scottsboro Boys* highlights the discomfort created when musicals, which are thought to be "just entertainment," take on difficult subject matter like race. The show's

The cast of *The Scottsboro Boys* performs the opening number in the original off-Broadway Vineyard Theatre production. *Credit:* © Joan Marcus

creators are fearless in pairing Broadway razzmatazz with difficult material. The number called "Electric Chair," for example, has three of the Scottsboro boys perform a tap-dance routine inspired by the jolts from an electric chair as they experience nightmares imagining their deaths by electrocution. It is stunning choreography as staged by Susan Stroman, but many in the audience felt uneasy, to say the least. That's to be expected and is, I'm sure, the desired response, but the feeling in my own body as I watched was strange. I was repulsed and horrified by what I saw, the threat of electrocution hanging over these wrongly accused individuals, and yet there was tap dancing and all my synapses, which have been conditioned by years of watching musical theater, were still excited. Are we supposed to clap after such a number? I did, but in some way it felt wrong. I wanted to acknowledge the performers, but the subject matter is so dark, I felt as if I were somehow applauding the electric chair itself and all it represented. The rest of the show wasn't any easier. The opening number, "Hey, Hey, Hey, Hey!," which sets up the minstrel show concept, is full of purposely racist humor; I felt guilty when I laughed at the jokes. The entire show became an awkward dance. One stunning production number follows another, but the content is unrelentingly grim:

the boys are found guilty over and over again; some die in jail; brothers are separated from each other. The show seems to be everything that a Broadway musical should and shouldn't be. *The Scottsboro Boys* is a great work because it pushes the boundaries of what a musical can say and do. It turns the form of musical theater against itself, enacting and deconstructing it at the same time. While it's a shame that *The Scottsboro Boys* had a short life, one can only hope that future regional productions will keep the work alive and that other musical theater artists will find inspiration in it and create shows of equal depth and honesty.

The privileging of whiteness in the American musical doesn't seem to be going away anytime soon. But if anyone is to blame for that, it's us, the audience. Most of us are not producers, composers, or lyricists, so we might feel there's little we can do, but perhaps it is with our wallets that we can effect change, using our money to support shows that give voice to nonwhite writers and stories. We can choose to buy a ticket to *The Scottsboro Boys* and not *Mamma Mia!* For those of us who are white, we must also take ownership of the privilege that comes with whiteness, rather than remain complicit with its invisibility. The Broadway musical has been the domain of whiteness for over one hundred years, but it only maintains that power as long as whiteness remains unspoken and hidden. By talking about this issue and seeing how whiteness operates in the theater, perhaps we can bring about some change in the current century and turn the American musical into the truly all-American art form that it aspires to be.

Notes

OVERTURE

1. The categories for the Golden Globe Awards divide films into "Drama" and "Comedy or Musical," thereby emphasizing the notion that musicals are somehow inherently lightweight. Regardless of how dramatic, serious, and even depressing the musical *Les Misérables* might be, for the 2013 Golden Globe Awards, it was nominated in the category of "Best Motion Picture: Comedy or Musical."

2. Gerald Mast, *Can't Help Singin': The American Musical on Stage and Screen* (Woodstock, NY: Overlook Press, 1987), 1.

3. W.E.B. Du Bois, *The Souls of Black Folk* (1903; New York: Penguin, 1996), 1.

4. Stuart J. Hecht, *Transposing Broadway: Jews, Assimilation, and the American Musical* (New York: Palgrave Macmillan, 2011), 5.

5. Hecht goes on to argue that musicals are "democratic" because they "feature a broad range of characters, each with at least one distinctive song that reflects who they are and what they believe" (ibid., 8). That musicals contain a variety of characters is true, but a diversity of character traits does not necessarily mean ethnic or racial diversity, a component that is clearly missing from most musicals.

6. I should clearly note that there is an important history of musicals *about* African Americans as well. The history has been well told by Allen Woll in his definitive *Black Musical Theatre* (New York: Da Capo Press, 1989). That said, many of these musicals, like African Americans themselves, have experienced marginal treatment in the canon of the American musical. Such shows, like *Shuffle Along* (1921) and *Blackbirds of 1928*, entertained mainly black audiences and were not seen by the larger white theatergoing public. In many cases, copies of African American musical theater scripts and/or cast recordings are either nonexistent or difficult to find. While other musicals about the black experience in America have graced the Broadway stage, including some musicals written by white creators like *Hallelujah, Baby!* (1967), such shows have always been in the minority on Broadway.

7. Andrea Most's *Making Americans: Jews and the Broadway Musical* (Cambridge, MA: Harvard University Press, 2004) might drive one to want to distinguish between Jewish identity and white identity, a history that itself is quite nuanced and also treated in this book, insofar as the creation of these musicals often enabled Jewish Americans to become white.

8. Richard Dyer, *White: Essays on Race and Culture* (London: Routledge, 1997), 1.

9. David Savran, *A Queer Sort of Materialism: Recontextualizing American Theater* (Ann Arbor: University of Michigan Press, 2003), 10.

10. Scott McMillin, *The Musical as Drama: A Study of the Principles and Conventions behind Musical Shows from Kern to Sondheim* (Princeton: Princeton University Press, 2006), 21.

11. Richard Dyer, "The Colour of Entertainment," in *Musicals: Hollywood and Beyond*, ed. Bill Marshall and Robynn Stilwell (Portland, OR: Intellect Books, 2000), 25.

12. Some examples of the "I want" song are *A Chorus Line*'s "I Hope I Get It," *Wicked*'s "The Wizard and I," and the "Prologue" of *Into the Woods*.

13. McMillin, *The Musical as Drama*, 76, emphasis added.

14. Arthur Laurents, music by Leonard Bernstein, lyrics by Stephen Sondheim, *West Side Story*, in *Romeo and Juliet/ West Side Story* (1956; New York: Dell, 1965), 137.

15. The whiteness studies scholar Ruth Frankenberg makes a strong case that whiteness is anything *but* invisible, so all-pervasive and hegemonic is it in society. While I agree with much of her argument, the concept of whiteness as "unmarked" or "invisible" seems to me to be a practical concept to hold on to, insofar as much of the work that still needs to be done in terms of remedying racial inequality is having white people see, acknowledge, and be cognizant of the power that is accorded whiteness in U.S. society. See Ruth Frankenberg's "The Mirage of an Unmarked Whiteness," in *The Making and Unmaking of Whiteness*, ed. Birgit Brander Rasmussen, Eric Klinenberg, Irene J. Nexica, and Matt Wray (Durham, NC: Duke University Press, 2001), 72–96, for her complete argument.

16. Toni Morrison, *Playing in the Dark: Whiteness and the Literary Imagination* (New York: Vintage Books, 1992), 46.

17. For some key texts on white identity, see David Roediger's *The Wages of Whiteness* (1991) and *Working toward Whiteness* (2005), Matthew Frye Jacobson's *Whiteness of a Different Color* (1998), and Karen Brodkin's *How Jews Became White Folk and What That Says about Race in America* (1998).

18. George Lipsitz, *The Possessive Investment in Whiteness: How White People Profit from Identity Politics* (Philadelphia: Temple University Press, 1998), 20.

19. Mike Hill, *After Whiteness: Unmaking an American Majority* (New York: New York University Press, 2004), 1–7.

20. See Jill Dolan's *Utopia in Performance: Finding Hope at the Theater* (Ann Arbor: University of Michigan Press, 2005), for more on this.

21. Lipsitz, *The Possessive Investment in Whiteness*, vii–viii.

22. Musical theater studies exploded in the past few years with some noteworthy if uneven texts including John Bush Jones's *Our Musicals, Ourselves* (2003) and Raymond Knapp's *The American Musical and the Formation of National Identity* (2004), as well as numerous texts that look at the American musical through a variety of racial, gender, or sexual lenses.

23. For standard histories of the musical, see Richard Kislan's *The Musical: A Look at the American Musical Theater* (1995), Kurt Gänzl's *The Musical: A Concise History* (1997), and Andrew Lamb's *150 Years of Popular Musical Theatre* (2001).

24. Multiple texts have looked at the musical from the perspective of various ethnic, gender, or sexual minorities. These include Andrea Most's *Making Americans: Jews and the Broadway Musical* (2004), Stacy Wolf's *A Problem like Maria: Gender and Sexuality in the American Musical* (2002) and *Changed for Good: A Feminist History of the Broadway Musical* (2011), John Clum's *Something for the Boys: Musical Theater and Gay Culture* (1999), D. A. Miller's *Place for Us: Essay on the Broadway Musical* (1998), Alberto Sandoval-Sánchez's *José, Can You See? Latinos on and off Broadway* (1999), and Stuart Hecht's *Transposing Broadway: Jews, Assimilation, and the American Musical* (2011).

25. Raphaël Tardon, "Richard Wright Tells Us: The White Problem in the United States," trans. Keneth Kinnamon, *Action* (Paris), October 24, 1946, 10–11, rpt. in *Conversations with Richard Wright*, ed. Keneth Kinnamon and Michel Fabre (Jackson: University Press of Mississippi, 1993), 99.

26. Greg Kotis, *Urinetown* (New York: Faber and Faber, 1998), 99.

27. Ibid., 100.

28. Some critics might argue that shows such as *Parade* and *Caroline, or Change* closed not because of their thematic material but due to flaws in their content and structure, as well as uneven reviews. While those elements did play a role in the reception of such shows, equally harsh if not more damning criticisms have been leveled at *Mamma Mia!* (for its vapidness and thin book), *42nd Street* (for its uninspired revival), and *The Phantom of the Opera* (for its saccharine melodramatic plot). Whatever failings these latter shows might possess, they still contain a variety of hooks (upbeat music, dancing, and/or sets) that serve as major audience draws.

29. Bertolt Brecht, "A Short Organum for the Theatre" (1949), in *Brecht on Theatre: The Development of an Aesthetic*, ed. and trans. John Willett (New York: Hill and Wang, 1964), 180.

30. The 2002 musical *Hairspray* is a perfect example of this phenomenon.

31. Barbara J. Fields, "Ideology and Race in American History," in *Region, Race, and Reconstruction: Essays in Honor of C. Vann Woodward*, ed. J. Morgan Kousser and James M. McPherson (New York: Oxford University Press, 1982), 146.

32. Tin Pan Alley, for example, a collection of music publishing houses in New York in the early twentieth century, allowed young composers and song pluggers like Irving Berlin and George Gershwin to hawk their work to sheet music companies. The ability for talented upstarts, many of whom were Jewish immigrants, to break into the music business this way was unprecedented.

33. The Broadway League, "Touring Broadway Statistics," http://www.broadwayleague.com/index.php?url_identifier=touring-broadway-statistics, and "Broadway Season Statistics," http://www.broadwayleague.com/index.php?url_identifier=season-by-season-stats-1 (accessed January 22, 2012).

34. For that matter, musicals have become a major global business; shows as diverse as *The Lion King, Wicked,* and *Next to Normal* have been translated and produced in countries including Japan, China, Iceland, Germany, Argentina, and Mexico. The "brand" of Broadway and the spectacle of American theater thus make an impact that goes far beyond Times Square.

35. Brian O'Sullivan, e-mail to the author, December 2, 2011.

36. Ethan Mordden, *Beautiful Mornin': The Broadway Musical in the 1940s* (New York: Oxford University Press, 1999), 239, 240 (emphasis original).

37. Alberto Sandoval-Sánchez, *José, Can You See? Latinos on and off Broadway* (Madison: University of Wisconsin Press, 1999), 62.

38. President Barack Obama, for example, is called the country's first black president even though his mother is white and therefore he technically is of mixed-race heritage.

39. David Roediger, *Colored White: Transcending the Racial Past* (Berkeley: University of California Press, 2002), 15.

40. Peter Kolchin, "Whiteness Studies: The New History of Race in America," *Journal of American History* 89, no. 1 (June 2002), 158.

41. See Eric Lott's *Love & Theft: Blackface Minstrelsy and the American Working Class*, 15–37, for more on this.
42. I admit that much of my discussion here and throughout the book focuses on race as understood along a black/white racial line, to the potential marginalization of other racial groups in the United States. This slight isn't intentional so much as a reflection of 1) the sheer impact that African Americans, more than any other group aside from whites, have had on musical theater and entertainment in general and 2) the belief that the legacy of slavery, more than any other racialized act in this country, continues to have a lasting effect on the country's overall consciousness. While a handful of musicals, as we will see, deal with Hispanic, Asian, and Native American characters and/or feature work written by creators of those backgrounds, such cases are in the extreme minority in the American musical.
43. See Matthew Frye Jacobson, *Whiteness of a Different Color* (Cambridge, MA: Harvard University Press, 1999), 91–135.
44. Ibid., 12.

ONLY MAKE BELIEVE

1. Scott McMillin, "Paul Robeson, Will Vodery's 'Jubilee Singers,' and the Earliest Script of the Kern-Hammerstein *Show Boat*," *Theatre Survey* 41, no. 2 (November 2000): 62.
2. Erving Goffman, *The Presentation of Self in Everyday Life* (New York: Doubleday Anchor Books, 1959), 17.
3. For more on this topic, see Andrea Most's *Making Americans: Jews and the Broadway Musical* (Cambridge, MA: Harvard University Press, 2004).
4. For a Jewish reading of Ferber's work, including *Show Boat*, see Lori Harrison-Kahan's *The White Negress: Literature, Minstrelsy, and the Black-Jewish Imaginary* (New Brunswick, NJ: Rutgers University Press, 2011).
5. Robin Breon, "*Show Boat*: The Revival, the Racism," *Drama Review* 39, no. 2 (Summer 1995): 90–91.
6. McMillin, "Paul Robeson," 63. In a 2009 production of *Show Boat* that I saw at Signature Theatre in Arlington, Virginia, the African American actress playing Julie, Terry Burrell, was strangely put into what could be called whiteface makeup, so pale and powdery that she looked like a ghost.
7. Leslie Sanders, "American Scripts, Canadian Realities: Toronto's *Show Boat*," *Diaspora* 5, no. 1 (1996): 109.
8. Goffman, *The Presentation of Self*, 38.
9. Oscar Hammerstein II, *The Complete Lyrics of Oscar Hammerstein II*, ed. Amy Asch (New York: Knopf, 2008), 103.
10. McMillin, "Paul Robeson," 64.
11. Miles Kreuger, *Show Boat: The Story of a Classic American Musical*, rev. ed. (New York: Oxford University Press, 1977; New York: Da Capo Press, 1990), 211–212 (emphasis original).
12. The term has been an ongoing sore spot for black actors in the show since the beginning. As Todd Decker notes, some of the original performers of the show did not want to sing the word, and as late as 1988, for John McGlinn's complete and historic re-creation of *Show Boat* on CD for EMI, the entire black chorus that was engaged to perform decided to walk when McGlinn wouldn't change the opening. Instead a white chorus sang both the black and white chorus parts on the album. Todd

Decker, *Show Boat: Performing Race in an American Musical* (New York: Oxford University Press, 2013), 101–103, 209. Perhaps the closest parallel to this moment is a text with its own "classic/racist" dilemma: Mark Twain's *The Adventures of Huckleberry Finn* (1884). Jim, the slave, might be a "nigger" in Twain's world, but Twain was using satire and the "N-word" to make a statement about unequal race relations in nineteenth-century America, a point that has been lost on many contemporary readers, who simply see the book as racist. For more on this, see Jonathan Arac, *Huckleberry Finn as Idol and Target: The Functions of Criticism in Our Time* (Madison: University of Wisconsin Press, 1997).

13. Hammerstein, *Complete Lyrics*, 103.

14. Ibid., 104.

15. In the 1994 Broadway revival, director Hal Prince emphasized the work of the black stevedores by having them responsible for changing the set and moving set pieces in front of the audience, highlighting the fact that without their labor, nothing happens.

16. Hammerstein, *Complete Lyrics*, 104.

17. *Show Boat*, unpublished 1927 script, lyrics and book by Oscar Hammerstein II, music by Jerome Kern, 1927, Box 5, Folder 5, 1–15, Flo Ziegfeld–Billie Burke Papers, *T-Mss 1987–010, Billy Rose Theatre Division, New York Public Library for the Performing Arts.

18. Ibid., 1–15 to 1–16.

19. Hammerstein, *Complete Lyrics*, 104.

20. Ibid., 104–105.

21. Michael Rogin, *Blackface, White Noise: Jewish Immigrants in the Hollywood Melting Pot* (Berkeley: University of California Press, 1996), 102, 103.

22. Hugh Fordin, *Getting to Know Him: A Biography of Oscar Hammerstein II* (New York: Random House, 1977; New York: Ungar, 1986), 82.

23. Hammerstein, *Complete Lyrics*, 105.

24. Ibid.

25. Ibid., 108.

26. *Show Boat*, Flo Ziegfeld–Billie Burke Papers, 1–8–2.

27. Ibid., 1–6–5.

28. Edna Ferber, *Show Boat* (Garden City, NY: Doubleday, Page, 1926; New York: Gramercy Books, 2007), 80.

29. *Show Boat*, Flo Ziegfeld–Billie Burke Papers, 1–2–3.

30. Ibid., 1–4–4.

31. Ferber, *Show Boat*, 362.

32. M. NourbeSe Philip, *Showing Grit: Showboating North of the 44th Parallel* (Toronto: Poui Publications, 1993), 26.

33. *Show Boat*, Flo Ziegfeld–Billie Burke Papers, 1–2–3 to 1–2–4.

34. Hammerstein, *Complete Lyrics*, 106.

35. Gerald Mast, *Can't Help Singin': The American Musical on Stage and Screen* (Woodstock, NY: Overlook Press, 1987), 60.

36. *Show Boat*, Flo Ziegfeld–Billie Burke Papers, 1–2–5.

37. Peter Stanfield, "From the Vulgar to the Refined: American Vernacular and Blackface Minstrelsy in *Showboat*," in *Musicals—Hollywood and Beyond*, ed. Bill Marshall and Robynn Stilwell (Portland, OR: Intellect, 2000), 149.

38. Linda Williams, *Playing the Race Card: Melodramas of Black and White from Uncle*

Tom to O.J. Simpson (Princeton, NJ: Princeton University Press, 2001), 176 (emphasis original).

39. *Show Boat*, Flo Ziegfeld–Billie Burke Papers, 1–4–1.

40. Williams, *Playing the Race Card*, 176.

41. *Show Boat*, Flo Ziegfeld–Billie Burke Papers, 1–4–7.

42. As a side note, many critics have also faulted *Show Boat* directors and producers for not always casting a black actress in the role of Julie. It's a fair complaint, but one that seems to want to ground race in skin color, rather than realizing that the point of passing is that race is something more than skin color. The power of passing, after all, comes from the ways in which it destabilizes race by causing us to question where and why the lines among certain races are drawn.

43. *Show Boat*, Flo Ziegfeld–Billie Burke Papers, 1–4–18.

44. Hammerstein, *Complete Lyrics*, 116.

45. John McGlinn, "Notes on 'Show Boat,' " liner notes, *Show Boat*, compact disc, EMI, 1988, 28.

46. Indeed, just before working on *Show Boat*, Hammerstein (with composer Sigmund Romberg) completed the highly successful romantic operetta *The Desert Song*.

47. Decker, *Show Boat*, 84.

48. Mast, *Can't Help Singin'*, 62.

49. Barbara J. Ballard, "African-American Protest and the Role of the Haitian Pavilion at the 1893 Chicago World's Fair," in *Multiculturalism: Roots and Realities*, ed. C. James Trotman (Bloomington: Indiana University Press, 2002), 113.

50. For more on the African American response to the 1893 Chicago World's Fair and Williams and Walker, see chapter 5 in Louis Chude-Sokei, *The Last "Darky": Bert Williams, Black-on-Black Minstrelsy, and the African Diaspora* (Durham, NC: Duke University Press, 2006).

51. *Show Boat*, Flo Ziegfeld–Billie Burke Papers, 2–1–6.

52. Hammerstein, *Complete Lyrics*, 111.

53. Ibid.

54. Philip, *Showing Grit*, 39.

55. Hammerstein, *Complete Lyrics*, 111.

56. Camille F. Forbes, *Introducing Bert Williams: Burnt Cork, Broadway, and the Story of America's First Black Star* (New York: Basic Civitas Books, 2008), 30, 31.

57. Allen Woll, *Black Musical Theatre: From Coontown to Dreamgirls* (New York: Da Capo Press, 1989), 38.

58. *Show Boat*, Flo Ziegfeld–Billie Burke Papers, 2–3–5.

59. Ibid., 2–3–6.

60. Philip, *Showing Grit*, 34.

61. Like the work of the Jewish American composer Irving Berlin, who was known as "the Ragtime King" (not to be confused with the black composer Scott Joplin, "the King of Ragtime"), "ragging" was not really ragtime. In the case of Berlin, for example, his "ragtime" was not actually syncopated—the defining marker of such music—just lively and upbeat.

62. The song "It's Getting Hotter in the North" never made it into the production. In the original Broadway production, Norma Terris, the actress playing Magnolia, who doubled in the role of Kim, preferred to do imitations of famous individuals in this moment rather than sing "It's Getting Hotter in the North," despite the creators'

intentions. For the 1928 London production, the authors wrote another number, "Dance the Night Away." The original song was reinstated on the EMI complete recording of the show issued in 1988.

63. Decker, *Show Boat*, 220. See chapter 9, "Queenie's Laugh," in Decker's book for more on this topic.

PLAYING COWBOYS AND INDIANS

1. Jace Weaver, "Ethnic Cleansing, Homestyle," *Wicazo Sa Review* 10, no. 1 (Spring 1994): 27.

2. In Lynn Riggs's original play, the year is 1900, but given that *Oklahoma!* culminates in the moment in which Oklahoma actually becomes a state, we can place the action of the musical closer to 1907. For comparisons with Riggs's original play, see *Green Grow the Lilacs* in *The Cherokee Night and Other Plays* (Norman: University of Oklahoma Press, 2003).

3. David A. Chang, *The Color of the Land: Race, Nation, and the Politics of Landownership in Oklahoma, 1832–1929* (Chapel Hill: University of North Carolina Press, 2010), 2, 79.

4. In a 2010 production of *Oklahoma!* at Arena Stage in Washington, D.C., director Molly Smith cast the play multiracially to highlight the "all-Americaness" of this classic. Aunt Eller and Laurey were played by African American actors, and Curly was played by a Latino actor.

5. For more on this, see David Chang's introduction to *The Color of the Land*, 1–13.

6. Oscar Hammerstein II, book and lyrics, *Oklahoma!* (1942; New York: Applause, 2010), 11.

7. Ibid.

8. Other plays by Lynn Riggs *did* reference Native Americans, most specifically *The Cherokee Night* (1936).

9. Critic Jace Weaver offers a provocative reading of *Green Grow the Lilacs*, suggesting that perhaps Curly McClain, the cowboy, and other characters in the play are actually Native Americans. For more on this see Jace Weaver, *That the People Might Live: Native American Literatures and Native American Community* (New York: Oxford University Press, 1997), 99–101.

10. Frederick Jackson Turner, "The Significance of the Frontier in American History," in *Debating Diversity: Clashing Perspectives on Race and Ethnicity in America*, 3rd ed., ed. Ronald Takaki (New York: Oxford University Press, 2002), 44, 40.

11. Gary Gerstle, *American Crucible: Race and Nation in the Twentieth Century* (Princeton, NJ: Princeton University Press, 2001), 16.

12. Matthew Frye Jacobson, *Whiteness of a Different Color: European Immigrants and the Alchemy of Race* (Cambridge, MA: Harvard University Press, 1998), 219.

13. Gerstle, *American Crucible*, 42.

14. Hammerstein, *Oklahoma!*, 81.

15. Gerstle, *American Crucible*, 19.

16. For more on this, see Andrea Most, *Making Americans: Jews and the Broadway Musical* (Cambridge, MA: Harvard University Press, 2004), 107–118.

17. Laura Z. Hobson's book *Gentleman's Agreement* (1947), which would become a popular film that same year and win the Oscar for Best Picture, features the supporting character Dave Goldman, a Jew who returns home to the United States after fighting overseas in World War II only to encounter anti-Semitism.

18. Hammerstein, *Oklahoma!*, 117–119.
19. Michael Freedland, *Irving Berlin* (New York: Stein and Day, 1983), 168.
20. William Brasmer, "The Wild West Exhibition: A Fraudulent Reality," in *American Popular Entertainment: Papers and Proceedings of the Conference on the History of American Popular Entertainment*, ed. Myron Matlaw (Westport, CT: Greenwood Press), 213.
21. Sarah Blackstone, "Simplifying the Native American: Wild West Shows Exhibit the 'Indian,'" in *Staging Difference: Cultural Pluralism in American Theatre and Drama*, ed. Marc Maufort (New York: Peter Lang, 1995), 11.
22. Laura Browder, *Slippery Characters: Ethnic Impersonators and American Identities* (Chapel Hill: University of North Carolina Press, 2000), 61.
23. Dorothy and Herbert Fields, *Annie Get Your Gun* (New York: Samuel French, 1952), 10.
24. Irving Berlin, *The Complete Lyrics of Irving Berlin*, ed. Robert Kimball and Linda Emmet (New York: Knopf, 2001), 385.
25. Fields, *Annie Get Your Gun*, 31–32.
26. Ibid.
27. Berlin, *Complete Lyrics*, 30.
28. Cf. Andrea Most's argument in the chapter "The Apprenticeship of Annie Oakley," in *Making Americans*, 119–152. She writes, "As if in direct response to *Oklahoma!* this play rejects claims of naturalness, instead firmly and unequivocally insisting that America is *theater*, and that only those who understand and embrace America's inherent theatricality are destined for success" (119).
29. This number was filmed for the movie with Betty Hutton, but the sequence was not used. The song lives on as a DVD extra today.
30. Berlin, *Complete Lyrics*, 396.
31. Most, *Making Americans*, 124.
32. Berlin, *Complete Lyrics*, 387.
33. Fields, *Annie Get Your Gun*, 35.
34. Ibid., 61.
35. Ibid., 92.
36. Ibid., 67–68.
37. Berlin, *Complete Lyrics*, 393.
38. Peter Antelyes, "'Haim Afen Range': The Jewish Indian and the Redface Western," *MELUS* 34, no. 3 (Fall 2009): 17.
39. Stephen Holden, "Pop View; Irving Berlin's American Landscape," *New York Times*, May 10, 1987, http://www.nytimes.com/1987/05/10/arts/pop-view-irving-berlin-s-american-landscape.html?scp=1&sq=Irving%20Berlin%27s%20American%20landscape&st=cse.
40. This Indian-Jewish connection was not limited to vaudeville. In the first quarter of the twentieth century, Yiddish American culture exhibited strong interest in Native American culture. Yiddish writer Yehoash translated Longfellow's epic poem *Hiawatha* into Yiddish in 1910, thereby linking the narrative of a disappearing Native American culture with the nativist aspirations of American Jews. Yiddish culture also saw an 1895 short Yiddish play called *Tsvishn Indianer* (*Among Indians*); an epic Yiddish poem, *Kentucky* (1925) by I. Y. Schwartz; and multiple short stories by Yiddish writer Sheen Daixel that feature Indian characters. The Yiddish novelist Isaac Raboy

made a whole career writing books about Jews on the western frontier including *In der vayter vest* (1918), *Herr Goldenbarg* (1923), and *Der yidisher kauboy* (1942). In 1920, the Yiddish journal *Shriftn* dedicated an entire issue to Yiddish translations of Indian verse. There was even some Hebrew American writing that represented Native Americans, and while not always realistic in their depictions, the writers used Native Americans as metaphors: "Indians stood for the possibility of co-existence with nature . . . or the loss of some human authenticity crushed by the forces of modernism," writes Stephen Katz. Stephen Katz, *Red, Black, and Jew: New Frontiers in Hebrew Literature* (Austin: University of Texas Press, 2009), 77. See also Rachel Rubinstein, *Members of the Tribe: Native Americans in the Jewish Imagination*, 45–56, for more on this phenomenon.

41. Robert Baral, *Revue: The Great Broadway Period*, rev. ed. (New York: Fleet Press, 1970), 48.
42. The song itself seems to have been lost.
43. Blanche Merrill, *Fanny Brice's Comedy Songs* (New York: Mills Music, 1939), 8–11.
44. Berlin, *Complete Lyrics*, 391–392.
45. John Chapman, "Merman Scores Bull's-Eye with Every Berlin Number in 'Annie,'" review of *Annie Get Your Gun*, book by Dorothy and Herbert Fields, music and lyrics by Irving Berlin, directed by Joshua Logan, Imperial Theatre, New York, *Daily News*, May 17, 1946.
46. Berlin, *Complete Lyrics*, 391.
47. Folder 53–54, Tamiris, Helen, 1905–1966, Helen Tamiris Collection, (S) *MGZMC-Res. 24, Jerome Robbins Dance Division, New York Public Library for the Performing Arts.
48. Alexander Williams, review of *Annie Get Your Gun*, book by Dorothy and Herbert Fields, music and lyrics by Irving Berlin, directed by Joshua Logan, Shubert Theatre, Boston, *Boston Herald*, April 3, 1946.
49. Most, *Making Americans*, 138.
50. Fields, *Annie Get Your Gun*, 85.

TROUBLE IN NEW YORK CITY

1. "Landmark Symposium: *West Side Story*," *Dramatists Guild Quarterly* (Autumn 1985): 13 (emphasis added). *Abie's Irish Rose* was the long-running 1922 Broadway play about a Jewish man and Irish woman who strike up an interfaith relationship.
2. Arthur Laurents, "Musical Origins," Playbill, *West Side Story*, September 30, 1957, 17.
3. Some of the original music in the archives still shows lyrics being attributed to both Bernstein and Sondheim. Only after Washington did Bernstein propose that Sondheim take full credit for the lyrics.
4. Matthew Frye Jacobson, *Roots Too: White Ethnic Revival in Post–Civil Rights America* (Cambridge, MA: Harvard University Press, 2006), 35.
5. Mark Horowitz, "*West Side Story*," lecture, Gettysburg College, Gettysburg, PA, June 17, 2008.
6. Box 81, Folder 1, Jerome Robbins Papers, (S) *MGZMD 130, Jerome Robbins Dance Division, New York Public Library for the Performing Arts.
7. Ibid.
8. Undated script, Box 73, Folder 10 (1955), Leonard Bernstein Collection, Music Division, Library of Congress.

9. Craig Zadan, *Sondheim & Co.*, 2nd ed. (New York: Harper & Row, 1986), 15.

10. Box 81, Folder 1, Jerome Robbins Papers, (S) *MGZMD 130, Jerome Robbins Dance Division, New York Public Library for the Performing Arts.

11. Box 81, Folder 5, Jerome Robbins Papers, (S) *MGZMD 130, Jerome Robbins Dance Division, New York Public Library for the Performing Arts.

12. Arthur Laurents, music by Leonard Bernstein, lyrics by Stephen Sondheim, *West Side Story* in *Romeo and Juliet / West Side Story* (1956; New York: Dell, 1965), 180.

13. Arthur Laurents, *Original Story By: A Memoir of Broadway and Hollywood* (New York: Knopf, 2000), 358.

14. Keith Garebian, *The Making of "West Side Story"* (Toronto: ECW Press, 1995), 31.

15. Laurents had explored this racial shift himself in his play *Home of the Brave* (1945), about the anti-Semitism a soldier faces in the military. The plot was changed for the 1949 movie version, in which the solider is no longer Jewish but black, reflecting a shift from religion and white ethnicity to race as defined by skin color.

16. Laurents, *Original Story By*, 337–338.

17. Leonard Bernstein, *Findings* (New York: Simon and Schuster, 1982), 145.

18. These newspaper articles can be found in Box 46, Folder 13, Jerome Robbins Papers, (S) *MGZMD 130, Jerome Robbins Dance Division, New York Public Library for the Performing Arts.

19. One would surmise that the play Laurents was referencing was Arthur Miller's *A View from the Bridge*, which premiered in September 1955.

20. Arthur Laurents to Leonard Bernstein and Jerome Robbins, July 19, [1955?], Box 101, Folder 1, Jerome Robbins Personal Papers, (S)*MGZMD 182, Jerome Robbins Dance Division, New York Public Library for the Performing Arts.

21. Jerome Robbins to Arthur Laurents, October 6, 1955, Box 101, Folder 1, Jerome Robbins Personal Papers, (S)*MGZMD 182, Jerome Robbins Dance Division, New York Public Library for the Performing Arts.

22. Laurents wrote to Robbins, "I read The Changelings but was not, I fear, very impressed. Still, I got a phrase out of it for the musical—as you will notice." Box 101, Folder 1, Jerome Robbins Personal Papers, (S)*MGZMD 182, Jerome Robbins Dance Division, New York Public Library for the Performing Arts.

23. In fact, another early but discarded name for the musical was *Gangway!*

24. Garebian, *Making of "West Side Story,"* 41–42.

25. Laurents, *Original Story By*, 328.

26. Cheryl Crawford to Arthur Laurents, April 11, 1957, Roger L. Stevens Collection, Music Division, Library of Congress.

27. Garebian, *Making of "West Side Story,"* 42.

28. Meredith Willson, *The Music Man* (New York: G. P. Putnam's Sons, 1958), 31, 36.

29. Scott Miller calls *The Music Man* a "savage satire," but he never really supports his assertion. Scott Miller, *Deconstructing Harold Hill: An Insider's Guide to Musical Theatre* (Portsmouth, NH: Heinemann, 1999), 73. Brooks Atkinson, in his December 20, 1957, *New York Times* review, said he enjoyed the musical very much but thought it leaned toward being a cartoon. John Chapman, though, in the *New York Daily News*, felt that the Americana elements were "presented fondly and respectfully." John Chapman, "'The Music Man' One of the Best Musical Comedies of Our Time," *New York Daily News*, December 20, 1957, 60.

30. Willson, *The Music Man*, 52.

31. Ibid, 52–53. The seemingly fictitious words Eulalie utters are actually part of an old Gaelic counting system known as *"Yan Tan Tethera,"* used to count sheep in Britain.

32. Ibid., 103.

33. Ibid., 28.

34. Scott Miller writes that Willson "was himself born in Iowa in 1902. He studied at the Juilliard School of Music and played for a while with the John Philip Sousa Band and the New York Philharmonic Orchestra." Miller, *Deconstructing Harold Hill*, 74.

35. Carol J. Oja, *"West Side Story* and *The Music Man*: Whiteness, Immigration, and Race in the US during the Late 1950s," *Studies in Musical Theatre* 3, no. 1 (2009): 19.

36. Ibid., 15.

37. Nathan Glazer and Daniel Patrick Moynihan, *Beyond the Melting Pot: The Negroes, Puerto Ricans, Jews, Italians, and Irish of New York City* (Cambridge, MA: MIT Press, 1963), 13.

38. Rachel Rubin and Jeffrey Melnick, *Immigration and American Popular Culture: An Introduction* (New York: NYU Press, 2007), 91–92.

39. Glazer and Moynihan, *Beyond the Melting Pot*, 23.

40. Arthur Laurents to Jerome Robbins, n.d., Box 101, Folder 1, Jerome Robbins Personal Papers, (S)*MGZMD 182, Jerome Robbins Dance Division, New York Public Library for the Performing Arts.

41. Box 81, Folder 2, Jerome Robbins Papers, (S) *MGZMD 130, Jerome Robbins Dance Division, New York Public Library for the Performing Arts.

42. Frances Negrón-Muntaner, *"Feeling Pretty: West Side Story* and Puerto Rican Identity Discourses," *Social Text* 63 (Summer 2000): 91.

43. Qtd. in Nigel Simeone, *Leonard Bernstein: West Side Story* (Burlington, VT: Ashgate, 2009), 3.

44. Garebian, *Making of "West Side Story,"* 13; Walter Kerr, "'West Side Story' Returns," review of *West Side Story*, book by Arthur Laurents, music by Leonard Bernstein, lyrics by Stephen Sondheim, directed by Jerome Robbins, Minskoff Theatre, New York, *New York Times*, February 15, 1980.

45. Wolcott Gibbs, "Hoodlums and Heiresses," review of *West Side Story*, book by Arthur Laurents, music by Leonard Bernstein, lyrics by Stephen Sondheim, directed by Jerome Robbins, Winter Garden Theatre, New York, *New Yorker*, October 5, 1957, 64.

46. Rubin and Melnick, *Immigration*, 89, 98, 102, 103, 106.

47. Laurents, *West Side Story*, 137.

48. Arthur Laurents, "The Growth of an Idea," *New York Herald Tribune*, August 4, 1957.

49. Laurents, *West Side Story*, 176.

50. Box 81, Folder 2, Jerome Robbins Papers, (S) *MGZMD 130, Jerome Robbins Dance Division, New York Public Library for the Performing Arts.

51. Keith Garebian quotes *West Side Story*'s original Tony, Larry Kert, as stating during his audition process for the show: "But every day you read that Leonard Bernstein is looking for a six-foot, blond, Polish tenor. I'm a five-foot-eleven, dark, Jewish baritone!" Garebian, *Making of "West Side Story,"* 108.

52. Matthew Frye Jacobson, *Whiteness of a Different Color: European Immigrants and the Alchemy of Race* (Cambridge, MA: Harvard University Press, 1999), 110–111.

53. Puerto Ricans possessed U.S. citizenship rights as guaranteed under the Jones Act of 1917.

54. Alberto Sandoval-Sánchez, *José, Can You See? Latinos on and off Broadway* (Madison: University of Wisconsin, 1999), 64, 65, 66.

55. Meredith Willson, *But He Doesn't Know the Territory* (New York: G. P. Putnam's Sons, 1959), 184.

56. Willson, *The Music Man*, 53, 60.

57. Laurents, *West Side Story*, 137.

58. Stephen Sondheim, *Finishing the Hat: Collected Lyrics (1954–1981) with Attendant Comments, Heresies, Principles, Grudges, Whines, and Anecdotes* (New York: Knopf, 2010), 34–35.

59. Ibid., 34.

60. Ibid., 33–34. The music to "Mix!" was later recycled by Bernstein in the second movement of his choral work *The Chichester Psalms*.

61. Ibid., 31.

62. Garebian, *Making of "West Side Story,"* 55.

63. Laurents, *West Side Story*, 152.

64. Emphasis added, Box 81, Folder 2, Jerome Robbins Papers, (S) *MGZMD 130, Jerome Robbins Dance Division, New York Public Library for the Performing Arts.

65. Laurents, *West Side Story*, 179.

66. Ibid., 164, 165.

67. Leonard Bernstein to Jerome Robbins, October 29, 1955, Box 72, Folder 14, Jerome Robbins Personal Papers, (S) *MGZMD 182, Jerome Robbins Dance Division, New York Public Library for the Performing Arts.

68. George Stevens, *Conversations with the Great Moviemakers of Hollywood's Golden Age at the American Film Institute* (New York: Knopf, 2006), 491.

69. Sondheim, *Finishing the Hat*, 42.

70. Laurents, *West Side Story*, 217.

71. Ibid., 154, 155, 161.

72. Qtd. in Garebian, *Making of "West Side Story,"* 50. A quick explanation of Robbins's confusion: the traditional way to change scenery in theater was to close the traveler curtains in the front of the stage or to bring in a shallow drop so that a scene could be played in front of the curtains or drop in what was known as "in one," so that behind the curtains, stagehands could change the set for the next scene.

73. Laurents, *West Side Story*, 162.

74. Ibid., 200.

75. Wayne Robinson, "Willson's 'Music Man' on Shubert Stage," review of *The Music Man*, book, music, and lyrics by Meredith Willson, directed by Morton da Costa, Shubert Theatre, Philadelphia, PA, *Evening Bulletin*, n.d. (from clippings file).

76. Brooks Atkinson, review of *The Music Man*, book, music, and lyrics by Meredith Willson, directed by Morton da Costa, Majestic Theatre, New York, *New York Times*, December 20, 1957.

77. John Chapman, "Happy Days Here Again," *Sunday News*, December 29, 1957.

CARBON COPIES

1. Allen Woll's *Black Musical Theatre* is an outstanding history of such shows from the 1890s through the 1980s.

2. Angela Pao, *No Safe Spaces: Re-casting Race, Ethnicity, and Nationality in American Theater* (Ann Arbor: University of Michigan Press, 2010), 176.

3. Richard Schechner, "Race Free, Gender Free, Body-Type Free, Age Free Casting," *TDR* 33, no. 1 (Spring 1989): 6.

4. Michael Omi and Howard Winant, *Racial Formation in the United States*, 2nd ed. (New York: Routledge, 1994), 54.

5. Charles Isherwood, "Tovah Feldshuh at the Paper Mill: Top o' the Mornin', Dolly!," review of *Hello, Dolly!*, book by Michael Stewart, music and lyrics by Jerry Herman, directed by Mark S. Hoebee, Paper Mill Playhouse, Millburn, NJ, *New York Times*, June 13, 2006.

6. John Chapman, "Pearl Bailey, Cab Calloway & Co. Make a Brand-New Hit of 'Dolly!,'" review of *Hello, Dolly!*, book by Michael Stewart, music and lyrics by Jerry Herman, directed by Lucia Victor, St. James Theatre, New York, *New York Daily News*, November 13, 1967.

7. Walter Bailey, "Pearl Bailey–Cab Calloway 'Hello, Dolly!,'" *Philadelphia Tribune*, November 4, 1967.

8. Ragni Lantz, "Hello, Dolly!," *Ebony*, January 1968, 89.

9. Channing and Bailey became friends through the show. Not only did Channing show up for Bailey's opening, but the two teamed up for a popular 1969 TV special called *Carol Channing & Pearl Bailey on Broadway*.

10. Ted Poston, "Woman in the News: Pearl Bailey. Her Co-Star Was the President," *New York Post*, Weekend Magazine, n.d. (from clippings file).

11. Jackie Robinson, "'Hello, Dolly!' Something Else," *New York Amsterdam News*, March 9, 1968, 17.

12. Richard P. Cooke, "Pearl as Dolly," review of *Hello, Dolly!*, book by Michael Stewart, music and lyrics by Jerry Herman, directed by Lucia Victor, St. James Theatre, New York, *Wall Street Journal*, November 14, 1967.

13. Jesse H. Walker, "'Hello, Dolly!' Is Now 'Hello, Pearlie!,'" review of *Hello, Dolly!*, book by Michael Stewart, music and lyrics by Jerry Herman, directed by Lucia Victor, St. James Theatre, New York, *New York Amsterdam News*, November 18, 1967, 20.

14. Clive Barnes, "All-Negro 'Hello, Dolly!' Has Its Premiere," review of *Hello, Dolly!*, book by Michael Stewart, music and lyrics by Jerry Herman, directed by Lucia Victor, St. James Theatre, New York, *New York Times*, November 13, 1967.

15. Qtd. in Edwin Bolwell, "Dolly Levi Now Finds Her Match in Pearl Bailey," *New York Times*, July 29, 1967.

16. Lantz, "Hello, Dolly!," 89.

17. Mel Gussow, "Casting by Race Can Be Touchy," *New York Times*, August 1, 1976.

18. Richard Dyer, "The Colour of Entertainment," in *Musicals—Hollywood and Beyond*, ed. Bill Marshall and Robynn Stilwell (Portland, OR: Intellect Books, 2000), 26.

19. Tom Prideaux, "A Big New Deal for 'Dolly'—Hello Pearl," *Life*, December 8, 1967.

20. Kevin Kelly, "A Great New 'Dolly' to Say Hello To," review of *Hello, Dolly!*, book by Michael Stewart, music and lyrics by Jerry Herman, directed by Lucia Victor, St. James Theatre, New York, *Boston Globe*, November 14, 1967, 59 (emphasis added).

21. Poston, "Woman in the News: Pearl Bailey" (emphasis original).

22. Lantz, "Hello, Dolly!," 86.

23. Pao, *No Safe Spaces*, 184.

24. Hobe Morrison, review of *Hello, Dolly!*, book by Michael Stewart, music and lyrics by Jerry Herman, directed by Lucia Victor, Minskoff Theatre, New York, *Variety*, November 12, 1975.

25. Martin Gottfried, "Bailey's 'Hello, Dolly!' a Lusterless Pearl," review of *Hello, Dolly!*, book by Michael Stewart, music and lyrics by Jerry Herman, directed by Lucia Victor, Minskoff Theatre, *New York Post*, New York, November 7, 1975, 34.

26. Martin Gottfried, review of *The Pajama Game*, music by Richard Adler and Jerry Ross, book by George Abbott and Richard Bissell, lyrics by Richard Adler and Jerry Ross, directed by George Abbott, Lunt-Fontanne Theater, New York, *Women's Wear Daily*, December 10, 1973.

27. Douglas Watt, "'Pajama Game' in Brisk Revival," review of *The Pajama Game*, music by Richard Adler and Jerry Ross, book by George Abbott and Richard Bissell, lyrics by Richard Adler and Jerry Ross, directed by George Abbott, Lunt-Fontanne Theatre, New York, *Daily News*, December 10, 1973.

28. Clive Barnes, "'The Pajama Game' Returns," review of *The Pajama Game*, music by Richard Adler and Jerry Ross, book by George Abbott and Richard Bissell, lyrics by Richard Adler and Jerry Ross, directed by George Abbott, Lunt-Fontanne Theatre, New York, *New York Times*, December 10, 1973.

29. Gottfried, review of *The Pajama Game*, December 10, 1973.

30. Walter Kerr, "Hey There, What Happened?," review of *The Pajama Game*, music by Richard Adler and Jerry Ross, book by George Abbott and Richard Bissell, lyrics by Richard Adler and Jerry Ross, directed by George Abbott, Lunt-Fontanne Theatre, New York, *New York Times*, December 16, 1973.

31. Martin Gottfried, " 'Guys and Dolls' Suffers in the Black Version," review of *Guys and Dolls*, music and lyrics by Frank Loesser, book by Abe Burrows and Jo Swerling, directed by Billy Wilson, Broadway Theatre, New York, *New York Post*, July 22, 1976.

32. Bernard Carragher, "A Philadelphia Story," *New York Sunday Times*, August 2, 1976.

33. Jacqueline Trescott, "Robert Guillaume: The Leading Guy," *Washington Post*, May 6, 1976.

34. Howard Kissel, review of *Guys and Dolls*, music and lyrics by Frank Loesser, book by Abe Burrows and Jo Swerling, directed by Billy Wilson, Broadway Theatre, *Women's Wear Daily*, July 23, 1976.

35. Gottfried, " 'Guys and Dolls' Suffers in the Black Version."

36. Charles Michener, "Almost-Nicely," review of *Guys and Dolls*, music and lyrics by Frank Loesser, book by Abe Burrows and Jo Swerling, directed by Billy Wilson, Broadway Theatre, New York, *Newsweek*, August 2, 1976.

37. Mel Tapley, "Guys and Dolls: Black Actors on Broadway Proving Themselves," *New York Amsterdam News*, November 6, 1976.

38. Stephen Gayle, " 'Guys & Dolls' Black & Box Office," *New York Post*, August 28, 1976.

39. Hari, review of *Guys and Dolls*, music and lyrics by Frank Loesser, book by Abe Burrows and Jo Swerling, directed by Billy Wilson, Forrest Theatre, Philadelphia, *Variety*, March 31, 1976.

40. Trescott, "Robert Guillaume."

41. Judy Klemesrud, " 'Guys and Dolls' Comes Back Black," *New York Times*, July 18, 1976.

42. John Beaufort, "All-black 'Guys and Dolls,' " review of *Guys and Dolls*, music and lyrics by Frank Loesser, book by Abe Burrows and Jo Swerling, directed by Billy Wilson, Broadway Theatre, New York, *Christian Science Monitor*, July 26, 1976.

43. Klemesrud, " 'Guys and Dolls' Comes Back Black."

44. Joh Simon, "Dudes and Chicks," review of *Guys and Dolls*, music and lyrics by Frank Loesser, book by Abe Burrows and Jo Swirling, directed by Billy Wilson, Broadway Theatre, New York, *New Leader*, September 13, 1976.

45. Pao, *No Safe Spaces*, 186–187.
46. Gottfried, "'Guys and Dolls' Suffers in the Black Version."
47. Marilyn Stasio, "'Guys and Dolls' Comes Back—All Black and Beautiful," *Cue*, August 21–28, 1976, 12.
48. Brendan Gill, "Noo Yawk," review of *Guys and Dolls*, music and lyrics by Frank Loesser, book by Abe Burrows and Jo Swerling, directed by Billy Wilson, Broadway Theatre, New York, *New Yorker*, August 2, 1976, 53.
49. Ibid. (emphasis original).
50. Jessica B. Harris, "'Guys and Dolls' Most Exciting on B'way," *New York Amsterdam News*, July 31, 1976. The marquee info comes from a photo in this article.
51. Ernest Leogrande, "'Guys and Dolls' in the Black," review of *Guys and Dolls*, music and lyrics by Frank Loesser, book by Abe Burrows and Jo Swerling, directed by Billy Wilson, Broadway Theatre, New York, *Daily News*, July 22, 1976.
52. Gloria Goodale, "'Guys and Dolls' Celebrates 50th," *Christian Science Monitor*, April 26, 2002.
53. Hobe Morrison, review of *Timbuktu!*, music and lyrics by Robert Wright and George Forrest, book by Luther Davis, directed by Geoffrey Holder, Mark Hellinger Theatre, New York, *Variety*, March 8, 1978,.
54. Barbara Lewis, "'Timbuktu': Exotic Showcase for Black Stars," *New York Amsterdam News*, January 7, 1978.
55. Mel Gussow, "From Timbuktu to Here, a New 'Kismet' Is on Its Way," *New York Times*, August 26, 1977.
56. Luther Davis, "The Million Dollar Telephone Call," *Timbuktu!* Playbill.
57. Henry Weil, "'Timbuktu' Dazzles but Styles Clash," review of *Timbuktu!*, music and lyrics by Robert Wright and George Forrest, book by Luther Davis directed by Geoffrey Holder, Mark Hellinger Theatre, New York, *New York Tribune*, March 2, 1978.
58. Angela Pao discusses the National Asian American Theatre Company's all-Asian production of the very Jewish William Finn musical *Falsettoland* and concludes that despite the seemingly inherent disjunction between cast and subject matter, the musical was actually well served by this interpretation. Pao, *No Safe Spaces*, 204–212.
59. Frank Rich, "David Merrick Presents 'Oh, Kay!'," review of *Oh, Kay!*, music by George Gershwin, lyrics by Ira Gershwin, book by Guy Bolton and P. G. Wodehouse, directed by Dan Siretta, Richard Rodgers Theatre, New York, *New York Times*, November 2, 1990.
60. David Richards, review of *Oh, Kay!*, music by George Gershwin, lyrics by Ira Gershwin, book by Guy Bolton and P.G. Wodehouse, directed by Dan Siretta, Richard Rodgers Theatre, New York, *New York Times*, November 11, 1990.
61. Abiola Sinclair, "'Oh, Kay' a Solid Hit," review of *Oh, Kay!*, music by George Gershwin, lyrics by Ira Gershwin, book by Guy Bolton and P. G. Wodehouse, directed by Dan Siretta, Richard Rodgers Theatre, New York, *New York Amsterdam News*, November 17, 1990. Some white critics did rave about the show as well, including Clive Barnes in the *New York Post*, November 2, 1990.
62. Toni Morrison, *Playing in the Dark: Whiteness and the Literary Imagination* (New York: Vintage Books, 1992), 12.
63. Bob Weiner, "Black Is Not Always Beautiful," *Soho Weekly News*, July 22, 1976.
64. William H. Sun, "Power and Problems of Performance across Ethnic Lines: An Alternative Approach to Nontraditional Casting," *TDR* 44, no. 4 (Winter 2000): 92.

65. Clinton Turner Davis, "Non-Traditional Casting (an open letter)," *African American Review* 31, no. 4 (Winter 1997): 594.

66. August Wilson, "The Ground on Which I Stand," *American Theatre* 13, no. 7 (September 1996), *Academic Search Premier*, EBSCO*host* (accessed December, 31, 2012).

67. Robert Brustein, "Subsidized Separatism," *American Theatre* 13, no. 8 (October 1996), *Academic Search Premier*, EBSCO*host* (accessed December, 31, 2012).

68. Schechner, "Race Free, Gender Free, Body-Type Free, Age Free Casting," 9.

69. All-black productions of plays traditionally thought of as "white" continue to be produced on Broadway, including *On Golden Pond* (2005) starring James Earl Jones and Leslie Uggams; *Cat on a Hot Tin Roof* (2008) starring James Earl Jones, Terrence Howard, and Phylicia Rashad; and *A Streetcar Named Desire* (2012) starring Blair Underwood and Nicole Ari Parker.

A CHORUS LINE

1. Mervyn Rothstein, "After 15 Years (15!), 'A Chorus Line' Ends," *New York Times*, April 30, 1990.

2. Other examples of concept musicals include *Company* (1970), which is about marriage and relationships, and *Follies* (1971), about older chorus girls and their husbands recalling their days in the Follies. Both shows have music and lyrics by Stephen Sondheim and choreography (and in the case of *Follies* codirection) by Michael Bennett.

3. James Kirkwood and Nicholas Dante, book; Marvin Hamlisch, music; Edward Kleban, lyrics, *A Chorus Line* (1975; New York: Applause Books, 1995), 31.

4. For more on the original session, see Robert Viagas, Baayork Lee, and Thommie Walsh, *On the Line: The Creation of "A Chorus Line"* (New York: William Morrow, 1990).

5. Ken Mandelbaum, *"A Chorus Line" and the Musicals of Michael Bennett* (New York: St. Martin's Press, 1989), 100–101.

6. Kirkwood and Dante, *A Chorus Line*, 23, 25, 27.

7. Ibid., 28.

8. Ibid., 98.

9. This might seem a strange assertion given that Paul's monologue is all about his gayness and sexuality, but it's a tortured monologue, one that he can only share with Zach when all the other dancers have left the stage. After all, one of the first lyrics that Paul sings early in the show is "What will I say when he calls on me?" Paul is clearly worried and hesitant about having to reveal this uncomfortable part of his identity.

10. Other incarnations of the Follies existed past 1931 after Ziegfeld himself had died.

11. Linda Mizejewski, *Ziegfeld Girl: Image and Icon in Culture and Cinema* (Durham, NC: Duke University Press, 1999), 2, 115.

12. Of course, the Follies did feature Jewish performers like Fanny Brice and black performers like Bert Williams, and many composers and lyricists who worked for Ziegfeld, like Irving Berlin, were Jewish, but the chorus line would maintain its pristine Anglo-Saxon whiteness despite these minority contributions.

13. Kirkwood and Dante, *A Chorus Line*, 7.

14. Berkeley was a Ziegfeld choreographer and put his own mechanized spin on the Ziegfeld Girl. For more on this connection, see Joel Dinerstein's *Swinging the Ma-*

chine: Modernity, Technology, and African American Culture between the World Wars (Amherst: University of Massachusetts Press, 2003).

15. Tom Sutcliffe, "Numbers Up," *Time Out London*, July 23–29 1976, 10 (emphasis original).

16. Michael Feingold, "Believing the Myth," review of *A Chorus Line*, book by James Kirkwood and Nicholas Dante, music by Marvin Hamlisch, lyrics by Edward Kleban, conceived, choreographed, and directed by Michael Bennett, New York Shakespeare Festival, New York, *Village Voice*, June 2, 1975.

17. The following quotations from "I Hope I Get It" are from Kirkwood and Dante, *A Chorus Line*, 9, 12, 13, 22.

18. This same emotion is conveyed in another Ed Kleban song, "Self Portrait," that made it into the Kleban bio-musical *A Class Act* (2000).

19. Josephine Lee, "Racial Actors, Liberal Myths," *XCP: Cross-Cultural Poetics* 13 (2003): 94.

20. Box 3, Folder 9, Edward Kleban Papers, *T-Mss 1988–007, Billy Rose Theatre Division, New York Public Library for the Performing Arts.

21. Mandelbaum, *A Chorus Line*, 130–131.

22. Box 3, Folder 9, Edward Kleban Papers, *T-Mss 1988–007, Billy Rose Theatre Division, New York Public Library for the Performing Arts.

23. Herbert J. Gans, "Symbolic Ethnicity: The Future of Ethnic Groups and Cultures in America," in *On the Making of Americans: Essays in Honor of David Riesman*, ed. Herbert J. Gans et al. (Philadelphia: University of Pennsylvania Press, 1979), 215.

24. Werner Sollors, *Beyond Ethnicity: Consent and Descent in American Culture* (New York: Oxford University Press, 1986), 20.

25. Michael Novak, *The Rise of the Unmeltable Ethnics* (New York: Macmillan, 1972), 47–48.

26. Mary C. Waters, "The Costs of a Costless Community," in *New Tribalisms: The Resurgence of Race and Ethnicity*, ed. Michael W. Hughey (New York: New York University Press, 1998), 273, 277, 282.

27. Dan Sullivan, "Getting a Kick out of 'Chorus Line,'" *Los Angeles Times*, July 4, 1976.

28. Kirkwood and Dante, *A Chorus Line*, 61.

29. Frank Rich, introduction to Kirkwood and Dante, *A Chorus Line*, xiv.

30. Kirkwood and Dante, *A Chorus Line*, 97.

31. Ibid., 105 (emphasis original).

32. Qtd. in Bruce Lambert, "Rockettes and Race: Barrier Slips," *New York Times*, December 26, 1987.

33. Kirkwood and Dante, *A Chorus Line*, 110, 112, 113–114, 115, 122.

34. Samuel G. Freedman, preface to Kirkwood and Dante, *A Chorus Line*, vii.

35. Mandelbaum, *A Chorus Line*, 170–171.

36. Scott McMillin, *The Musical as Drama: A Study of the Principles and Conventions behind Musical Shows from Kern to Sondheim* (Princeton, NJ: Princeton University Press, 2006), 99–100.

37. Jack Kroll with Constance Guthrie, "Broadway's New Kick," *Newsweek*, December 1, 1975, 70.

38. Waters, "The Costs of a Costless Community," 286.

39. Harry Newman, "Holding Back: The Theatre's Resistance to Non-Traditional Casting," *Drama Review* 33, no. 3 (Fall 1989): 35.

40. For more about the politics of color-blind casting, see Angela C. Pao, *No Safe Spaces: Re-casting Race, Ethnicity, and Nationality in American Theater* (Ann Arbor: University of Michigan Press, 2010), 42–63.
41. Mandelbaum, *A Chorus Line*, 217–218.

EVERYTHING OLD IS NEW AGAIN

1. *Cats* premiered on London's West End in 1981 and landed in New York in 1982. It won the Tony Award for Best Musical in 1983.
2. Bernard Rosenberg and Ernest Harburg, *The Broadway Musical: Collaboration in Commerce and Art* (New York: New York University Press, 1993), 42.
3. A perfect example of this economic model of producing the contemporary Broadway musical is Stephen Sondheim's *Sweeney Todd* (1979). Despite the high praise that the show garnered from critics and audiences, when it closed two years after opening, it closed at a loss, having never recouped its initial investment. Thus, in the lingo of theatrical producing, *Sweeney Todd* is technically considered a "flop." On a further note, in Philadelphia, where I grew up, the once vibrant seasons of touring shows were virtually replaced in the late eighties and early nineties by six-month sit-downs of *Les Misérables* and *The Phantom of the Opera* that tied theaters up for stretches at a time.
4. Jeffrey C. Goldfarb, "When the Stage Turns to Reruns," *Christian Science Monitor*, August 19, 1980 (emphasis added).
5. The pilot episode (2007) of the hit 1960s-set TV show *Mad Men* concludes with a rendition of *My Fair Lady*'s "On the Street Where You Live." The song's classic status is meant to nostalgize the sixties, but this nostalgia, which evokes notions of love and happiness, is quickly compromised by the fact that we know that the show's protagonist, Don Draper, is having an affair that casts a shadow over his home's supposed domestic bliss.
6. Other examples of this genre include *My One and Only*, a Gershwin revue from 1983, and *Crazy for You* (1992), a "new" Gershwin musical based loosely on *Girl Crazy*. Yet another "new" Gershwin property, entitled *Nice Work if You Can Get It* (2012), loosely based on *Oh, Kay!*, premiered on Broadway in 2012.
7. Frank Rich, "What Ails Today's Musicals?," *New York Times*, November 14, 1982.
8. Fredric Jameson, "Postmodernism and Consumer Society," in *The Anti-Aesthetic: Essays on Post-Modern Culture*, ed. Hal Foster (Seattle: Bay Press, 1989), 114 (emphasis original).
9. Rebecca Ann Rugg, "What It Used to Be: Nostalgia and the State of the Broadway Musical," *Theater* 32, no. 2 (Summer 2002): 46.
10. Another great example of this genre would be the 2002 Tony Award–winning Best Musical *Hairspray*, based on the 1988 John Waters film of the same name, which nostalgizes the 1960s civil rights movement in ways that are highly entertaining and overly simplistic.
11. J. Hoberman, *42nd Street* (London: BFI Publishing, 1993), 76.
12. Photos from the original Broadway production reveal at least one African American woman in the chorus in a nonfeatured role, but that seemed to be the extent of the show's racial diversity.
13. Howard Kissel, *David Merrick: The Abominable Showman* (New York: Applause Books, 1993), 14–15.

14. John Beaufort, "'42nd Street'—The Shortest Distance between Two Eras," review of *42nd Street*, book by Michael Stewart and Mark Bramble, music by Harry Warren, lyrics by Al Dubin, directed by Gower Champion, Winter Garden Theatre, New York, *Christian Science Monitor*, September 18, 1980.

15. Hoberman, *42nd Street*, 67; William H. Young and Nancy K. Young, *Music of the Great Depression* (Westport, CT: Greenwood Press, 2005), 91.

16. Hoberman, *42nd Street*, 67–68.

17. Richard Barrios, *A Song in the Dark: The Birth of the Musical Film*, 2nd ed. (New York: Oxford University Press, 2010), 366.

18. Hoberman, *42nd Street*, 11.

19. Mark Bramble and Michael Stewart, book; music by Harry Warren, lyrics by Al Dubin, *42nd Street*, Tams-Witmark Music Library, 1-2-19.

20. Stanley Kauffmann, "Nimble Feet, Fumbling Hands," review of *42nd Street*, book by Michael Stewart and Mark Bramble, music by Harry Warren, lyrics by Al Dubin, directed by Gower Champion, Winter Garden Theatre, New York, *Saturday Review*, n.d. 1980 (from clippings file), 88.

21. Bramble and Stewart, *42nd Street*, 1-1-1.

22. When *42nd Street* was revived on Broadway in 2001, it played with the songbook again, this time adding "I Only Have Eyes for You," also from *Dames*.

23. Alan Woods, "Consuming the Past: Commercial American Theatre in the Reagan Era," in *The American Stage: Social and Economic Issues from the Colonial Period to the Present*, ed. Ron Engle and Tice L. Miller (New York: Cambridge University Press, 1993), 257.

24. Frank Rich, review of *42nd Street*, book by Michael Stewart and Mark Bramble, music by Harry Warren, lyrics by Al Dubin, directed by Gower Champion, Winter Garden Theatre, New York, *New York Times*, August 26, 1980.

25. John Simon, "And Still Champion," review of *42nd Street*, book by Michael Stewart and Mark Bramble, music by Harry Warren, lyrics by Al Dubin, directed by Gower Champion, Winter Garden Theatre, New York, *New York Magazine*, September 8, 1980, 75.

26. Hoberman, *42nd Street*, 13.

27. See chapter 5 in Joel Dinerstein's *Swinging the Machine* (2003) for more on this phenomenon.

28. Bramble and Stewart, *42nd Street*, 2-4-10.

29. Ibid., 1-6-38.

30. By 1997, even the world of prostitution in 1980s Times Square would be fodder for a musical, evoked and nostalgized by creators Cy Coleman, Ira Gasman, and David Newman in *The Life*.

31. Bramble and Stewart, *42nd Street*, 2-6-22 (emphasis original), 2-8-31.

32. Ibid., 2-3-7 (emphasis original).

33. Bramble and Stewart, *42nd Street*, 2-6-23; Barrios, *A Song in the Dark*, 363.

34. Allan J. Lichtman, *White Protestant Nation: The Rise of the American Conservative Movement* (New York: Atlantic Monthly Press, 2008), 356.

35. Paul Krugman, "Republicans and Race," *New York Times*, November 19, 2007.

36. Herman Schwartz, "Affirmative Action," in *Minority Report: What Has Happened to Blacks, Hispanics, American Indians, and Other Minorities in the Eighties*, ed. Leslie W. Dunbar (New York: Pantheon Books, 1984), 62.

37. Michael Omi and Howard Winant, *Racial Formation in the United States*, 2nd ed. (New York: Routledge, 1994), 130.
38. As Tommy Tune saw it, "I didn't want to do a pastiche and I didn't want to do a period piece. I wanted it to be more vibrant than that." John Harris, "The Making of *The Will Rogers Follies*," *TheaterWeek*, May 13, 1991, 18.
39. Peter Stone, book; Cy Coleman, music; Betty Comden and Adolph Green, lyrics, *The Will Rogers Follies: A Life in Revue*, Tams-Witmark Music Library, 1993, 10.
40. Ibid.
41. Ibid., 68.
42. Ibid., 12.
43. Ibid.
44. Ibid.,13.
45. "Agreement on Casting of 'Will Rogers,'" *New York Times*, June 18, 1992; Alex Witchel, "On Stage, and Off," *New York Times*, December 27, 1991.
46. Stone, *Will Rogers Follies*, 21.
47. Ibid., 8.
48. Alex Witchel, "Portrayal of Indians in 'Rogers,'" *New York Times*, May 24, 1991.
49. Stone, *Will Rogers Follies*, 34.
50. Michèle LaRue, "The Scenic View," *Backstage*, May 17, 1991, 35.
51. Stone, *Will Rogers Follies*, 81–82 (emphasis original).
52. Ibid., 82.
53. Paul Meloccaro, e-mail to CASTRECL mailing list, April 1, 2000, http://mailman. mit.edu/mailman/private/castrecl/2000-April/001810.html. CASTRECL is an e-mail LISTSERV for individuals interested in the history, production, and collection of cast recordings. Its membership/audience is made up of performers, musical theater historians, laypeople, and record producers.
54. Peter Stone, *Annie Get Your Gun*, Production Script, March 4, 1999, unpublished, I–Prologue–1.
55. Rich Orloff, "Old Musicals, New Librettos," *Dramatist*, July/August 2001, 33.
56. Qtd. in Patrick Pacheco, "Play by Play: Revivals No Folly for Musical Master Stone," *Newsday*, December 31, 1998.
57. The Rodgers and Hammerstein favorite Juanita Hall (from *South Pacific*) was actually African American, but she somehow read as "Chinese" for the purposes of the show.
58. Qtd. in Misha Berson, "A 'Drum' with a Difference," *American Theatre* (February 2002): 17.
59. Qtd. in Dan Bacalzo, "A Different Drum: David Henry Hwang's Musical 'Revisal' of *Flower Drum Song*," *Journal of American Drama and Theatre* 15, no. 2 (Spring 2003): 73.
60. A case in point: there are often stories of the organization shutting down or threatening to shut down stage productions of *The Sound of Music* that try to make the stage version more like the movie by having Maria and the children sing "My Favorite Things" instead of Maria and Mother Superior as was originally written. While they have often allowed the inclusion of the two songs written for the film, "I Have Confidence" and "Something Good," the show must otherwise be performed as in the original stage production.
61. Edward Albee seems to be the worst manipulator of this with play titles such as

Edward Albee's Who's Afraid of Virginia Woolf? and the extremely awkward title of his soon to be newest play, *Edward Albee's Laying an Egg.*

62. Orloff, "Old Musicals," 36.

63. Qtd. in Bacalzo, "Different Drum," 75.

64. The first major Broadway revival of the 1965 musical *On a Clear Day You Can See Forever* opened on Broadway in 2011 starring Harry Connick Jr., but this was no simple revival; rather, the director, Michael Mayer, with the assistance of the book writer, Peter Parnell, completely rewrote the book, turning the lead character Daisy into a gay man named David. Songs were repurposed and characters changed around. To call the show a revival would not be accurate; this was essentially a new musical. The results, sadly, were rather mixed from the critics' point of view.

65. Bacalzo, "Different Drum," 79–80.

66. The playwright Joe DiPietro provided a revised book for a 2004 production of the Rodgers and Hammerstein flop *Allegro* at Signature Theatre in Arlington, Virginia, with the blessing of the Rodgers and Hammerstein Organization.

67. The 1995 revue *Smokey Joe's Café* featured a mainly African American cast but hailed the work of the Jewish rock-and-roll greats Jerry Leiber and Mike Stoller. *Black and Blue*, a revue of black music from the 1920s and 1930s, played Broadway for slightly over two years from 1988 to 1991, while *Ain't Misbehavin'* (1978) celebrated the music of Fats Waller. In both these cases, the music evoked was hardly baby boomer.

EXIT MUSIC

1. "Stephen Sondheim Takes Issue with Plan for Revamped Porgy and Bess," *New York Times*, August 10, 2011, http://artsbeat.blogs.nytimes.com/2011/08/10/stephen-sondheim-takes-issue-with-plan-for-revamped-porgy-and-bess/ (accessed January 29, 2012).

2. Patrick Healy, "'Porgy': No New Scene, Some Hard Feelings," *New York Times*, November 14, 2011, http://www.nytimes.com/2011/11/15/theater/the-gershwins-porgy-and-bess-is-less-changed-for-broadway.html (accessed January 29, 2012).

3. The Encores! Great American Musicals in Concert series at City Center in New York capitalizes on precisely this fact, producing concert versions of older, classic musicals that have been lost or forgotten. Encores! has always privileged the scores, though, taking great care to provide full orchestras and, when possible, the original orchestrations for these works, but producing the shows with truncated librettos (often adapted by the playwright David Ives).

4. Everett Evans, "Lin-Manuel Miranda Is Broadway's Golden Boy," *San Francisco Chronicle*, August 8, 2008, http://www.chron.com/entertainment/article/Lin-Manuel-Miranda-is-Broadway-s-golden-boy-1772369.php (accessed January 29, 2012).

5. In an interesting spin, a 2008 Broadway revival of *West Side Story*, directed by the original librettist, Arthur Laurents, took the audacious tactic of translating part of the show's original libretto and some of its songs into Spanish. Laurents felt that this would help contemporize the show and level the playing field for the Sharks, allowing them to communicate in their native tongue. The individual called on to translate songs like "I Feel Pretty" was Lin-Manuel Miranda, the composer/lyricist of *In the Heights,* who had the challenging task of trying to preserve Stephen Sondheim's internal-rhyming lyrics in Spanish. The production earned mixed reviews, and the

concept of using Spanish, at least to me, while inspired, never seemed to play out in ways that made sense or enriched the show.

6. Heidi Rodewald, Stew's wife, who also performed in the show's band, co-wrote the score with Stew.

7. *The Wiz* premiered in 1975 and *Dreamgirls* in 1981. *Once on This Island*, which was an original Caribbean-infused black musical but was based on the novel *My Love, My Love* by Rosa Guy, came to Broadway in 1990. In 1995, Savion Glover starred in *Bring in 'da Noise, Bring in 'da Funk*, a musical revue that told the story of African American life through dance.

8. *The Scottsboro Boys* premiered at the Vineyard Theater off-Broadway in 2010, followed by a regional run at the Guthrie in Minneapolis; then it came to Broadway. Many other shows that are by and about nonwhites have followed a similar trajectory, starting off-Broadway or in regional theaters. With slightly less risk involved, such venues can be testing grounds for new work and garner the reviews necessary to transfer a show to a Broadway house.

9. The show also features a twelfth actor, an African American woman, who serves as an observer of what transpires and who also portrays the role of Rosa Parks in the final scene.

Bibliography

Antelyes, Peter. "'Haim Afen Range': The Jewish Indian and the Redface Western." *MELUS* 34, no. 3 (Fall 2009): 15–42.

Arac, Jonathan. *"Huckleberry Finn" as Idol and Target: The Functions of Criticism in Our Time*. Madison: University of Wisconsin Press, 1997.

Bacalzo, Dan. "A Different Drum: David Henry Hwang's Musical 'Revisal' of *Flower Drum Song*." *Journal of American Drama and Theatre* 15, no. 2 (Spring 2003): 71–83.

Ballard, Barbara J. "African-American Protest and the Role of the Haitian Pavilion at the 1893 Chicago World's Fair." In *Multiculturalism: Roots and Realities*, ed. C. James Trotman, 108–124. Bloomington: Indiana University Press, 2002.

Baral, Robert. *Revue: The Great Broadway Period*. Rev. ed. New York: Fleet Press, 1970.

Barrios, Richard. *A Song in the Dark: The Birth of the Musical Film*. 2nd ed. New York: Oxford University Press, 2010.

Berlin, Irving. *The Complete Lyrics of Irving Berlin*. Ed. Robert Kimball and Linda Emmet. New York: Knopf, 2000.

Bernstein, Leonard. *Findings*. New York: Simon and Schuster, 1982.

Berson, Misha. "A 'Drum' with a Difference." *American Theatre* 19, no. 2 (February 2002): 14–18, 76.

Blackstone, Sarah. "Simplifying the Native American: Wild West Shows Exhibit the 'Indian.'" In *Staging Difference: Cultural Pluralism in American Theatre and Drama*, ed. Marc Maufort, 9–17. New York: Peter Lang, 1995.

Brasmer, William. "The Wild West Exhibition: A Fraudulent Reality." In *American Popular Entertainment: Papers and Proceedings of the Conference on the History of American Popular Entertainment*, ed. Myron Matlaw, 207–214. Westport, CT: Greenwood Press, 1979.

Brecht, Bertolt. "A Short Organum for the Theatre." 1949. In *Brecht on Theatre: The Development of an Aesthetic*, ed. and trans. John Willett, 179–208. New York: Hill and Wang, 1964.

Breon, Robin. "*Show Boat*: The Revival, the Racism." *Drama Review* 39, no. 2 (Summer 1995): 86–105.

Brodkin, Karen. *How Jews Became White Folks and What That Says about Race in America*. New Brunswick, NJ: Rutgers University Press, 1998.

Browder, Laura. *Slippery Characters: Ethnic Impersonators and American Identities*. Chapel Hill: University of North Carolina Press, 2000.

Brustein, Robert. "Subsidized Separatism." *American Theatre* 13, no. 8 (October 1996): 26–27, 100–107.

Chang, David A. *The Color of the Land: Race, Nation, and the Politics of Landownership in Oklahoma, 1832–1929*. Chapel Hill: University of North Carolina Press, 2010.

Chude-Sokei, Louis. *The Last "Darky": Bert Williams, Black-on-Black Minstrelsy, and the African Diaspora*. Durham, NC: Duke University Press, 2006.

Clum, John M. *Something for the Boys: Musical Theater and Gay Culture*. New York: St. Martin's Press, 1999.

Davis, Clinton Turner. "Non-Traditional Casting (an open letter)." *African American Review* 31, no. 4 (Winter 1997): 591–594.

Decker, Todd. *"Show Boat": Performing Race in an American Musical*. New York: Oxford University Press, 2013.

Deloria, Philip. *Playing Indian*. New Haven, CT: Yale University Press, 1998.

Dinerstein, Joel. *Swinging the Machine: Modernity, Technology, and African American Culture between the World Wars*. Amherst: University of Massachusetts Press, 2003.

Dolan, Jill. *Utopia in Performance: Finding Hope at the Theater*. Ann Arbor: University of Michigan Press, 2005.

Dramatists Guild. "Landmark Symposium: *West Side Story*." *Dramatists Guild Quarterly* 7, no. 3 (Autumn 1985): 11–25.

Du Bois, W.E.B. *The Souls of Black Folk*. 1903. New York: Penguin, 1996.

Dyer, Richard. "The Colour of Entertainment." In *Musicals: Hollywood and Beyond*, ed. Bill Marshall and Robynn Stilwell, 23–30. Portland, OR: Intellect Books, 2000.

———. *White: Essays on Race and Culture*. New York: Routledge, 1997.

Ferber, Edna. *Show Boat*. 1926. A facsimile of the first edition. New York: Gramercy Books, 2007.

Fields, Barbara J. "Ideology and Race in American History." In *Region, Race, and Reconstruction: Essays in Honor of C. Vann Woodward*, ed. J. Morgan Kousser and James M. McPherson, 143–177. New York: Oxford University Press, 1982.

Fields, Dorothy, and Herbert Fields. *Annie Get Your Gun*. 1946. New York: Samuel French, 1952 [?].

Forbes, Camille F. *Introducing Bert Williams: Burnt Cork, Broadway, and the Story of America's First Black Star*. New York: Basic Civitas Books, 2008.

Fordin, Hugh. *Getting to Know Him: A Biography of Oscar Hammerstein II*. 1977. Reprint, New York: Ungar Publishing Company, 1986.

Frankenberg, Ruth. "The Mirage of an Unmarked Whiteness." In *The Making and Unmaking of Whiteness*, ed. Birgit Brander Rasmussen, Eric Klinenberg, Irene J. Nexica, and Matt Wray, 72–96. Durham, NC: Duke University Press, 2001.

Freedland, Michael. *Irving Berlin*. New York: Stein and Day, 1983.

Freedman, Samuel G. Preface to *A Chorus Line: The Book of the Musical*, by James Kirkwood and Nicholas Dante. Music by Marvin Hamlisch. Lyrics by Edward Kleban. New York: Applause Books, 1995.

Gans, Herbert J. "Symbolic Ethnicity: The Future of Ethnic Groups and Cultures in America." In *On the Making of Americans: Essays in Honor of David Riesman*, ed. Herbert J. Gans et al., 193–220. Philadelphia: University of Pennsylvania Press, 1979.

Gänzl, Kurt. *The Musical: A Concise History*. Boston: Northeastern University Press, 1997.

Garebian, Keith. *The Making of "West Side Story."* 1995. Reprint, Oakville, ON: Mosaic Press, 1998.

Gerstle, Gary. *American Crucible: Race and Nation in the Twentieth Century*. Princeton, NJ: Princeton University Press, 2001.

Glazer, Nathan, and Daniel Patrick Moynihan. *Beyond the Melting Pot: The Negroes, Puerto Ricans, Jews, Italians, and Irish of New York City*. Cambridge, MA: MIT Press, 1963.

Goffman, Erving. *The Presentation of Self in Everyday Life*. New York: Doubleday Anchor Books, 1959.

Hammerstein, Oscar II. *The Complete Lyrics of Oscar Hammerstein II.* Ed. Amy Asch. New York: Knopf, 2008.

———. *Oklahoma! The Complete Book and Lyrics of the Broadway Musical.* 1942. New York: Applause Books, 2010.

Harrison-Kahan, Lori. *The White Negress: Literature, Minstrelsy, and the Black-Jewish Imaginary.* New Brunswick, NJ: Rutgers University Press, 2011.

Hecht, Stuart J. *Transposing Broadway: Jews, Assimilation, and the American Musical.* New York: Palgrave Macmillan, 2011.

Hill, Mike. *After Whiteness: Unmaking an American Majority.* New York: New York University Press, 2004.

Hoberman, J. *42nd Street.* London: BFI Publishing, 1993.

Hobson, Laura Z. *Gentleman's Agreement.* New York: Simon and Schuster, 1947.

Hwang, David Henry. *Flower Drum Song.* Music by Richard Rodgers. Lyrics by Oscar Hammerstein. New York: TCG, 2003.

Jacobson, Matthew Frye. *Roots Too: White Ethnic Revival in Post–Civil Rights America.* Cambridge, MA: Harvard University Press, 2006.

———. *Whiteness of a Different Color: European Immigrants and the Alchemy of Race.* Cambridge, MA: Harvard University Press, 1999.

Jameson, Fredric. "Postmodernism and Consumer Society." 1982. In *The Anti-Aesthetic: Essays on Post-Modern Culture,* ed. Hal Foster, 111–125. Seattle: Bay Press, 1989.

Jones, John Bush. *Our Musicals, Ourselves: A Social History of the American Musical Theatre.* Lebanon, NH: University Press of New England, 2003.

Katz, Stephen. *Red, Black, and Jew: New Frontiers in Hebrew Literature.* Austin: University of Texas Press, 2009.

Kirkwood, James, and Nicholas Dante. *A Chorus Line: The Book of the Musical.* Music by Marvin Hamlisch. Lyrics by Edward Kleban. 1975. New York: Applause Books, 1995.

Kislan, Richard. *The Musical: A Look at the American Musical Theater.* Rev. and expanded ed. New York: Applause Books, 1995.

Kissel, Howard. *David Merrick: The Abominable Showman.* New York: Applause Books, 1993.

Knapp, Raymond. *The American Musical and the Formation of National Identity.* Princeton, NJ: Princeton University Press, 2004.

Kolchin, Peter. "Whiteness Studies: The New History of Race in America." *Journal of American History* 89, no. 1 (June 2002): 154–173.

Kotis, Greg. *Urinetown.* New York: Faber and Faber, 1998.

Kreuger, Miles. *"Show Boat": The Story of a Classic American Musical.* Corrected ed. 1977. Reprint, New York: Da Capo Press, 1990.

Lamb, Andrew. *150 Years of Popular Musical Theatre.* New Haven, CT: Yale University Press, 2001.

Laurents, Arthur. *Original Story By: A Memoir of Broadway and Hollywood.* New York: Knopf, 2000.

———. Music by Leonard Bernstein. Lyrics by Stephen Sondheim. *West Side Story.* 1956. In *Romeo and Juliet/ West Side Story.* New York: Dell, 1965.

Lee, Josephine. "Racial Actors, Liberal Myths." *XCP: Cross-Cultural Poetics* 13 (2003): 88–110.

Lichtman, Allan J. *White Protestant Nation: The Rise of the American Conservative Movement.* New York: Atlantic Monthly Press, 2008.

Lipsitz, George. *The Possessive Investment in Whiteness: How White People Profit from Identity Politics*. Philadelphia: Temple University Press, 1998.

Lott, Eric. *Love and Theft: Blackface Minstrelsy and the American Working Class*. New York: Oxford University Press, 1993.

Mandelbaum, Ken. *"A Chorus Line" and the Musicals of Michael Bennett*. New York: St. Martin's Press, 1989.

Mast, Gerald. *Can't Help Singin': The American Musical on Stage and Screen*. Woodstock, NY: Overlook Press, 1987.

McMillin, Scott. *The Musical as Drama: A Study of the Principles and Conventions behind Musical Shows from Kern to Sondheim*. Princeton, NJ: Princeton University Press, 2006.

————. "Paul Robeson, Will Vodery's 'Jubilee Singers,' and the Earliest Script of the Kern-Hammerstein *Show Boat*." *Theatre Survey* 41, no. 2 (November 2000): 51–70.

Merrill, Blanche. *Fanny Brice's Comedy Songs*. New York: Mills Music, 1939.

Miller, D. A. *Place for Us: Essay on the Broadway Musical*. Cambridge, MA: Harvard University Press, 1998.

Miller, Scott. *Deconstructing Harold Hill: An Insider's Guide to Musical Theatre*. Portsmouth, NH: Heinemann, 1999.

Mizejewski, Linda. *Ziegfeld Girl: Image and Icon in Culture and Cinema*. Durham, NC: Duke University Press, 1999.

Mordden, Ethan. *Beautiful Mornin': The Broadway Musical in the 1940s*. New York: Oxford University Press, 1999.

Morrison, Toni. *Playing in the Dark: Whiteness and the Literary Imagination*. New York: Vintage Books, 1992.

Most, Andrea. *Making Americans: Jews and the Broadway Musical*. Cambridge, MA: Harvard University Press, 2004.

Negrón-Muntaner, Frances. "Feeling Pretty: *West Side Story* and Puerto Rican Identity Discourses." *Social Text* 63 (Summer 2000): 83–106.

Newman, Harry. "Holding Back: The Theatre's Resistance to Non-Traditional Casting." *TDR* 33, no. 3 (Fall 1989): 22–36.

Novak, Michael. *The Rise of the Unmeltable Ethnics*. New York: Macmillan, 1972.

Oja, Carol J. "*West Side Story* and *The Music Man*: Whiteness, Immigration, and Race in the US during the Late 1950s." *Studies in Musical Theatre* 3, no. 1 (2009): 13–30.

Orloff, Rich. "Old Musicals, New Librettos." *Dramatist*, July/August 2001, 24–36.

Pao, Angela. *No Safe Spaces: Re-casting Race, Ethnicity, and Nationality in American Theater*. Ann Arbor: University of Michigan Press, 2010.

Philip, M. NourbeSe. *Showing Grit: Showboating North of the 44th Parallel*. Toronto: Poui Publications, 1993.

Rich, Frank. Introduction to *A Chorus Line: The Book of the Musical*, by James Kirkwood and Nicholas Dante. Music by Marvin Hamlisch. Lyrics by Edward Kleban. New York: Applause Books, 1995.

Riggs, Lynn. *"The Cherokee Night" and Other Plays*. Foreword by Jace Weaver. Norman: University of Oklahoma Press, 2003.

Roediger, David. *Colored White: Transcending the Racial Past*. Berkeley: University of California Press, 2002.

————. *The Wages of Whiteness: Race and the Making of the American Working Class*. 1991. Rev. ed. New York: Verso, 1999.

———. *Working toward Whiteness: How America's Immigrants Became White: The Strange Journey from Ellis Island to the Suburbs.* New York: Basic Books, 2005.

Rogin, Michael. *Blackface, White Noise: Jewish Immigrants in the Hollywood Melting Pot.* Berkeley: University of California Press, 1996.

Rosenberg, Bernard, and Ernest Harburg. *The Broadway Musical: Collaboration in Commerce and Art.* New York: New York University Press, 1993.

Rubenstein, Rachel. *Members of the Tribe: Native Americans in the Jewish Imagination.* Detroit: Wayne State University Press, 2010.

Rubin, Rachel, and Jeffrey Melnick. *Immigration and American Popular Culture: An Introduction.* New York: New York University Press, 2007.

Rugg, Rebecca Ann. "What It Used to Be: Nostalgia and the State of the Broadway Musical." *Theater* 32, no. 2 (Summer 2002): 44–55.

Sanders, Leslie. "American Scripts, Canadian Realities: Toronto's *Show Boat.*" *Diaspora* 5, no. 1 (Spring 1996): 99–117.

Sandoval-Sánchez, Alberto. *José, Can You See? Latinos on and off Broadway.* Madison: University of Wisconsin Press, 1999.

Savran, David. *A Queer Sort of Materialism: Recontextualizing American Theater.* Ann Arbor: University of Michigan Press, 2003.

Schechner, Richard. "Race Free, Gender Free, Body-Type Free, Age Free Casting," *TDR* 33, no. 1 (Spring 1989): 4–12.

Schwartz, Herman. "Affirmative Action." In *Minority Report: What Has Happened to Blacks, Hispanics, American Indians, and Other Minorities in the Eighties,* ed. Leslie W. Dunbar, 58–75. New York: Pantheon Books, 1984.

Simeone, Nigel. *Leonard Bernstein: "West Side Story."* Burlington, VT: Ashgate, 2009.

Sollors, Werner. *Beyond Ethnicity: Consent and Descent in American Culture.* New York: Oxford University Press, 1986.

Sondheim, Stephen. *Finishing the Hat: Collected Lyrics (1954–1981) with Attendant Comments, Heresies, Principles, Grudges, Whines, and Anecdotes.* New York: Knopf, 2010.

Stanfield, Peter. "From the Vulgar to the Refined: American Vernacular and Blackface Minstrelsy in *Showboat.*" In *Musicals—Hollywood and Beyond,* ed. Bill Marshall and Robynn Stilwell, 147–156. Portland, OR: Intellect, 2000.

Stevens, George, Jr. *Conversations with the Great Moviemakers of Hollywood's Golden Age at the American Film Institute.* New York: Knopf, 2006.

Sun, William H. "Power and Problems of Performance across Ethnic Lines: An Alternative Approach to Nontraditional Casting." *TDR* 44, no. 4 (Winter 2000): 86–95.

Tardon, Raphaël. "Richard Wright Tells Us: The White Problem in the United States." Trans. Keneth Kinnamon. *Action* (Paris), October 24, 1946, 10–11. Reprinted in *Conversations with Richard Wright,* ed. Keneth Kinnamon and Michel Fabre, 99–105. Jackson: University Press of Mississippi, 1993.

Turner, Frederick Jackson. "The Significance of the Frontier in American History." In *Debating Diversity: Clashing Perspectives on Race and Ethnicity in America,* 3rd ed., ed. Ronald Takaki, 39–54. New York: Oxford University Press, 2002.

Viagas, Robert, Baayork Lee, and Thommie Walsh. *On the Line: The Creation of "A Chorus Line."* New York: William Morrow, 1990.

Waters, Mary C. "The Costs of a Costless Community." In *New Tribalisms: The Resurgence of Race and Ethnicity,* ed. Michael W. Hughey, 273–295. New York: New York University Press, 1998.

Weaver, Jace. "Ethnic Cleansing, Homestyle." *Wicazo Sa Review* 10, no. 1 (Spring 1994): 27–39.

———. *That the People Might Live: Native American Literatures and Native American Community.* New York: Oxford University Press, 1997.

Williams, Linda. *Playing the Race Card: Melodramas of Black and White from Uncle Tom to O.J. Simpson.* Princeton, NJ: Princeton University Press, 2001.

Willson, Meredith. *But He Doesn't Know the Territory.* New York: G. P. Putnam's Sons, 1959.

———. *The Music Man.* New York: G. P. Putnam's Sons, 1958.

Wilson, August. "The Ground on Which I Stand." *American Theatre* 13, no. 7 (September 1996): 14–16.

Wolf, Stacy. *Changed for Good: A Feminist History of the Broadway Musical.* New York: Oxford University Press, 2011.

———. *A Problem Like Maria: Gender and Sexuality in the American Musical.* Ann Arbor: University of Michigan Press, 2002.

Woll, Allen. *Black Musical Theatre: From "Coontown" to "Dreamgirls."* 1989. Reprint. New York: Da Capo Press, 1989.

Woods, Alan. "Consuming the Past: Commercial American Theatre in the Reagan Era." In *The American Stage: Social and Economic Issues from the Colonial Period to the Present,* ed. Ron Engle and Tice L. Miller, 252–266. New York: Cambridge University Press, 1993.

Young, William H., and Nancy K. Young. *Music of the Great Depression.* Westport, CT: Greenwood Press, 2005.

Zadan, Craig. *Sondheim & Co.* 2nd ed. New York: Harper & Row, 1986.

Permissions

"Oh, What a Beautiful Mornin', " lyrics by Oscar Hammerstein II, music by Richard Rodgers
Copyright © 1943 by WILLIAMSON MUSIC
Copyright Renewed
International Copyright Secured. All Rights Reserved. Reprinted by Permission.

"Oklahoma," lyrics by Oscar Hammerstein II, music by Richard Rodgers
Copyright © 1943 by Williamson Music
Copyright Renewed
International Copyright Secured All Rights Reserved Used by Permission.

"Ol' Man River," lyrics by Oscar Hammerstein II, music by Jerome Kern
Copyright © 1928 Universal–Polygram International Publishing Inc.
Copyright Renewed
All Rights Reserved. Used by Permission
Reprinted with Permission of Hal Leonard Corporation

"Where's the Mate for Me?" lyrics by Oscar Hammerstein II, music by Jerome Kern
Copyright © 1928 Universal–Polygram International Publishing Inc.
Copyright Renewed
All Rights Reserved. Used by Permission
Reprinted with Permission of Hal Leonard Corporation

"You Are Love," lyrics by Oscar Hammerstein II, music by Jerome Kern
Copyright © 1928 Universal–Polygram International Publishing Inc.
Copyright Renewed
All Rights Reserved. Used by Permission
Reprinted with Permission of Hal Leonard Corporation

"Confidence" and "Token," lyrics by Edward Kleban
Copyright © 2013 by Linda Kline
International copyright secured. All rights reserved.

"Hello Twelve, Hello Thirteen, Hello Love," lyrics by Edward Kleban, music by Marvin Hamlisch
© 1975 (renewed) Edward Kleban and SONY/ATV Music Publishing LLC
All rights for Edward Kleban controlled by Wren Music Co.
All rights for SONY/ATV Music LLC administered by SONY/ATC Music Publishing LLC, 8 Music Square West, Nashville, TN 37203
All Rights Reserved
Reprinted with Permission of Hal Leonard Corporation

"I Hope I Get It," lyrics by Edward Kleban, music by Marvin Hamlisch
© 1975 (renewed) Edward Kleban and SONY/ATV Music Publishing LLC
All rights for Edward Kleban controlled by Wren Music Co.
All rights for SONY/ATV Music LLC administered by SONY/ATC Music Publishing LLC, 8 Music Square West, Nashville, TN 37203
All Rights Reserved
Reprinted with Permission of Hal Leonard Corporation

"One," lyrics by Edward Kleban, music by Marvin Hamlisch
© 1975 (renewed) Edward Kleban and SONY/ATV Music Publishing LLC
All rights for Edward Kleban controlled by Wren Music Co.
All rights for SONY/ATV Music LLC administered by SONY/ATC Music Publishing LLC, 8 Music Square West, Nashville, TN 37203
All Rights Reserved
Reprinted with Permission of Hal Leonard Corporation

"I'm an Indian," lyrics by Blanche Merrill, music by Jack Edwards and Leo Edwards
Copyright © 1921 Renewed 1949 EMI Mills Music Inc. (ASCAP)
All rights administered by EMI Mills Music Inc.
Exclusive print rights controlled and administered by Alfred Music Publishing Co., Inc.
All Rights Reserved
Used By Permission

West Side Story, lyrics by Stephen Sondheim, music by Leonard Bernstein
© Copyright 1956, 1957, 1958, 1959 by Amberson Holdings LLC and Stephen Sondheim. Copyright renewed.
Leonard Bernstein Music Publishing Company LLC, publisher. Boosey & Hawkes, agent for rental.
International copyright secured.
Reprinted by permission of Boosey & Hawkes, Inc.

"Ya Got Trouble," lyrics and music by Meredith Willson
© 1957, 1958, 1966 (Renewed) Frank Music Corp. and Meredith Willson Music
All Rights Reserved
Reprinted with Permission of Hal Leonard Corporation

Letters and materials from the Jerome Robbins Papers reprinted by permission of the Robbins Rights Trust.

Material reprinted from the Helen Tamiris Papers. Permission granted by Michael P. Gibbons.

Index

About the Author

Warren Hoffman has worked in the arts as a producer, dramaturg, literary manager, and theater critic for over ten years. He holds a Ph.D. in American literature from the University of California–Santa Cruz and has taught at multiple universities. In 2009, he published his first book, *The Passing Game: Queering Jewish American Culture.*